Songs of Resilience

Songs of Resilience

Edited by

Andy Brader

Songs of Resilience, Edited by Andy Brader

Meaningful music making for life Series, Book 3,
Series Editors Steve C Dillon & Elizabeth Mackinlay

This book first published 2011

Cambridge Scholars Publishing

12 Back Chapman Street, Newcastle upon Tyne, NE6 2XX, UK

British Library Cataloguing in Publication Data
A catalogue record for this book is available from the British Library

ISBN (10): 1-4438-2652-9, ISBN (13): 978-1-4438-2652-5

TABLE OF CONTENTS

ACKNOWLEDGMENTS

First and foremost I acknowledge the authors who contributed their work and experience to this book. I thank them for their diligence and perseverance. Prior to acceptance each chapter was blind refereed by a panel of international experts in the field. A special note of thanks goes to the reviewers for their careful work and thoughtful feedback. I also thank the staff at Queensland University of Technology for their support and Gretchen Coombs in particular for sub-editing the book.

We are privileged to have the artwork of Vincent Serico on the front cover. The snake representation in this painting is part of a series that engages with the struggle between colonial and Indigenous values. I am extremely grateful to Vincent's estate and the Australasian CRC for Interaction Design for their support.

Evolutionary science will go someway towards explaining the book's snake design cover. I was invited to edit this volume after reading about resilient snakes in Australia. Biologists have shown that the toxic cane toad has placed evolutionary pressure on snakes to adapt their body shape. Certain species of snake have grown longer, an adaptation that makes them better able to survive their toxic meal. The most remarkable aspect of this adaptation is the speed at which it took place. These changes in body length have arisen over the past seventy years since farmers introduced the cane toad to Australia. These snakes have evolved to become resilient to cane toad's poison because of their desire to thrive. Each snake derives its physical capacity for resilience in response to the conditions to which it is exposed; its access to, and availability of resources – in the snake's case - natural and environmental ones. Similarly this book seeks to show how musicians, as members of ecological human systems, are evolving to master the sophisticated amalgamation of statistical and qualitative indicators with their music practices. Like the snake successful music practitioners will adapt to become more effective at helping others' thrive in adverse conditions. Over time, they will document social and individual gains in well-being and happiness more effectively.

PREFACE

Not only have measures of well-being and happiness ceased to rise with economic growth but, as affluent societies have grown richer, there have been long-term rises in rates of anxiety, depression and numerous other social problems (Wilkinson & Pickett, 2010 p.5)

This is a quantifiable research statement presented in a recent scholarly book aimed at general readers. In that book – *The Spirit Level* – peer-reviewed articles from reputable economics and health professors support the statement above with overwhelming international, large-scale statistical evidence. As a whole, their evidence clearly shows that for the first time in human history the poor are, on average, fatter than the rich; that developed countries with high income disparity display a propensity towards isolation and mental illness amongst individuals, whilst those countries with closer income equality consistently score higher on happiness and well-being indicators. Although this causality debate requires more careful scrutiny of data, the inference that a strong correlation exists between national and state based income inequality and major health and social problems is beyond reasonable dispute.

The Spirit Level's research findings have implications for musicians, artists, health, education and social work practitioners who work in both rich and developing countries to sing songs of resilience. Whether they like it or not, these large-scale statistical comparisons of health and social indicators signal the backdrop against which funding applications are to be justified, won, and lost. The politicians in most countries nowadays, whether large or small, rich or poor, recognise the importance of promoting artistic and cultural events, which bring citizens together peacefully and voluntarily. Most national, federal, and state governments also subsidised a mixture of public/private partnerships for such gatherings through their social, cultural and economic policies.

Creative practitioners whose work (paid or voluntary) intersects with these policies and funding arrangements can all benefit from ascertaining, and reporting on, the levels of well-being, happiness, and equally depression, distrust, and anxiety in their local region and respective countries. As *The Spirit Level* further disseminates this statistical analysis, aligned with what

Schultz & Northridge (2004) call the "Social Determinants of Health", these indicators will become increasingly significant measures of successful music projects.

Many skilled practitioners manage to demonstrate that sustained musical activities can contribute to reductions in anxiety, depression and numerous social problems, and they are well established in networks throughout the globe. Some of them have contributed to this book. They continue to show us that an ability to focus the outcomes of a music project toward a health, education or social intervention is complicated because it can often detract from artistic intention, group dynamics and the like. Yet the well-connected authors in this book believe in their own and others' ability to share expertise in order to find a common-ground where evidence-based research, storytelling and music making sit alongside one another in a collegial manner.

This book, the third in the **Meaningful Music-Making For Life** series, is intended as a call to action for creative practitioners to report on musical successes against reputable indicators in meaningful ways. All musicians know what they do – musically that is – can act as a source of power and inspiration. And in modern societies musicians certainly serve several purposes. But I for one wish more of the general public were aware of health, education and social researchers reporting quantifiable benefits associated with music, and artistic activity generally. This book goes someway towards filling that gap as it documents a series of music practices that report on successes using statistics, narratives, case studies and songs to reflect their resilient attributes. Yet as the editor of this volume I acknowledge that certain things – the musical character and lyrical content of songs for instance - cannot be measured and analysed without losing some of the meaning individuals and groups attached to them.

Twelve chapters were carefully chosen because they represent part of the rich tapestry of resilient music making. Part one offers two review chapters. The first conceptual chapter draws on my own reflections of practitioners aiming to secure and sustain funding for music services that enhance individual and communal resilience. Chapter two presents a psychological review of the contemporary literature on resilience to investigate what we actually mean by wellbeing, quality of life, and resilience. It asks important questions about these constructs validity across domains of scientific research.

I presented an early version of chapter two by Lemerle and Stewart to the rest of the contributors as a conceptual framework that could prove beneficial in their documentation of songs. The book's second section contains the remaining practice-led chapters that all respond to Lemerle and Stewart's provocative review using contemporary and historical songs of resilience from Sweden, the United States, Vanuatu, Australia and England. More than half of the book's contributors are music practitioners for whom this book represents their first publication, and for some of those English is not their first language.

Song of Resilience online

Early in 2009 Steve Dillon (series editor) and I made a concerted effort to increase the online audio-visual documentation of songs of resilience through a free web service. Supported by the Save-to-Disc Network this WIKI encourages registered users to upload and publish evidence of their songs of resilience online. That developing resource now supports this book as a form of complementary evidence that cannot be represented through text alone. I invite readers to explore the additional audio-visuals supporting each chapter, and more importantly to join us by adding to the collection.

http://songsofresilience.wikispaces.com

References

Schultz, A. and Northridge, M.E. (2004). Social Determinants of Health. *Health Ed & Beh*, 31(4): 455-471.

Wilkinson, R. & Pickett, K. (2010) The Spirit Level. Penguin Books. London.

PART ONE:

REVIEW -
A SOCIOLOGIST'S REFLECTIONS
AND A PSYCHOLOGICAL LITERATURE
REVIEW

CHAPTER ONE

PRODUCING BETTER OUTCOMES:
MUSIC AND PUBLIC SERVICES

ANDY BRADER

Introduction

Plato made the following observation about the qualities of music:

> For the modes of music are never disturbed without unsettling of the most
> fundamental political and social conventions. Republic 424b-c. (Hamilton,
> 1961, reprint)

Music has played an important role in social life for thousands of years,
and its varied forms of communication have significantly influenced the
types of public services reported in this book. It is now time for practitioners
and academics to sing songs of resilience that reinvigorate the public's
understanding of the positive role music can play in all of our lives, and
for public services to better resource music projects. The last twenty years
have seen major advances in studies of music and its affects on the brain's
neuroplasticity, but as yet no one has managed to provide a comprehensive
response to Oliver Sachs' (2006) question: why does music, for better or
worse, have so much power? This book seeks to demonstrate the power of
those music making experiences that bridge the gap between the physical
and social sciences across commercial, social and cultural contexts.

Developing resilience through varied modes of music is the common
theme of this book's chapters. Internationally renowned and early career
academics have collaborated with practitioners to sing songs of resilience;
some of which are narratives that report on the effects of music practices
for an individual or general population, and some are based on a specific
approach, genre or service. Others are quite literally "songs" that
demonstrate aspects of resilience in action. These chapters offer one way
to gain a clearer understanding of how songs play an important role in the

development of innovative public policy reform across health, education and social services.

In populist terms resilience depicts a capability to bounce back from an adverse experience, but the essays before you examine the concept from distinctive musical modes and perspectives. Detailed research literature on theories of resilience, mostly in the psychology of health and education, has deepened our understanding of how individuals access appropriate resources that assist them in their attempts to bounce back (Ungar, 2008, Stewart et al., 2004; Luthar, 2006). Despite theoretical and ideological differences between these approaches to resilience and how they might inform the public policy reform agenda, they share arguments based on an ecological view of human systems. Resilience and public sector reform literature both argue that the roles information, buildings, roads, infrastructure and facilities play in successful health, education and social service outcomes are often underestimated and misrepresented. Subsequently, a costly education invention that reports on its own success can falsely attribute positive outcomes solely to their intervention without acknowledging the overlapping nature of other services that contributed to the success of said education intervention. Let us take the case of senior citizens in need of basic computer literacy training – they are recipients of ecologically linked public services that are not immediately recognisable in educational interventions. The quality of local libraries, community centres and training providers also make important contributions to those senior citizens' educational achievements, and it is proper recognition of these networked relationships in the reporting of outcomes that is central to ecological understandings of human systems.

In to order make ecological arguments about the value of publicly funded musical activities, the traditional conception of the public sector as set of large, cumbersome institutions that redistribute tax revenues towards essential services must change (James, 2009). According to policy think tanks and political analysts, the future of publicly funded institutions such as hospitals, schools, housing and welfare services in social democratic societies is dependant upon the success of new delivery strategies that focus on co-production processes and outcomes in collaboration with clients (Carey, 2009; Dunston, 2009). Leading figures in policy reform argue that the new direction of public services will have a fundamental concern with relationships, interaction and mutuality (Clark & Newman, 2009; Leadbetter, 2004, 2007). These concerns have been central to the work of music practitioners for many years, and more recently in online social media networks (Grinnell, 2009).

This book documents projects that have redistributed public funds to engage people from diverse backgrounds in some form of musical relationship. Based on their engagement with these communities, music practitioners and academics offer valuable insights about relationships, interaction and mutuality that should inform these public service reforms. The rest of this chapter ties together my professional and conceptual reflections with the experiences of academics and practitioners who aim to secure and sustain funding for music services that enhance individual and communal well being.

Music and resilience

The following chapters form a persuasive chorus of social practices that advocate the use of music to help build the capacity for resilience in individuals and groups. As a whole they demonstrate that publicly funded music projects, some of which aim to build resilience, share common features aligned with an ecological view of reform in health, education and social work systems. I hope to make this connection between music, resilience and public services explicit by posing the following questions:

Do music projects in education, health and social services build a measurable capacity for resilience amongst individuals?

Can we replicate these projects' outcomes to develop a capacity for resilience in diverse cultural groups?

Does the shared use of the term resilience help to secure funding for innovative musical activities that provide tangible health, education and social outcomes?

In order to discuss the challenges facing public services, they need to be set in the context of book's main focus - the role of music in building an individual and group capacity for resilience. Some definitions are required from specialists in each area to make these connections explicit.

Denora (2003) suggests the active properties of music have shifted our focus from the music and society paradigm towards socio-musical research, which posits the "socialising role of music in its broadest sense" (p.175). I define music as a socialising medium of communication where humans orchestrate instruments to create patterns with sound and silience. These sounds and silences are often arranged as songs, both literal and metaphoric, which include organised and intentional performances, spontaneous outbursts, rehearsals, recordings and listening activities. I am well aware that this definition is biased, culturally and historically available to English speakers, and along with my questions, it is applicable to most art forms. I intend it to accommodate different perspectives of music as well as the dominant western understanding – itself multiple and contested. I intend this definition to further inform practitioners' ability to discern more tangible outcomes for people who currently participate in socio-musical activities.

Ungar (2008) outlines a three-part definition of resilience that speaks directly to social workers, nurses, teachers, youth and community developers as well as those people facing adversities with whom they work in collaboration. Ungar argues that most theories of resilience have focused on characteristics of individuals, but currently these theories are better understood from an ecological perspective that implicates those mandated to help in the process of intervening. He states:

> First, resilience is the capacity of individuals to navigate their way to resources that sustain well being; second, resilience is the capacity of individuals' physical and social ecologies to provide these resources; and third, resilience is the capacity of individuals and their families and communities to negotiate culturally meaningful ways for resources to be shared (2008. p. 23).

In the next chapter Lemerle and Stewart expand on this definition to include the availability and accessibility of resources required by individuals, families and communities in public health systems. Ungar makes a similar point when he describes the matrix of service providers and community resources that support wellbeing. Yet the second part of Ungar's definition, which refers to ecologies, does not fully acknowledge the persistence of structural inequalities that fuel unequal access to resources, nor the micro level power relations between local clients and their service providers. Ungar's definition is strong, but like previous individualistic theories of resilience, it underplays the powers that markets and communities bring to bear on an individual's ability to navigate their way towards appropriate resources.

As a sociologist I take my view of power from Touraine (2000) who argues that we live in a period of de-modernisation, where all human subjects have to develop their own strategies to reconcile the power that markets and communities exert upon them. In this context the capacity to access resources that provide individuals with the capabilities to realise resilience is repeatedly thwarted by the interplay between overarching forces of macro level market conditions and micro level communities of practice. How frustrating it must be for a person experiencing mental anguish to have a practitioner inform them about resources that may help him/her, only to find their access repeatedly blocked by economic and cultural variants that they interpret as beyond their control.

The literature emanating from the field of critical social policy since the mid 1970s (see Titmus' 1974 residual model of welfare) continues to highlight severe cycles of deprivation experienced by marginalised groups in western societies and how this reproduction can act as a self-fulfilling prophecy. More recently this line of argument has been reinvigorated by health and economic statistical analysts, who argue that increases in income inequality are socially corrosive to public health (Wilkinson & Pickett, 2010). If the capacity for resilience in action depends upon access to appropriate resources, then micro and macro power relations must be acknowledged and reconciled. But who is responsible for making resources both available and appropriate? Public services in health, education and social work certainly have a major role to play in creating, outsourcing and signposting suitable resources, but these providers cannot be held responsible for the myriad of structural and cultural barriers that may hinder group or individual access.

Although inevitable problems arise when we unpack definitions of music and resilience, there are benefits to bringing these concepts together with the ongoing debate about public service reform. I believe that linking these debates engenders a common language amongst health, education and social work practitioners that could extend resources for music projects which increase participants' capacity for resilience.

It is interesting to note that this book's contributors had never described or conceived of their work as "songs of resilience" until the editors invited them to do so. A most fascinating feature of this edited collection is how authors have interpreted and responded to the research literature on resilience using distinct technical registers. All the chapters report on academics and practitioners advocating for music's ability to heal and connect humanity by using justifications based on their own and others' experiences. For example, the language of a socio-cultural perspective that derives from Vygotskian education theory and the language of socio-ecological perspectives used in public health literature could have both framed this book to argue that social, cultural and environmental factors have been neglected in traditional fields of positivist research and practice. Further examples of divergent terminology in education, health and social work perspectives refer to the names given to resources available to individual and groups. The resources to which Ungar's definition and the public health literature refer are commonly called capitals in sociology literature (see Bourdieu, 2001, forms of capital – social, cultural, symbolic, institutional, or Adam Smith for a much earlier exposition of human capital). It is open to debate whether the language of resources, capitals or currencies is most salient, but until there is a general agreement about which concept to use consistently the problem of evaluating outcomes remains unresolved. I would add to this ongoing debate that consolidating language patterns to report on outcomes which attract and sustain public funding is just one of many solutions. The future version of resources, capitals, or currencies that manages to reach a consensus across disciplines, and accommodates an assessment of macro and micro power relations in action, will have a level of clarity that outweighs current definitions.

Multi-faceted musical activities in public services

The policy-funding-practice nexus remains complex and requires more contextual description here as it links resilience building activities with all public services, but especially those designed to respond in times when citizens face severe adversity. Admittedly, public services do not carry universal meaning and my understanding of what constitutes them will differ from readers who reside in countries without a historical link to the welfare state model. At a base level, however, my argument should resonate with any reader interested in the effective redistribution of tax revenues towards those citizens in need of additional support.

Since the mid 1990s the theme running through my work has been popular music production in education, youth and community settings across local and national policy contexts. In both a practitioner and academic capacity I have co-produced publicly funded projects (as an employee and volunteer) for fifteen years, where humans interact with and through technologies related to music, education and social justice. In the UK and Australia I have witnessed many policy attempts to regenerate marginalised communities, and I continue to analyse the political shifts and dominant positions within such public policies whilst also applying for funding to implement and evaluate innovative music projects locally.

My participation in and theorising of these public services relate to what some academics call a crisis of legitimacy for governments charged with the delivery of public services in networked societies. Castells (1999) argues that national governments are too large to make a difference locally and too small to affect global change without sharing sovereign power (see Habermas, 1975, for an earlier exposition of the crisis of legitimacy for nation-states). Most western governments have recognised their crisis of legitimacy, and have moved strategically towards more decentralised and regional decision making. This move acknowledges that governments cannot deliver public services in ecological terms without working in collaboration with citizens as co-producers.

The current reform of public policy, funding and services is a delicate balancing act that requires consideration of and consultation with several stakeholders. Important music projects within this reform agenda present cutting edge action research projects that evaluate the effects these resilience-building activities have on individuals and groups. The questions I presented in the previous section arise from framing music projects in this way, and fundamentally they are about the currency of the term "resilience" and its uses in reporting the outcomes of public services that involve musical activity.

Of course public services encapsulate levels of complexity that this synopsis will not discuss. There are however general trends in proposed reforms that cross traditional political boundaries and commentaries from key policy think tanks (e.g., Demos and other "think tanks"), academic journals (e.g., Critical Social Policy) and politicians of all persuasions (e.g., Liberal, Labour, Conservative, Green, Independent) agree that a whole-systems approach to public services is the future, and that it will be organised poles apart from the fiscal model of social policy outlined in the Beveridge Report of 1942 (Abel-Smith, 1992). Whilst the use of information and communication technologies provides us with an almost infinite range of joined-up possibilities, the current vision of reform remains focused on the efficient allocation of scarce resources. For example, Leadbetter (2009) describes the future of smart public sector reform as a move away from services where governments do things "for" and "to" it citizens towards a co-production model. This is hardly a new concept for those who engage disadvantaged communities with musical activities, and in response, practitioners have outlined some of the specific problems with youth participation in such social work reform (Brader, 2010; Carey, 2009), but still acknowledge the general reform agenda as necessary. In order to engage with this debate, and to argue that musical activities have an important role to play in these ongoing discussions with government, I summarise the direction of this reform agenda in three areas.

First, public services dealing with acute health, education and social needs demand "conversations at critical junctures, not just transactions" (Leadbetter, 2009, p.2). The dominant policy discourse supporting this reform agenda states that better outcomes depend on the quality of this interaction. Those espousing this agenda argue that instead of simply providing a hospital bed or schooling service, most people in crisis want to discuss all their options with a knowledgeable professional. Accordingly, public health professionals should follow up the unfortunate conversation, "you have X condition and require Y treatment", with in-depth discussions that inform clients about the possible combination of service options.

In terms of music related activities, this could involve a purposeful conversation with a mental health client about the individual benefits of music therapy and the social benefits of participating in a group activity. Both options require a concerted resource allocation for that mental health patient, yet the type, cost and outcomes of these resources vary dramatically. Whilst one client might build their capacity for resilience through an informal music group, another might require costly one-to-one therapy sessions to arrive at a satisfactory and sustainable outcome. Regardless of the outcome's cost there are several musical options available for mental-health clients that require conversations, not just transactions. Stephen Clift and his colleagues argue in chapter six that amateur singing groups perform a proactive health function, which provide a measureable difference to participants' sense of wellbeing and quality of life. These issues – about the preventative role music can play in producing better health, education and social outcomes – rarely form part of the public service reform debate, but they should.

Second, government policies of the future will aim to create a greater sense of capability in consumers of public services. A popular example taken from this debate focuses on recuperative care for the elderly, where the aim is not to continue provision, but to withdraw it over time. Many education and juvenile justice strategies share a parallel concern with this example; they try to re-engage and/or rehabilitate those at-risk and youth offenders with mainstream norms and values. In the future this capability to resume a former lifestyle, or adhere to mainstream norms and values, is presumably accomplished through more informative conversations at critical junctures.

This focus on increasing consumer capability in the pursuit of better outcomes also refers to self-help and at-home solutions that provide combinations of face-to-face and technologically mediated modes of delivery. Take the case of the child with a speech impediment who is offered outpatient care after intensive therapy sessions facilitated in a local education setting. As the capability to sing has been well documented as a suitable coping strategy for those who stutter (Colcord & Adams, 1979), it would be appropriate in this situation for a health care professional to help their client access information about singing groups and other relevant resources through whatever technology is available.

Third, scaling new solutions for large populations is a major interest for governments and it is inevitable that the public servants who administer them will encounter the brunt of client complaints. Traditionally, increases in public spending implied institutional investments made on our behalf, in buildings, facilities and wage increases. Nowadays the ecological and networked basis of all complex human systems means that investment in one part (usually a visible part) of the network is particularly difficult to evaluate because it affects and is influenced by other parts. Leadbetter (2009) cites the statistics of fires in homes, which have fallen dramatically over the last ten years because of relational variables such as cheap smoke alarms, less smokers and more accessible information about flammable materials. The traditional government solution to the reduction of fires in homes was to invest in more fire engines, which are expensive, inflexible infrastructure assets with high-fixed costs locked into multi year finance arrangements.

According to Leadbetter, historically most public service investment has been in metaphoric, reactive fire engines. In the current economic environment a wise institutional investment of public funds would opt for the solution that has the most ecological breadth and scope. The cases presented in this book offer examples of ecologically minded investments in users and providers of musical activities and their micro level resources, which together can provide the conditions necessary to sustain the capacity for resilience amongst individuals and groups.

In terms of musical activity that builds a capacity for resilience, I argue that this notion of ecological public services has the potential to account for outcomes within which music has played an often-invisible part. It is now widely accepted that the quality of information, buildings, roads, infrastructures and facilities play a large part in successful health, education and social service outcomes, but they are rarely acknowledged in evaluations of current schemes. Take a mundane, but crucial example of role that musical activity plays in the delivery of key public services. If we include listening to music as a well-being activity that nurses have documented as a beneficial health intervention (McCaffrey & Locsin, 2002), then the number of public services using music as part of their delivery mode increases exponentially. Presenting citizens with social opportunities to listen to music in youth and community centres, schools, aged-care and prison facilities, hospitals, public recreation areas and festivals is a good use of public funds, which is a difficult, but not an impossible task to evaluate. This ecological argument for scaling up and decentralising public services through co-production serves the interests of those advocating increases in funding for musical activity because it makes the (often auxiliary) uses of music more visible.

Music has saturated social life to the extent that we often forget how much we are exposed to it on a daily basis. Take a minute to consider this all encompassing concept of music and the number of uses it has within major and ancillary public services such as health, education and social work. Then consider this expanded view of the role music plays in social life alongside public health research, which shows that the vast majority of positive health outcomes actually happen at home or five minutes from home at the pharmacy or local doctors. This view of reform in public health resources, focused on home and community based systems, is slowly replacing the traditional view of public service funding, so that fire engines and other large physical investments are peripheral, not central costs. If this reform agenda becomes a reality and public services of the 21st century start allocating more resources from a "needs and outcomes" perspective, and less via the visible institutions such as hospitals and schools, then socio-musical activity that builds the capacity for resilience has a bright future. Such a move towards a more efficient, needs-based public sector relegates the "to and for" and promotes services "with and by" clients in collaborative, interactive relationships built on mutual benefits.

The evaluation problem

Successful long-term solutions for public services will learn to identify the complex type and nature of adversities to which individuals and groups are exposed. In a crude distinction these experiences of adversity take two major forms – those that are insurmountable and those that are not. Adverse conditions that can be overcome are also referred to as structural experiences of social exclusion or marginalisation (see Byrne, 1999), they are often simultaneous, overlapping and ephemeral, and they are frequently reported to produce what seems like a single continuous negative experience for many individuals. Public service providers have a history of treating these adverse experiences as static states of being that somehow remain constant through time and space so that an individual's experience of adversity is not reflected accurately by the public systems providing access to social and economic resources (Brader, 2010).

These forms are distinct from the chronic type of adversity in which a physical or mental condition has obvious no cure (see chapter nine where Donald DeVito's depicts Autism Spectrum Disorder as an enduring form of adversity). According to Lawford & Eiser (2001), the nature and frequency of adverse experiences determine the types of life skills necessary to adapt and traverse that experience, whilst also determining the specific resources that may be accrued. The implication for those providing publicly funded socio-music activities is that individuals and groups with health, education and social issues, which tend to overlap and change frequently, require iterative assessments of need; the solutions have to be ongoing, flexible and measurable over time and across different spaces.

The traditional fiscal model that funds and delivers health, education and social work provisions are being challenged from several angles: cultural studies, sociology, social and positive psychology, community organisations, public health promoters, narrative arts and alternative therapies. Active practitioners in these fields are making significant inroads into public policy and funding, and especially in private healthcare where several non-medical therapies are now accepted as legitimate. Large-scale research studies agree that the published literature lacks an overview of rigorous empirical studies, which summarise and compare successful music-based projects claiming to build a capacity for resilience (Sachs, 2006). Those reviews that have managed to address such concerns have organised their reports around themes associated with primary medical outcomes. It would appear many researcher/practitioner teams are involved with their own musical specialities in ways that inadvertently overlook the collection of valuable formative and summative assessments that support ongoing research into music's multiple and recurrent value as a social practice. For example, there are possibilities for music projects, funded and delivered through the public health sector, to agree upon a set of risk/protective factors and map their progress against an education project that uses the same terminology to report on distinct but related outcomes. Elements of this crossover between education and health initiatives exist in this book (Lemerle & Stewart chapter two, Harris et al., chapter four) but these examples have also encountered difficulties when trying to report on outcomes using the appropriate discipline terminology. A shared language would offer both sectors opportunities to report on improved outcomes that build the capacity for resilience and provide larger, longitudinal datasets that strengthen the claims each sector makes about the role music played in these outcomes. In short, the type of research reviews required cannot proceed without some agreement on common terms of reference.

From my perspective three terms require more detailed investigation and resolution: 1) Risk factors 2) Protective factors and 3) Resources. I assert that trans-discipline working definitions of these terms need to be agreed upon as the basis of research questions, data gathering and reporting, in order for there to be a comprehensive evaluation of music's ability to assist individuals and groups build a capacity for resilience. This definition must incorporate an analysis of local and global power relations that affect individuals and groups' abilities to create and access appropriate resources. Viewing the entire public sector as part of an ecological system necessitates that these terms be defined in ways that all stakeholders can report upon, understand and relate.

Risk factors have been dominant indicators in education, health and social work for more than two decades now. These well-established concepts change according to the time and space in which they are investigated. The way researchers and practitioners interpret risk factors often transform the overall direction of their project and the reported outcomes. This leads to inconsistencies across disciplines that report on divergent research outcomes, particularly in studies about strategies to overcome adversities. As a concept risk has been criticised for being overly individualistic (see Beck, 1992, and Douglas, 1992) and in this context it could lead a research team to report attribution errors about perceived risks from medical or education perspectives. For example, Abbot-Chapman's (2008) research demonstrates that support and protective factors are adult-centric concepts, which assume that young people engaged in "risky" activities do not "trust" in the ways that adults expect.

Similarly, protective factors in policy and practice have been criticised for not fully incorporating informal support networks (Brader, 2010; Rutter, 1990), thus attributing any positive outcomes to an intentional and formalised health, education or social work intervention. Protective factors and certain family and social resources are often used interchangeably to depict qualities that fend off adversities. To properly evaluate the positive benefits of diverse music activities that claim to build a capacity for resilience, these inconsistencies in terminology need resolution so there can be a general consensus about how we identify, intervene and report on risk and protective factors.

We also need to agree on what it means for individuals and groups to access resources. As mentioned before, the theories used by several education researchers (Grenfell, 1996; Albright & Luke, 2007) use Bourdieu's later work (2001) to argue that economic, social and cultural forms of capital have shaped our understanding of resources in modern societies. Both embodied and objective states of these capital forms have expanded to now include symbolic, institutional, psychological and organisational subtypes. Regardless of the exact typology and its relationship to Bourdieu's concepts of field, habitus and doxa, there is a direct correlation between the ways academics talk about the acquisition, development, decline, use and access to resources that build the capacity to resilience, and this notion of capitals. When disciplines display divergent ways of explaining the same phenomena, and respond in contrasting ways to those facing persistent adversities, they often compound rather than alleviate inequitable access to resources. Neither this nor the following chapters can resolve this important issue, so I encourage readers to ask questions about their own interests and specialist areas whilst reading this book. Take time to consider the in/visible networks of power relations between music, resilience, public services, risk and protective factors, capitals and resources within your field of practice.

Discussion

Reformed public policy in its broadest sense aims to produce proactive, efficient solutions in collaboration with citizens, and innovative music projects certainly have a role to play here. Despite current attempts to reform political and social conventions of the day, traditional models of funding musical activity in health, education and social work prevail, and there is a lack of coherence in the growing number of approaches challenging them. To sustain funding that allows resilience to flourish amongst individuals and groups, socio-music projects need to evaluate their outcomes in a more structured fashion that does not comprise nor over formalise their flexible modes of delivery and diverse practices. Promoting this critical mass of work and research surrounding music without homogenising the diversity of practices presents an arduous mission.

Music continues to prosper as an artform, commercially and as a social practice in formal, non-formal and informal modes. Physical and social sciences remain fascinated by its effectiveness and prolific appeal, which has made music adaptable and amenable to technological advances in commercial, governmental and community fields. From classical to rock to hip-hop, we have witnessed the articulation of rebellion and critique through music. Sachs, DeNora and contributors to this book advocate for musical activity as a legitimate form of socialisation in and of itself. Yet history reminds us that musicians are generally resistant and sceptical towards being enrolled in the delivery and marketing of products and services other than their own. We know that music already plays an ancillary role in many public services, and that it is gaining ground as a form of therapy and alternative education in its own right. What then is the best way forward for those interested in improving the status and acceptance of music, and the arts more generally, in public service reform?

I started this chapter with Sachs' question – why does music have so much power? Whilst Sachs talks of music's impact on the individual, and DeNora its ubiquity within everyday social life, I have argued that its power is derived from its ability to traverse and connect the networks of individuals and groups, in and through, markets and communities. Producing better outcomes for those experiencing both ephemeral and continuous adverse conditions requires music practitioners to communicate and document the development of sustainable resources that lead to a resilience-building capacity. These resources are present in physical, virtual, individual, social, cultural, and economic forms; it is proper and right for musicians, practitioners and academics to work with their peers, colleagues and clients to identify and capitalise upon the (in) visible values they provide.

References

Abbott-Chapman, J., C. Denholm, et al. (2008). Social support as a factor inhibiting teenage risk-taking: views of students, parents and professionals. Journal of Youth Studies 11(6): 611-627.

Abel-Smith, B (1992). The Beveridge Report: Its origins and outcomes. Blackwell Synergy - International Social Security Review, Volume 45 Issue 1-2 Page 5-16, January 1992. Retrieved 2008-05-19.

Albright, J. & Luke, A. Eds. (2007). *Pierre Bourdieu and Literacy Education.* London: Routledge/Erlbaum.

Beck, U. (1992). The Risk Society: Towards a new modernity. London: Sage.

Bourdieu, P. (2001). The forms of capital. In M. Granovetter & R. Swedberg (Eds.), The Sociology of Economic Life: (2nd ed., 96-111).

Brader, A. (2010). *Youth Identities: Time, Space & Social Exclusion.* Saarbrucken: Lambert Academic Publishing.

Carey, M. (2009). Critical Commentary: Happy Shopper? The Problem with Service User and Carer Participation. British Journal of Social Work 39(1): 179.

Castells, M. (1999). The Information Age: Economy, Society and Culture Volumes I, II, and III." Journal of Planning Education and Research 19: 211.

Clarke, J. & Newman, J. (2009). Elusive Publics: knowledge, power and public service reform. In: Gewirtz, Sharon ed. *Changing teacher professionalism: International trends, challenges, and ways forward.* UK: Routledge, pp. 43–53.

Colcord, R. D. and M. R. Adams (1979). Voicing duration and vocal SPL changes associated with stuttering reduction during singing. Journal of Speech, Language and Hearing Research 22(3): 468.

DeNora, T. (2003). Music sociology: getting the music into the action. British Journal of Music Education 20(02): 165-177.

Douglas, M. (1992). *Risk and Blame: Essays in cultural theory.* London: Routledge.

Rutter, M. (1990). Psychosocial resilience and protective mechanisms. Risk and protective factors in the development of psychopathology 3, 49-74.

Dunston, R., A. Lee, et al. (2009). Co-Production and Health System Reform–From Re-Imagining To Re-Making. Australian Journal of Public Administration 68(1): 39-52.

Grenfell, M. (1996). *Bourdieu and Education*. London: Falmer.

Grinnell, C. K. (2009). From Consumer to Prosumer to Produser: Who Keeps Shifting My Paradigm? (We Do!). Public Culture 21(3), 577.

Habermas, J. (1975). *Legitimation crisis*. Boston: Beacon Press.

Hallam, S. (2001). "The Power of Music. The strength of music's influence on our lives." The Performing Right Society: MCPS-PRS Alliance.

Hamilton, Huntington & Cairns (1961). *The Collected Dialogues of Plato Including the Letters*. New York: Pantheon Books, 340, 1294-95, 665-66, 643-44, 1174-75.

James, O. (2009). Evaluating the Expectations Disconfirmation and Expectations Anchoring Approaches to Citizen Satisfaction with Local Public Services. Journal of Public Administration Research and Theory 19(1), 107.

Lawford, J. & Eiser, C. (2001). Exploring links between the concepts of Quality of Life and Resilience. Pediatric Rehabilitation 4(1): 209-216.

Leadbeater, C. (2004). Personalisation through participation: a new script for public services. London: DEMOS.

Leadbeater, C. and H. Cottam (2007). The User Generated State: Public Services 2.0. Public Matters: The renewal of the Public Realm, London: Politicos: 95–116.

Luthar, S. (2006). Resilience in development: a synthesis of research across five decades. In Cicchetti, D. & Cohen, D.J. (Ed). (2006). Developmental Psychopathology, Vol 3: Risk, disorder, and adaptation (2nd ed.). Hoboken, NJ, US: John Wiley & Sons.

McCaffrey, R. & Locsin R. (2002). Music listening as a nursing intervention: a symphony of practice. Holistic nursing practice 16(3): 70.

Sacks, O. (2006). The power of music. Brain 129 (10), 2528.

Stewart, D; Sun, J; Patterson, C; Lemerle, K; & Hardie, M. (2004). Promoting and building resilience in primary school communities: Evidence from a comprehensive "health promoting school" approach. International Journal of Mental Health Promotion 6 (3): 26-33.

Titmuss, R. (1974). *Social Policy*. London: Allen & Unwin.

Ungar, M. (2008). Putting Resilience Theory into action. In Liebenberg & Ungar, *Resilience in Action*. University of Toronto Press, Toronto pp.16

CHAPTER TWO

RESILIENCE:
THRIVING BEYOND ADVERSITY

KATE LEMERLE AND DONALD E STEWART

Introduction

For much of the past century the scientific study of human endurance and capacity for achieving self-actualisation has largely been ignored within the field of psychology. Instead our fascination for understanding mental pathology such as depression and anxiety continues to outpace research that addresses wellbeing and its determinants. Many health outcomes are now known to emerge from interactions between behavioural patterns and social norms such as dietary choices, personal characteristics that include genetic heritage and psychological dispositions, and contextual factors such as music, dance, and folklore which shape normative beliefs (Stokols, 1996; Berkman & Kawachi, 2000). These cultural influences pervade every aspect of one's development – from individual identity formation to patterns of daily living – exposing individuals (and particularly children) to potential opportunities to acquire and sustain the psychological resources essential for optimal functioning. Fundamental to these is resilience, the individual's capacity to respond adaptively to adversity, which is largely shaped by interactions between the individual and multiple social contexts to which they are exposed. These include physical institutions, such as schools and religious institutions, and conceptual or ideological institutions, such as the values that derive from socialisation practices or culturally-sanctioned traditions (Lerner, Dowling & Anderson, 2003; Park & Huebner, 2005).

In this chapter, we review the contemporary literature about resilience within the context of the emerging field of positive psychology. Central to this perspective is recognition of the interlocking systems that shape human developmental outcomes and psychosocial functioning, pioneered by Bronfenbrenner (1979) and broadly referred to as the ecological model. Positive developmental outcomes such as resilience are essential for thriving or attaining optimal human functioning, but until recently the cultural conditions within the various settings that influence human development have received scant consideration in relation to mental health (Clauss-Ehlers, 2008). In the words of Linley and Joseph (nd), a holistic psychology "...works[s] to promote optimal functioning across the full range of human functioning from disorder and distress to health and fulfilment" (p. 4). Whilst they do not disregard research that helps us understand human pathology, exponents of the positive psychology movement argue that the empirical evidence base derived from rigorous scientific research into positive mental health must be expanded. Additionally, comprehensive theoretical frameworks that explain the psychological mechanisms that characterize optimal human functioning across various contexts must be developed. In particular, we need to broaden our understanding of how culture, a core element of social systems, shapes essential mental health outcomes such as resilience.

When he took over as president of the American Psychological Association (APA) in 1998, Martin Seligman called for an investment in research of those psychological variables that contribute to wellbeing and optimal human functioning. Between 2000-2008 the body of positive psychology literature grew exponentially (Figure 1). Despite Seligman's call for a more integrative approach to explaining human behaviour, only 0.13% of the total literature covered in PsycINFO during the past decade reflects this emerging field (Schui & Krampen, 2010), and it is still far outpaced by publications in the traditional, clinical, realm of psychology as demonstrated by Linley and Joseph's (2004a) comparison of publication trends for depression, anxiety and psychological wellbeing between 1978 and 2003 (Figure 2).

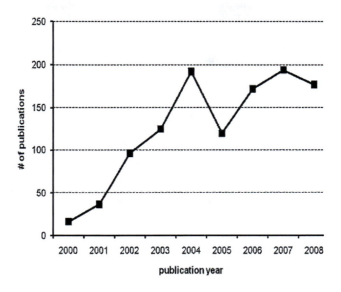

Figure 1. **Development of absolute numbers of publications on positive psychology (2000-2008) (Schui & Krampen, 2010).**

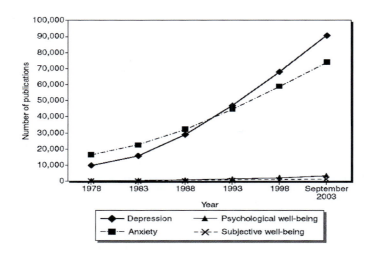

Figure 2. **Publication Trends 1978 - 2003 (Linley & Joseph, 2004a)**

Integral to ecological models of positive mental health outcomes must be a deeper appreciation for the interactions between cultural conditions within the various settings that influence human development and psychosocial functioning (Clauss-Ehlers, 2008). This view is echoed in a recent World Health Organization publication (WHO, 2009) promoting the view that social systems expose individuals to varying levels of resources or capital that determine the availability of protective factors to which the individual has access, from the macro level (policy and regulatory institutions), through the meso level (organizations and agencies with resources and power) and finally micro level (individuals, families and friends living in communities). At each level, the individual has access to various forms of capital, or psycho-social resources that promote and support adaptive functioning. The social relationships and social structures in individuals' lives provide social capital; cultural capital refers to resources produced and valued – based on norms and practices of a given culture; and psychological capital refers to levels or measures of psychological wellbeing or mental health including levels of self-efficacy, self-esteem, coping skills for managing stress, and psychological attachments. In combination, they provide the individual with "cultural health capital," defined by Shim (2010) as one's repertoire of cultural skills, interpersonal competencies, attitudes and behaviours, and interactional styles, cultivated by socializing agents and which, when deployed, may result in more optimal health.

Lower social and cultural capital is related to lower human capital (Furstenberg, 2006; Gannon, nd), and whilst elements of these capitals are widely investigated, the extent to which cultural capital equips the individual with "character strengths" or virtues that enable one to find meaning in adversity, recover from challenging circumstances (resilience) and experience thriving (human psychological growth), is poorly understood (Schensul, 2009). For example, the potential for activities such as singing and dancing that contribute to cultural life and determine resiliency pathways remains largely unexplored.

Peterson and Seligman's (2004) *Handbook and Classification of Character Strengths and Virtues* describes and classifies virtues and human strengths endorsed by almost every culture across the world (e.g., wisdom, courage, humanity, justice, temperance and transcendence), and now provides a well structured classification system from which empirical investigations into the associations between human, social and cultural capital can proceed (Seligman, Steen, Park & Peterson, 2005). However, we have much yet to learn about how these character strengths and virtues are developed, the relative parts they play in building our capacity for surviving and thriving, and the extent to which social and cultural forces influence their development and expression.

As an example, wellbeing is generally viewed as a description of a person's life situation (McGillivray, 2007) but it can also be defined according to national economic indicators such as gross domestic product (GDP), or in ecological terms as environmental degradation, both of which are described as "objective measures" (Conceição & Bandura, nd). Likewise, the term "quality of life" has been widely adopted by different disciplines, referring to subjective indicators such as wellbeing and satisfaction with life along with objective indicators like functional status (Galloway, 2005; Haas, 2007). Galloway notes the lack of consistency across a vast literature in which these constructs are defined as both uni- and multi-dimensional; as either subjective or a combination of the subjective and objective; and where distinctions are made between the cognitive and emotional, social, economic or environmental aspects of each. Additionally, the emerging literature now considers a raft of variables with potential to moderate or mediate the pathways contributing towards an individual's resilience.

Resilience as a social and behavioural construct

With a series of longitudinal studies beginning in 1953, Murphy and Moriarty (1976) provided one of the earliest psychological investigations of children's capacity to cope despite obstacles. Through tracking the responses to stress of 128 normal infants as they progressed into adolescence, they observed that there was considerable variation in children's thresholds for responsiveness to stressors, as well as the stage at which they began to draw on recovery factors, and the manner in which they were able to use these recovery factors. For example, some children displayed greater capacity than others for seeking and accepting help from the environment in order to master stressful life events, and some children were able to integrate life skills, such as help-seeking, quickly into their repertoire of coping resources whilst others needed to work hard at applying various life skills. Their conclusion was that a wide range of capacities developed during childhood (such as trust, autonomy and initiative) provides a kind of inoculation effect, but that resilience was a dynamic construct forever changing in response to external and internal conditions.

The next major development in this field came with Werner and Smith's publication of the findings from the Kauai Longitudinal Study in 1982. Similar to the earlier study, they found that children's capacity to master stage-specific developmental issues successfully was determined by the nature of their transactions with the environment over time. Werner and Smith realised that although children exposed to risk factors had a higher rate of adverse outcomes than the normal population, nonetheless, roughly about one third of young people succeeded and thrived regardless of the seriousness of the adversity. They began to study the factors that underlie resilience, or the capacity to thrive despite adversity, and whether it could be strengthened by deliberate strategies. In particular, they built on earlier sociological investigations of how interactions between environment (referred to as structural factors) and individual characteristics (referred to as agency factors) help to determine one's resilience at different life stages.

Since Werner and Smith's study, Garmezy, Masten, and Tellegen (1984) developed three models to explain the impact of stress on the quality of adaptation: the compensatory model, the challenge model, and the protective factor or immunity versus vulnerability model. They described a compensatory factor as a variable that has a direct and independent influence on a risk factor, thereby neutralizing it. Their challenge model proposed that a stressor (i.e., risk factor) provides a challenge that, when overcome, strengthens competence thereby becoming a potential enhancer of successful adaptation, provided the stressor is not excessive. Their third proposition was that protective factors may moderate the effect of exposure to risk thereby reducing the probability of a negative outcome; that is, resilience emerges from the synergy between risk and protective factors.

Bissonnette (1998) refers to an essential triplet of protective factors, including 1) the dispositional attributes of the individual such as autonomy and optimistic outlook; 2) familial characteristics such as positive styles of attachment and emotional support from at least one caregiver who encourages and reinforces mastery and accomplishment; and 3) external support factors such as a positive environments which may include aspects of cultural traditions. She argues that one's cognitive appraisals are determined by the extent of perceived control over events; commitment to find meaning in all of life's circumstances and events, as well as to enhance one's place in the world through serving others, and the capacity to cope with uncertainty and change as a form of challenge (Bissonnette, 1998).

Masten (1994, p. 5) integrated these models into an operational definition of resilience as "a pattern over time, characterized by good eventual adaptation despite developmental risk, acute stressors, or chronic adversities." The resilient person was characterized as one with various internal strengths or assets coupled with access to environmental resources such as supportive adults, collectively known as protective factors (Rutter, 1987; Garmezy, 1991; Gore & Eckenrode, 1994) which could be derived from:

> ➤ innate biologically mediated traits (Curtis & Cicchetti, 2003) such as the set point for mood level, a genetically determined range for the brain's metabolism of mood states or self-regulation (Lyubomirsky, in Reich, Zautra & Hall, 2010);
> ➤ access to mentors who facilitate the acquisition of a repertoire of learned competencies or coping life skills either through structured teaching or modelling (Rutter, 1987; Werner, 1994; Kinsella et al., 1996; Fuller, 1998; Nastasi & Bernstein, 1998; Bengal, Strittmatter & Willmann, 1999);
> ➤ cultural practices such as socialisation behaviours within families which determine attachment experiences, as well as broader systemically-based processes that affect self-regulation of arousal (e.g., mourning rituals, beliefs in spiritual figures that influence sense of safety and security and provide meaning and purpose in life) (Hughes et al., 2006; Brown, 2008; Nicolas et al., 2008; Yee et al., ND; Masten & Wright, in Reich, Zautra, & Hall, 2010).

Rutter's (1987) conclusion that an individual's resilience directly arises from the interplay between individual vulnerabilities ameliorated by internal or external protective factors after exposure to one or more risk factors, which in ordinary circumstances would lead to a maladaptive outcome, became the predominant definition for much of the next two decades. This can be seen in the burgeoning research during the 1980s and 1990s attempting to identify and classify biological and contextual threats linked to poor mental health outcomes, as well as defining the relative significance of singular life events, such as parental divorce or life-threatening illness, in comparison to situational stressors such as poverty (Gore & Eckenrode, 1994) or accumulated stressors or risk factors. Luthar's review aptly describes this development as the locus of resilience, acknowledging that an individual's resilience may be derived from external circumstances rather than solely from innate characteristics (Cicchetti & Cohen, 2006).

Luthar and Cicchetti's (2000) extensive research with vulnerable adolescents was important for its emphasis on the notion that resilience is not a fixed construct or by-product of "good" developmental pathways, but a dynamic process influenced by interactions between protective and vulnerability factors and an adversity condition in the environment. These include: acute or prolonged abuse, exposure to challenging socio-cultural factors such as social disadvantage, or extreme events such as natural disasters. Interestingly, the focus on contextually determined risk factors – those unique to specific settings such as families and neighbourhoods – had, by the beginning of the decade, established itself as dominant in psychological research with barely any attention given to investigating contextually determined protective factors, or those features of settings that enhanced human capacity for thriving and flourishing.

Most recently, several large-scale international studies have unequivocally demonstrated the importance of social environments for health and wellbeing, especially in relation to the formative influences of various dimensions of the social environment on children's physical and psychological health. For example, findings from the Health Behaviour of School-aged Children (HBSC) research project over the past 10 years confirm that the more diverse the mix of internal and external protective factors that can be accumulated, particularly through the adolescent years, the more likely young people are to be able to cope with adverse situations and, in some circumstances, thrive on them even when they live in poorer circumstances (Morgan et al, 2007, p.23). This claim has been supported by new streams of research that have evolved from socio-ecological models of health such as Antonovsky's (1987) theory of salutogenesis.

Antonovsky's research with Holocaust survivors isolated sets of indicators that differentiated people who survived seemingly unimaginable odds with relatively intact psychological wellbeing compared with those who experienced prolonged post-traumatic stress disorder. He proposed that regardless of the severity of the stressors, people develop the capacity for resilience by drawing on what he called "generalised resistance resources" (GRRs) (Antonovsky, 1987, p.19). He later defined GRRs as "property of a person, a collective or a situation … [that] facilitated successful coping with the inherent stressors of human existence" (Antonovsky, 1996, p.15).

This definition is consistent with theories of psychological health about the availability of human and social capital that look towards the resources, capacities, strengths and productive human investment of groups and societies. Luthans, Luthans and Luthans (2004) summarised these links between "positive psychological capital" (p. 46), which they define as comprising the four positive psychological capacities of confidence, hope, optimism, and resilience, and attainment of various beneficial outcomes including academic and work performance. Aspects of this finding have been consistently replicated in the literature, as illustrated in Fergusson's (2006) systematic review of children's wellbeing and social capital (resources derived from interpersonal relationships) recently acknowledged by the OECD report, *The Well-being of Nations: The Role of Human and Social Capital* (2001) as fundamental to the success of a nation.

The question remains, however, whether resilience (the capacity to "bounce back" adaptively in response to adversity) and thriving (the capacity for exponential growth as a consequence of adversity) are one and the same, and whether their developmental trajectories vary in accordance to a single adverse event, such as a natural disaster or life-threatening experience, compared with prolonged or persistent adversity such as chronic disability or membership of a minority group held in low regard by the dominant group(s).

According to Tedeschi and Calhoun (1995), the potential for positive change following trauma and adversity is determined by one's capacity for positive reappraisal of the circumstances (e.g., learned helplessness is replaced by learned optimism). Lepore and Revenson (2006) refer to this as "reconfiguration resilience" in which changes in an individual's cognitions, beliefs and behaviours following an adverse experience improved their participants' capacity to adapt more readily after subsequent challenges. Internal cognitive reprocessing of adverse events (e.g., finding meaning in life's circumstances through religion, spirituality or membership of a cultural or social movement), referred to as "cognitive switching" by Brown and Ryan (2003), is now recognised to have not only psychological benefits but also results in positive health outcomes including reductions in physiological arousal to stress (Lazarus & Folkman, 1984) as well as structural and functional brain changes. For example, a recent neuroimaging study showed that affect labelling (applying linguistic processing of the emotional aspects of an evocative image either by talking or writing) produces less amygdala activity than perceptual processing of the emotional aspects of the same image (Lieberman, et al., 2007). Put simply, talking or writing about feelings may dampen the response of the amygdala, thus helping to alleviate emotional distress.

Despite still being in its infancy, neuroimaging research offers scientific evidence that interventions based on cognitively reappraising life events or circumstances can not only alter thinking patterns but can also have an impact on brain circuitry and neurological structures associated with complex mental functions. Brown and Ryan (2003) in an associated discussion of "mindfulness training" define mindfulness as an inherent mental capacity to regulate attention intentionally upon consciousness and its contents, which may in turn "moderate the impact of potentially distressing psychological content through the mental operation of stepping back from thoughts, emotions, and sensations" (p.4). It is a process of cognitive switching. They claim that each of us has the potential to expand our capacity to use this technique and bring about new ways of perceiving and thinking about situations. Mindfulness training shows considerable potential for facilitating recovery and growth from extreme life events, often referred to as "adversarial growth" (Linley & Joseph, 2004; Tedeschi & Calhoun, 2004), and may play a part in resilience.

Resilience and post traumatic growth

There is a growing body of literature on growth experiences in the aftermath of traumatic events known as Post Traumatic Growth (PTG). Fredrickson, Tugade, Waugh and Larkin (2003) found that for some individuals, trauma fuels thriving, a construct gaining significance within the positive psychology movement and which seems to share phenomenological characteristics with PTG. But opinions remain mixed concerning the place of resilience in relation to both PTG and thriving (Hobfoll et al.(2009). In addition, no explanation has yet been proposed for the various trajectories that individuals follow after exposure to trauma or adversity, and the extent to which thriving or languishing can be influenced by contextual factors such as cultural practices, beliefs or values.

Jang and LaMendola (2007) investigated post traumatic growth in a collectivist culture, using the Chinese version of the Post Traumatic Growth Inventory (PTGI) to investigate 640 Taiwanese survivors of "921," a devastating earthquake with a magnitude of 7.6 on the Richter scale that occurred on September 21 (hence "921"), 1999. The earthquake caused 2,423 deaths and 11,305 injuries, and more than 100,000 people were left homeless. Taiwan displays a collectivist culture strongly influenced by religious traditions and spirituality where notions of living harmoniously with nature are a predominant way of life, and natural disasters are generally considered the will of the gods. In addition to the

PTGI, 28 individuals including 16 survivors, six service providers, and six volunteers, most of whom reported loss of loved ones or property damage, were interviewed to find out whether or not they reported religious affiliation, a measure of spirituality, before and after the 921 Earthquake. Spirituality, which is reported to be a critical component of PTG (Pargament, Desai, & McConnell, in Calhoun & Tedeschi, 2006), was measured by participant reports of continuous religious affiliation. Those who reported continuous religious affiliation scored significantly higher on the PTGI than those who reported no religious affiliation, t (496) = 4.63, p<.01, thereby confirming their hypothesis that spirituality has a significant relationship to post traumatic growth. This conclusion should be considered cautiously given that no comparison group of individualistic cultural background was used. Nevertheless, future research should pay heed to cultural traditions and the extent to which protective factors derived from traditional cultural values and practices can influence resilience and its variations (such as PTG).

In some circumstances, such as prolonged hardship associated with war, various cultural factors may influence PTG through the meaning ascribed to the adverse event. In such cases, the combined effects of duration of exposure and cultural significance may contribute to psychological outcomes. Hobfoll et al., (2009) provide the first longitudinal examination of trajectories of resilience and resistance to terrorist-related trauma with a cohort of Jews and Arabs in Israel. They differentiate between four possible trajectories following trauma: the chronic distress trajectory characterised by varying and persistent levels of distress; the delayed distress trajectory characterized by initial resistance that subsides and gives way to persistent distress; the resilience trajectory characterized by initial symptoms followed by rapid recovery to a relatively stable, healthy level of psychological functioning; and finally the resistance trajectory that refers to individuals who never develop symptoms of disorder. Resistance may provide some individuals who are pre-disposed, through genetic structure and/or environmental interventions, with the capacity to thrive in the face of adversity, although one may assume that the cultural significance or meaning ascribed to the adversity has a moderating effect. They found that some cultural factors, for example, being Jewish (ethnicity) and secular rather than traditionally religious, increased the likelihood of exhibiting the resistance trajectory with higher resistance associated with lower PTG. In addition, some social capital indicators (having majority status, higher income, and greater social support from friends) also contributed to resistance and resilience trajectories, which could be assumed to affect wellbeing.

Although Hall, Hobfoll, Canetti, Johnson, Palmieri & Galea (2010) found no link between wellbeing and post traumatic growth, the significant question here is whether the PTG-promoting events (or protective factors) were available before or after the trauma, and the extent to which these protective factors were related to more meaningful conditions such as religious beliefs or cultural values. Evidence that PTG is predicted, to some extent, by exposure post trauma to positive events and processes comes from Linley and Joseph's review (2004b), although this is not consistent with Hobfoll's (2007) finding of little or no benefit arising from prolonged attempts to find meaning or to thrive in the face of sustained traumatic experiences such as warfare. Furthermore, the part played by subjective wellbeing as a moderating variable and the extent to which cultural capital contributes to subjective wellbeing needs further investigation. Some evidence suggests that music and artistic activities promote health and subjective wellbeing or perceived quality of life (Kim & Kim, 2009).   Therefore, it would seem reasonable to conclude that cultural practices involving music, art and other creative outlets such as writing following adversity has potential to foster PTG and possibly strengthen resilience, although the only research of this to date has been within collectivist cultures.

Positive psychology, wellbeing and resilience

The role of subjective appraisals, such as wellbeing and quality of life, in the development of resilience was shown to be significant as a means of shifting attention to life's positives (cognitive shifting) and attainment of positive outcomes (goal orientation) by Sin and Lyubomirsky's (2009) meta-analysis of evidence-based interventions for fostering positive psychological resources. They found significant relationships between positive psychological strategies and enhanced wellbeing across forty-nine independent studies totalling 4,235 participants. In this meta-analysis, wellbeing was defined as positive feelings, positive behaviours, and positive cognitions including hedonic wellbeing (positive affect, life satisfaction, happiness), and eudaimonic wellbeing (self-acceptance, positive relations, autonomy, purpose in life). Effect sizes ranged from -.31 to .84 with 96% in the predicted direction. Their conclusion that positively oriented life-enhancing strategies benefit people is consistent with the resiliency literature of the 1980s and 1990s, (Werner & Smith, 1982;

Rutter, 1987; Masten, 1994), and the concept of "hardiness" that was originally proposed by Kobassa (1979).

Maginness (2007) has identified five streams of resiliency research including the developmental model, personality theories including hardiness and sense of coherence, biological models encompassing environmental influences on brain function, the positive psychology approach with flow theory and learned optimism, and the post traumatic growth model. Her study supported the notion that certain personality characteristics – easy temperament, humour, internal locus of control and interpersonal reserve – are common to individuals high in resiliency. Other characteristics, such as having the capacity to respond flexibly, to be persistent in searching for solutions to the situational demands and effective in decision-making, contributed to positive outcomes from challenging experiences. She referred to these as adaptive mechanisms and the ability to be proactive in finding meaning in adversity, such as using positive reframing of the problem to foster optimism or future-focus. Finally, she identified three motivational systems as significant – the appetitive, defensive and attentional systems. These are characterised by approach behaviour (meeting challenges head-on), an ability to put anxiety aside to respond to the situation at hand despite heightened arousal states, and secure early attachment relationships, which seemed to enhance neurological self-regulation. Six factors emerged from her research: reduced reactivity and recovery rates to stressors; effective and efficient responses to stressors; beliefs about self and world explanatory of the stressors; and confirming that resilience is a complex construct that cannot be explained by one model alone (p. 167). It is worth noting that she contextualises her model as a set of adaptive prosocial skills which evolve within the cultural context.

Unfortunately, few studies have considered the potential mediating roles of variables such as cultural belief systems on the subjective interpretations of traumatic events or the PTG trajectory, the contextual determinants of resilience, or the interactive and/or mediating effects of such variables within complex social systems. Hofstede's (2001) exploration of the differences in thinking and social action that exist among members of more than 50 modern nations has clearly established that social institutions such as the family and schools reinforce the value systems of their culture. These value systems are developed in early childhood and are expressed as the different values that predominate among people from different countries. The dominant value systems of each nation (the "national culture") are claimed to affect how people think, feel and act in response to external circumstances (Hofstede, 2001).

One of the few investigations of resilience in which these cultural distinctions were considered was Grotberg's (1995) International Resilience Project, which set out to learn what approaches are used by parents in 14 different cultures to promote resilience: do they draw on the same pool of resilience factors, or do they vary in the combinations of factors used to build children's capacity to withstand adversity? This groundbreaking study clearly identified relationships between culture and resilience factors. Although the number of responses per country was too small to determine cultural variations by country, Grotberg found that some cultures rely more on faith than on problem solving in facing adversity. Some cultures are more concerned with punishment and guilt while others readily discipline and reconcile. Some cultures expect children to be more dependent on others for help in adversity rather than becoming autonomous and more self-reliant.

These findings have more recently been recognised by Clauss-Ehlers (2008) who found that individuals engage a range of coping strategies that include coping through accessing socio-cultural supports in response to stressful life experiences. Adaptive coping (ACP) was positively correlated with use of unique socio-cultural supports (SCS) (r = .34, p<.01), which she defined as "socio-cultural coping" (p. 207). The cultural milieu, perhaps through storytelling, music, dance and mythology teaches the individual about socially and culturally relevant stressors, and how to attain his or her goals to respond adaptively and to enhance functionality (that is, to attain post traumatic growth). In the broad sense, evidence is beginning to form that indicates resilience has a socio-ecological foundation, and determinants at this level should be factored in to any discussions of this construct.

Socio-ecological models of human resilience

As noted at the start of this chapter, the notion of mental health protective factors derived from socio-cultural resources is not new, but it has recently gained credence as a result of its adoption by the WHO (Friedli, 2009). Growing out of Bronfenbrenner's (1977) ecological systems theory, the interactions between organisms and their environments are now widely acknowledged as determinants of health outcomes. Several streams of research investigating the contextual (or settings-based) processes that shape individual and population health status reflect the increasing interest in this model, which include the development of cultural change strategies to foster environmental conditions that support better health and optimise human wellbeing (Stokols, 1996). Numerous empirical studies have supported Bronfenbrenner's socio-ecological approach (Seeman & McEwan, 1996; Yen & Syme, 1999; Stahl & Rutten, 2000), a point clearly made in the recent WHO publication that provides an excellent summary of the evidence (WHO, 2009).

According to this framework, attainment of developmental potential is largely determined by the combined effects of accrued risks to which one is exposed (both innate and contextual), and those protective factors to which one has access and which may buffer those risks (Antonovsky, 1987; Alvarez-Dardet & Ashton, 2005). Whilst the environment can function as a source of danger or risk, it can also enable health behaviours, for example, by instituting laws requiring risk minimisation such as seatbelt wearing, and providing access to health resources such as primary health care. "Resilient locations" (WHO, 2009, p. 23), those settings that rate highly on health indicators relative to economic resources, weaken the impact of other contextual risk factors, which explains why poverty is more damaging to health in some contexts than in others. One such example involves communities with high levels of social capital, measured by norms of trust, reciprocity and participation that are known to provide a mental health buffering effect for individual health deficits (Friedli, 2009). In addition, mounting evidence suggests that the often-overlooked socio-ecological dimension of cultural capital may play an equally significant role in arming the individual as well as communities with protective resources essential for recovery and growth from adversity.

Although there have been many studies investigating the interactive effects between the components of resilience and various forms of capital, for example, human capital (such as parenting style) and social capital (such as quality of the local neighbourhood), there has been little attention paid to the cultural determinants of resilience (Ungar, 2005). Ungar has drawn attention to the lack of cultural relevance in both research design and interpretation of findings besetting much of the contemporary research on resilience. The Eurocentric dominance in the research has been criticised by Smith (2006) who questioned the relevance of theoretical models that are said to be universal explanations of the phenomenon without consideration of the implications arising from cultural socialisation practices. He argues that individuals are embedded within their societies, which inevitably play a substantial part in overall socialisation, and that cultural determinants play a primary role in the meaning ascribed to various contextual phenomena.

This point is clearly made by Grotberg's (1997) research in which clear cultural distinctions were found in resilience-promoting parenting strategies employed within Armenian, Namibian and Sudanese families. Whilst her three culturally distinct samples identified common facets of the notion of resilience as an important outcome for their children, the socialisation styles adopted to achieve this outcome varied widely, suggesting a significant influence of cultural determinants on the perception of resilience. It seems apparent that interactions between individuals and the many settings in which they operate form a type of fingerprint that differentiates one society from another, reflected in the society's culture (defined as customs, traditions, and the beliefs of the family and community), which ultimately determines psychosocial wellbeing and developmental maturation. Therefore, no discussion of resilience would be complete without consideration of key socialising settings and the part they play in shaping factors underpinning wellbeing and thriving (such as schools in developed nations).

Cultural capital within socio-ecological contexts - schools as a source of resilience

A number of studies of the part played by schools in promoting children's resilience have focused on contextual variables such as the school culture (Stewart, Sun, Patterson, Lemerle, & Hardie, 2004; Lemerle, 2005; Sun & Stewart, 2007). Most notable has been the Health Promoting Schools (HPS) approach which grew out of the World Health Organization's Global School Health Initiative in 1995. The distinguishing features of a Health Promoting School (HPS) are that it embraces a socio-ecological model of health and considers this essential for educational attainment; it integrates interventions that target multiple levels at which change occurs including school curriculum, management and policy-making, ethos, relationships and communication between all stakeholders (Weare & Markham, 2005). Socio-cultural differences between schools embracing the HPS model and those not doing so were shown by Lemerle's (2005) study, which compared responses from 468 teachers in 20 schools actively implementing the HPS approach with a control sample of 386 teachers in 19 schools rated low on HPS indicators. Mean scores on eleven school organisational health variables and four social capital variables were higher in the HPS schools (p < .001) (Table 1).

Table 1: Comparison of Organisational Health Variables in High and Low Health Promoting Schools.

	Low HPS (Mean)	High HPS (Mean)	t	df	p (2-tailed)
School Organisational Health Dimensions:					
School Morale	61.1	68.8	-5.17	797	.001
Supportive Leadership	62.5	70.8	-3.87	794	.001
Decision Authority	10.6	11.3	-4.86	798	.001
Macro Decision Authority	19.3	20.0	-3.15	798	.001
Role Clarity	65.2	69.1	-2.11	804	.04
Co Worker Support	22.0	23.2	-4.75	798	.001
Appreciation	48.8	54.5	-3.11	789	.001
Professional Growth	58.6	64.4	-3.60	806	.001
Goal Congruity	62.5	69.0	-4.08	806	.001
Curriculum Co-ordination	59.3	64.9	-3.31	804	.001
Student Orientation	74.9	79.7	-2.92	809	.001
Social Capital Dimensions:					
Value for Life	7.2	7.5	-3.12	799	.001
Social Proactivity	24.1	25.1	-3.39	798	.001
Trust	16.1	16.9	-3.15	790	.001
Tolerance for Diversity	7.1	7.5	-3.53	798	.001

Furthermore, differences in teachers' self-reported wellbeing and job commitment were found. For general self-rated mental health, 25.7% of teachers in High HPS reported "no problems" compared with 19.7% in Low HPS. Independent samples of t-tests indicated that differences between means for Psychosomatic Strain were statistically significant (t = 2.15, p = .03) between the two sets of schools. Teachers from High HPS reported less Psychosomatic Strain (Mean High HPS = 19.03, Mean Low HPS = 19.98). Reports of daily mental health problems were three times higher for teachers in low HPS schools (3.9% in Low HPS) compared with those in the high HPS sample (1.1% with daily problems in High HPS).

Whilst not collecting specific measures of resilience in teachers, this study provides evidence of contextual variables that are associated with a more resilience-enhancing culture in schools that are health promoting. The extent to which teachers' resilience is correlated with students' resilience is yet to be examined, but it is reasonable to extrapolate the findings from a similar program in the United States (Bernat, 2009) in which teachers' attitudes were found to be positively associated with students' resilience.

Results from this study suggest that teachers in schools that actively adopt the HPS approach are generally more resilient given their better mental health commitment to the job and overall self-rated health and wellbeing. This, in turn, can establish a "virtuous loop" or positive feedback system whereby the adoption of a specific set of organisational practices enhances various teacher outcomes associated with resilience, and this in turn has a resilience-enhancing effect on the students as has been clearly demonstrated by Stewart et al. (2005). In their study, 2580 students from Years 3, 5, and 7 (ages 8, 10, 12 years), 1291 parents/caregivers, and 422 school staff completed a HPS scale, student resilience scale, student protective factor scale and parents/caregivers social environment scale. Multivariate analysis of variances showed that HPS practices has significant effects on the students' self-rated resilience (F = 2.33, p <.01), protective factors (F = 2.83, p <.001) and perceptions of the school environment (F = 4.06, p < .001).

Our conclusions from these various studies are that organisational practices within schools indeed have the potential to profoundly influence the cultural environment of the school, which is associated with resilience in both the staff and the students. That being said, the pathways of influence between teachers, students, and other potential mediating variables such as parents' resilience and family climate have yet to be determined, particularly in relation to other cultural dimensions that might be operating such as curriculum content (for example, specific resilience-building programs that may have a direct influence as well as indirect influences such as cross-cultural traditions practiced within the school setting).

Conclusions

In the discussion above relating to individual development, PTG and the socio-ecological settings in which people live, a significant, yet possibly overlooked component of contemporary research into the developmental influences on resilience relates to cultural capital. Furthermore, as the research reviewed here indicates, the relative influences of various social and cultural determinants of post-traumatic growth are yet to be elucidated. The extent to which resilience and PTG operate along the same continuum and whether this varies according to social and cultural capital indicators is yet to be fully understood. A great deal more understanding is also needed to identify structural elements within social networks that optimise the resilience-promoting capacity of settings most likely to have a developmental impact on children and adults, among them, not only features of organisational or institutional practices, but also deeper elements of the embedded culture of the setting.

In this chapter we have reviewed the emergence of resilience as a field of study within the positive psychology movement, and we raise a number of questions related to the praxis, or the practical application of resilience theory. We have been particularly interested in young people and it is now firmly established in both Australian as well as international literature that the school environment is potentially a powerful influence on children's development of resilience (Wong et al., 2009). However a great deal more needs to be understood about the socio-cultural determinants of resilience within the school setting.

Whilst schools have access to a plethora of "resilience-building" programs and resources that aim or claim to be beneficial for promoting youth resilience (Bernard, 2004; Claxton, 2004; Fuller, 2001; Reivich & Shatte, 2003), many have not been subjected to rigorous standards of evaluation. We have found that many interventions employ only evaluations that are descriptive and formative in nature (AUSEINET, 1999). They depend on assumptions that have yet to be tested, for example, we found that many resilience-building programs targeting young people pay little if any heed to children's ethnicity and hence cultural traditions and values that might be challenged or undermined in the program. By promoting sets of competencies considered universally essential for resilience without consideration of their social or cultural relevance, these interventions may even undermine a child's existing repertoire of psychological, social or cultural assets being used to respond adaptively to challenging life conditions by assuming that only "western" life skills or traditions have meaning or value. This inevitably poses problems particularly for a diverse society such as Australia with a population of people from over 200 countries speaking more than 300 different languages, including Indigenous languages (DIAC 2007).

Additionally, many school-based programs fail to consider socio-cultural factors embedded within the school as a social system (for example, the relevance and meaning of school discipline policies in the context of a multicultural school population; or the relevance of music, art, dance, drama or song across the entire way of life of a community) or those external socio-cultural factors (such as family and neighbourhood social climate) that interact with the school environment.

We suggest that prevailing contemporary models of resilience ignore the reality that life skills are not universal but are determined by differing circumstances that present unique sets of risk and protective factors. There are various ways in which individuals respond to adversity depending on many uncontrollable or unpredictable contextual factors, such as social and cultural conditions and values, or the culturally-bound explanatory models of health associated with cultural identity. The type of adversity to which one is exposed, combined with one's interpretation of events or the meaning ascribed to them, determine the types of life skills necessary to adaptively traverse that experience, whilst also determining the specific forms of capital that may be accrued as a consequence of the experience itself (Lawford & Eiser, 2001). We propose that considerably more attention needs to be paid to such factors in both modelling explanatory frameworks for resilience, as well as applying these in the development of interventions designed to foster it.

References

Alvarez-Dardet, C. & Ashton, J R. (2005). Saluting good health. Journal of Epidemiology and Community Health, 59, 437.

Antonovsky, A. (1987). *Unravelling the Mystery of Health.* San Francisco: Jossey-Bass Publishers.

Antonovsky, A. (1996). The salutogenic model as a theory to guide health promotion. Health Promotion International, 11, 1, 11-18.

AUSEINET: The Australian Early Intervention Network for Mental Health in Young People. National Stocktake of Prevention and Early Intervention Programs – November 1999. Retrieved from http://auseinet.flinders.edu.au/resources/auseinet/stocktake2/st2_chapt 6.pdf

Beck A.T. (1991). Cognitive therapy: a 30-year retrospective. American Psychologist, 46,4, 368–375.

Bengal, J., Strittmatter, R. & Willmann, H. (1999). What Keeps People Healthy? The Current State of Discussion and the Relevance of

Antonovsky's Salutogenic Model of Health. Cologne, Federal Centre for Health Education.

Berkman, L. F. & Kawachi, I. (2000). *Social Epidemiology*. New York: Oxford University Press.

Bernard, M. (2004). *You Can Do It! Education*. Retrieved from http://youcandoit.com.au

Bernat, F. P. (2009). Youth resilience: Can schools enhance youth factors for hope, optimism and success? Women & Criminal Justice, 19, 3, 251 -266.

Bissonnette, M. (1998). Optimism, Hardiness, and Resiliency: A Review of the Literature. Prepared for the Child and Family Partnership Project. Retrieved from http://www.reachinginreachingout.com/documents/Optimism%20Hard iness%20and%20Resiliency.pdf

Bonanno, G. A., Galea, S., Bucciarelli, A. & Vlahov, D. (2007). What predicts psychological resilience after disaster? The role of demographics, resources, and life stress. *Journal of Consulting and Clinical Psychology*, 75, 671–682.

Bronfenbrenner, U. (1977). Toward an experimental ecology of human development. *American Psychologist*, July: 513-531.

—. (1979). *The ecology of human development: Experiments by nature and design*. Cambridge, MA: Harvard University Press.

—. (1994). Ecological Models of Human Development. In *International Encyclopedia of Education* Vol 3 (2nd Ed.). Oxford: Elsevier.

Brown, D. L. (2008). African American resiliency: examining racial socialization and social support as protective factors. *Journal of Black Psychology,* 34, 32-48.

Brown, K.W. & Ryan, R.M. (2003). The benefits of being present: Mindfulness and its role in psychological wellbeing. *Journal of Personality and Social Psychology*, 84, 4,822–848.

Calhoun, L. G. & Tedeschi, R.G. (2006). Handbook of Post Traumatic Growth. New Jersey: Lawrence Erlbaum.

Clauss-Ehlers, C.S. (2008). Sociocultural factors, resilience, and coping: Support for a culturally sensitive measure of resilience. *Journal of Applied Developmental Psychology*, 29, 197–212.

Claxton, G. (2004). Building learning power. Challenge: Public Service for the 21st Century. Retrieved from http://www.ps21.gov.sg/challenge/2004_08/ministries/building.html

Conceição, P. & Bandura, R. (ND). Measuring Subjective Wellbeing: A Summary Review of the Literature. United Nations Development Programme (UNDP). Retrieved from

http://www.undp.org/developmentstudies/docs/subjective_wellbeing_c
onceicao_bandura.pdf

Curtis, W.J. & Cicchetti. D. (2003). Moving research on resilience into the
21st century: theoretical and methodological considerations in
examining the biological contributors to resilience. *Development and
Psychopathology*, 15, 773-810.

DIAC Annual Report 2006-07. Retrieved from
http://www.immi.gov.au/about/reports/annual/200607/html/outcome2/
output2_4.htm

Eriksson, M. & Lindstrom, B. (2007). Antonovsky's sense of coherence
scale and its relation with quality of life: a systematic review. *Journal
of Epidemiology & Community Health*, 61,11, 938-944.

Ferguson, K. M. (2006). Social capital and children's wellbeing: a critical
synthesis of the international social capital literature. *International
Journal of Social Welfare*, 15, 2–18.

Foley D.L, Eaves L.J., Wormley B., Silberg J.L., Maes, H.H., Kuhn J, et
al. (2004). Childhood adversity, monoamine oxidase A genotype, and
risk for conduct disorder. *Archives of General Psychiatry*, 61, 738–
744.

Fredrickson, B., Tugade, M. M., Waugh, C. E. & Larkin, G. R. (2003).
What good are positive emotions in crises? A prospective study of
resilience and emotions following the terrorist attacks on the United
States on September 11th, 2001. *Journal of Personality and Social
Psychology*, 84, 365–376.

Friedli, Lynne. (2009). Mental health, resilience and inequalities. WHO
Regional Office for Europe. Retrieved from
http://www.capacity.org.uk/downloads/mental_health_inequalties.pdf

Fuller, A. (1998). From surviving to thriving: Promoting mental health in
young people. Melbourne: ACER Press.

—. (2001). Creating Resilient Learners. *Learning Matters*, 6, 3, 22- 25.

Furstenberg, F. F. (2006). Diverging Development: The Not-so-Invisible
Hand of Social Class in the United States. Paper presented at the
biennial meetings of the Society for Research on Adolescence, San
Francisco, CA, March 23-26, 2006. Retrieved from
http://transad.pop.upenn.edu/downloads/invisiblehand_final.rev.pdf

Galloway, S. (2005). Quality of Life and well-being: measuring the
benefits of culture and sport: Literature review and thinkpiece. Report
of the Scottish Executive Social Research. Retrieved from
http://www.scotland.gov.uk/Publications/2006/01/13110743/23

Gannon, T.N. (ND). Tangled webs in which they weave: social contexts
and adolescent mental health. Ph.D. Dissertation Proposal prepared for

the CHAS/Health Economics Workshop, Department of Sociology, University of Chicago. Retrieved from http://chess.bsd.uchicago.edu/ccehpe/hew_papers/winter_2005/Ganno n.pdf

Ganzel, B.L., Kim, P. Glover, G. H. & Temple, E. (2008). Resilience after 9/11: multimodal neuroimaging evidence for stress-related change in the healthy adult brain. *NeuroImage*, 40, 788–795.

Garmezy, N. (1991). Resiliency and vulnerability to adverse developmental outcomes associated with poverty. *American Behavioral Scientist*, 34, 4, 416-430.

Garmezy, N., Masten, A.S. & Tellegen, A. (1984). The study of stress and competence in children: a building block for developmental psychopathology. *Child Development*, 55, 1, 97-111.

Gore, S. & Eckenrode, J. (1994). Context and process in research on risk and resilience. In R. J. Haggerty, L. R. Sherrod, N. Garmezy, & M. Rutter (Eds.), *Stress, Risk, and Resilience in Children and Adolescents: Processes, Mechanisms, and Interventions* (pp. 19-63). New York: Cambridge University Press.

Grotberg, E. H. (1995). A Guide to Promoting Resilience in Children: Strengthening the Human Spirit. From the Early Childhood Development: Practice and Reflections series, Bernard Van Leer Foundation. Retrieved from http://resilnet.uiuc.edu/library/grotb95b.html

—. (1997). The International Resilience Project. Paper presented at the Annual Convention of the International Council of Psychologists, 55th, Graz, Austria July 14-18, 1997.

Hancock, T. (2001). People, partnerships and human progress: building community capital. *Health Promotion International*, 16, 3, 275-280.

Haas, B. (2007). Clarification and integration of similar Quality of Life concepts. *Journal of Nursing Scholarship*, 31, 3, 215 – 220.

Hobfoll, S. E., Hall, B. J., Canetti-Nisim, D., Galea, S., Johnson, R. J. & Palmieri, P. (2007). Refining our understanding of traumatic growth in the face of terrorism: moving from meaning cognitions to doing what is meaningful. *Applied Psychology: An International Journal*, 56, 345–366.

Hobfoll, S.E., Palmieri, P., Johnson, R.J., Canetti-Nisim, D., Hall, B.J. & Galea, S. (2009). Trajectories of resilience, resistance, and distress during ongoing terrorism: the case of Jews and Arabs in Israel. *Journal of Consulting and Clinical Psychology*, 77, 1, 138–148.

Hofstede, G. (2001). Culture's consequences: comparing values, behaviours, institutions and organizations across nations. California: Sage Publications.

Hughes, D., Rodriguez, J., Smith, E.P., Johnson, D.J., Stevenson, H.C. & Spicer, P. (2006). Parents' ethnic–racial socialization practices: A review of research and directions for future study. *Developmental Psychology*, 42, 5,747–770.

Jang,Li-ju & LaMendola, W. F. (2007). Social work in natural disasters: The case of spirituality and post-traumatic growth. *Advances in Social Work*, 8, 2, 305-316.

Kim, S. & Kim, H. (2009). Does cultural capital matter? Cultural divide and quality of life. *Social Indicators Research*, 93, 295–313.

Kinsella, K., Anderson, R. & Anderson, W. (1996) Coping skills, strengths and needs as perceived by adult offspring and siblings of people with mental illness: A retrospective study. *Psychiatric Rehabilitation Journal*, 20, 24-32.

Kobassa S.C. (1979). Stressful life events, personality, and health: an inquiry into hardiness. *Journal of Personality and Social Psychology*, 37, 1, 1-11.

Kobassa, S. C., Maddi, S. R. & Kahn, S. (1982). Hardiness and health: a prospective study. *Journal of Personality and Social Psychology*, 42, 168-177.

Lazarus, R. & Folkman, S. (1984). *Stress, Appraisal, and Coping*. New York: Springer.

Lemerle, K. (2005). Evaluating the Impact of the School Environment on Teachers' Health and Job Commitment: Is the Health Promoting School a Healthier Workplace? School of Public Health, Queensland University of Technology, Brisbane. Unpublished PhD thesis.

Lerner, R.M., Dowling, E.M. & Anderson, P.M. (2003). Positive youth development: Thriving as the basis of personhood and civil society. *Applied Developmental Science*, 7, 3, 172–180.

Lieberman, M.D. et al. (2007). Putting feelings into words: affect labeling disrupts amygdala activity in response to affective stimuli. *Psychological Sciences*, 18, 421–428.

Linley, P.A. & Joseph, S. (2004a). Applied positive psychology: A new perspective for professional practice. In P.A. Linley & S. Joseph (Eds.), *Positive Psychology in Practice* (pp. 3-12). Hoboken, NJ: Wiley.

Linley P. A. & Joseph, S. (2004b). Positive change following trauma and adversity: a review. *Journal of Traumatic Stress*, 17, 1, 11–21.

Luthans, F., Luthans, K. W. and Luthans, B. C. (2004). Positive psychological capital: going beyond human and social capital. *Business Horizons,* 47, 45–50.

Luthar, S. (2006). Resilience in development: a synthesis of research across five decades. In Cicchetti, D. & Cohen, D.J. (Ed.), *Developmental Psychopathology*, Vol 3: Risk, disorder, and adaptation (2nd ed.). Hoboken, NJ, US: John Wiley & Sons.

Luthar, S. & Cicchetti, D. (2000). The construct of resilience: implications for interventions and social policies. *Development and Psychopathology*, 12, 857-885.

Maginness, A. (2007). The development of resilience - a model. Thesis submitted for the degree of Doctor of Philosophy in Psychology, University of Canterbury, June 2007. Retrieved from http://ir.canterbury.ac.nz/bitstream/10092/1443/1/thesis_fulltext.pdf

Masten, A. (1994). Resilience in individual development: Successful adaptation despite risk and adversity. In M. C. Wang and E. W. Gordon (Eds.), *Educational resilience in inner-city America: Challenges and Prospects* (pp. 141-149). Hillsdale, NJ: Lawrence Erlbaum.

McGillivray, M. (2007). Human Well-being: Issues, Concepts and Measures. In Mark McGillivray (Ed.), *Human Well-Being: Concept and Measurement*. Basingstoke, UK: Palgrave MacMillan.

Morgan, A., Currie, C., Due, P., Gabhain, S.N., Rasmussen, M., Samdal, O. & Smith, R. (2007). Mental well-being in school-aged children in Europe: associations with social cohesion and socioeconomic circumstances. WHO Background Briefing Paper. Retrieved from http://www.euro.who.int/document/sed/hbsc_forum_2007_mental_well-being.pdf

Murphy, L. B. & Moriarty, A. E. (1976). *Vulnerability, coping and growth from infancy to adolescence*. Oxford, England: Yale University Press.

Nastasi, B. & Bernstein, R. (1998). Mini-series: Resilience applied the promise and pitfalls of school-based resilience programs. *School Psychology Review*, 27, 3, 217-32.

Nicolas, G., Helms, J. E., Jernigan, M. M., Sass, T., Skrzypek, A. & DeSilva, A. M. (2008). A conceptual framework for understanding the strengths of black youths. *Journal of Black Psychology,* 34, 3, 261-280.

OECD Centre for Educational Research and Innovation (2001). The Well-being of Nations: The Role of Human and Social Capital. Retrieved from http://www.oecd.org/dataoecd/36/40/33703702.pdf

Park, N. & Huebner, E.S. (2005). A cross-cultural study of the levels and correlates of life satisfaction among adolescents. *Journal of Cross-Cultural Psychology*, 36, 4, 444-456.

Peterson, C. & Seligman, M.E.P. (2004). *Character Strengths and Virtues: A Handbook and Classification*. Oxford University Press: New York.

Reich, J. W., Zautra, A. J. & Hall, J. S. (2010). *Handbook of Adult Resilience*. New York: The Guildford Press.

Reivich, K. & Shatte, A. (2003). The resilience factor: 7 key ways to finding your inner strength and overcoming life's hurdles. USA: Broadway Books.

Rutter M. (1979). Protective factors in children's responses to stress and disadvantage. *Annals of the Academy of Medicine Singapore,* 8, 3, 324-38.

—. (1987). Psychosocial resilience and protective mechanisms. *American Journal of Orthopsychiatry,* 57, 316-31.

Schensul, J. J. (2009). Community, culture and sustainability in multilevel dynamic systems intervention science. *American Journal of Community Psychology*, 43, 241–256.

Schui, G. & Krampen, G. (2010). Bibliometric analyses on the emergence and present growth of positive psychology. *Applied Psychology: Health and Wellbeing*, 2, 1, 52–64.

Seeman, T. E. & McEwan, B. S. (1996). Impact of social environment characteristics on neuroendocrine regulation. *Psychosomatic Medicine*, 58, 459-471.

Seligman, M.E.P., Steen, T.A., Park, N. & Petersen, C. (2005). Positive psychology progress: empirical validation of interventions. *American Psychologist*, 60, 5, 410–421.

Shim, J.K. (2010). Cultural health capital: a theoretical approach to understanding health care interactions and the dynamics of unequal treatment. *Journal of Health & Social Behavior*, 51, 1, 1-15.

Sin, N. L. & Lyubomirsky, S. (2009). Enhancing well-being and alleviating depressive symptoms with positive psychology interventions: A practice-friendly meta-analysis. *Journal of Clinical Psychology*, 65, 5, 467-487.

Stahl, T. & Rutten, A. (2000). The importance of the social environment for physically active lifestyle - results from an international study. Social Science and Medicine, 52, 1-10.

Stewart, D. E., Sun, J. & Patterson, C. R. (2005). Comprehensive Health Promotion in the School Community: The "Resilient Children and Communities' Project. Paper presented at the "Engaging Communities' Conference, Brisbane, Australia. Retrieved from http://www.engagingcommunities2005.org/abstracts/Stewart-Donald-final.pdf#search=%22%22resilient%20children%20and%20communiti es%22%22

Stewart, D., Sun, J., Patterson, C., Lemerle, K. & Hardie, M. (2004). Promoting and building resilience in primary school communities: Evidence from a comprehensive "health promoting school" approach. *International Journal of Mental Health Promotion*, 6, 3, 26-33.

Stokols, D. (1996). Translating social ecological theory into guidelines for community health promotion. *American Journal of Health Promotion*, 10, 4, 282-298.

Sun, J. & Stewart, D. (2007). How effective is the health-promoting school approach in building social capital in primary schools? *Health Education*, 107, 6, 556-574.

Tarter, R.E. and Vanyukov, M. (1999). In Maginness, A. (2007). The development of resilience - a model. Thesis submitted for the degree of Doctor of Philosophy in Psychology, University of Canterbury, June 2007, p. 11. Retrieved from
http://ir.canterbury.ac.nz/bitstream/10092/1443/1/thesis_fulltext.pdf

Tedeschi R.G. & Calhoun L.G. (1995). *Trauma and Transformation: Growing in the Aftermath of Suffering*. Thousand Oaks, CA; Sage Publications.

Tedeschi, R. G. & Calhoun, L. G. (2004). Posttraumatic growth: conceptual foundations and empirical evidence. *Psychological Inquiry*, 15, 1–18.

Ungar, M. (2005). Nurturing Hidden Resilience in At-Risk Youth in Different Cultures. Paper presented at the joint AACAP/CACAP Meeting, Toronto, October 2005.

Weare, K. & Markham, W. (2005). What do we know about promoting mental health through schools? *IUHPE Promotion and Education*, 12, 3-4, 14-18.

Werner, E. E. (1994). Overcoming the odds. *Developmental and Behavioral Pediatrics*, 15, 2, 131-136.

Werner, E. E. & Smith, R. S. (1982). Vulnerable but invincible: A longitudinal study of resilient children and youth. New York: McGraw-Hill.

Wong, M.C.S., Lee, A., Stewart, D., Sun., J., Cheng, F.F.K., Kan , W., & Ho, M. (2009). A comparative study on resilience level between WHO health promoting schools and other schools among a Chinese population. *Health Promotion International*, 24, 2, 149-155.

World Health Organisation (WHO, 2009). Health Impact Analysis. Retrieved from http://www.who.int/hia/evidence/doh/en

Yee, B.W.K., Debaryshe, B.D., Yuen, S., Kim, S.Y. & McCubbin, H. Asian American and Pacific Islander Families: Resiliency and Lifespan Socialisation in Cultural Context. Retrieved from http://uhfamily.hawaii.edu/Publications/journals/AAPIfamiliesBookCh apter.pdf

Yen, I. H. & Syme, S. L. (1999). The social environment and health, a discussion of the epidemiologic literature. *Annual Review of Public Health*, 20, 287-308. Retrieved from http://www.sagepub.com/upm-data/23185_Chapter_67.pdf

PART TWO:

SONGS OF RESILIENCE

CHAPTER THREE

SONGS FOR SURVIVAL:
EXPLORING RESILIENCE AND RESISTANCE
IN THE CONTEMPORARY SONGS
OF INDIGENOUS AUSTRALIAN WOMEN

KATELYN BARNEY AND LEXINE SOLOMON

Introduction

I do not profess to have lived a life any harder than the next person. I was 17 when my mother passed. It was a Saturday morning, a normal day of chores and then without any warning, my mother haemorrhaged. We were all shaken. The breast cancer won. My father had stopped coming home from his job on the railway and, as the eldest of seven, eventually I was left alone to raise my siblings. Many times my brothers and sisters have longed to hear stories about themselves to remember things from their childhood, but without parents there is no one to tell us. So one day I got this idea that I could record an album of songs to tell my siblings our story, remember our parents through songs and stories I carried through these years to tell them about "us" - that might answer their questions about life. (Lexine Solomon, journal entry, 28 November, 2009).

Indigenous Australian women who perform contemporary music have had diverse life experiences. Many have experienced traumatic and difficult life events, yet they emphasise that they remain resilient and strong despite a long colonial history of racial and sexual oppression. Drawing on our collaborative research together, as a non-Indigenous researcher (Barney) and Torres Strait Islander performer and researcher (Solomon) working with Indigenous Australian women performers, we consider how resilience is embedded in the contemporary songs of three Indigenous women and their on-going struggle to have their voices heard. Autoethnographic vignettes, song texts and poetry are used to weave separate narratives about the individual experiences of three Indigenous Australian women performers and how they use their songs to cope with adversity. Solomon also reflects on her own song writing through a series of journal entries throughout, included like the one at the start of this chapter, to consider the role of contemporary song in strengthening her own health and wellbeing. Conclusions will be drawn regarding the ways contemporary music functions in this context as a vehicle for resistance and resilience to empower Indigenous Australian women.

Resilience and resistance of Indigenous Australian women

Australia's colonial history, which included the forced removal of Aboriginal and Torres Strait Islander people from their land and culture, their subsequent experiences of alienation and the loss of power and control over their lives through policies of protection and assimilation, has been well documented (Reynolds, 1981; Moreton-Robinson, 2000). This history is not just in the distant past but is within Indigenous Australian people's living memories – the repercussions continue to impact their lives. Atkinson's (2002) research on generational trauma in Indigenous Australian communities illustrates that the trauma of colonisation has resulted in "a group of profoundly hurt people living with multiple layers of traumatic distress, chronic anxiety, physical ill-health, mental distress, fears, depressions, substance abuse, and high imprisonment rates" (2002, p.70).

In addition to this, Indigenous Australian women scholars emphasise that Indigenous Australian women experienced colonisation differently to men. Beherndt writes that colonisation meant that Indigenous Australian women experienced "invasion, dispossession, destruction of culture, abduction, rape, exploitation of labour and murder" (Beherndt, 1993, p.29). From the initial invasion, the Europeans viewed Aboriginal and Torres Strait Islander women as a part of the colonial conquest. Though Aboriginal women conveniently filled a multiplicity of roles including that of worker, it was her role as sexual partner (whether concubine or prostitute) that defined her (Beherndt, 1993, p.29). Huggins also notes "Aboriginal women experienced the added burden of sexual exploitation based on a white male assumption of superiority over both women and Aboriginal people" (Huggins 1998, p.16). Similarly, Moreton-Robinson argues that Indigenous women's perspectives are shaped variously by racism and sexism, a legacy of dispossession, a deep connection to land and continuing their "activism as mothers, sisters, aunts, daughters, grandmothers and community leaders, as well as negotiating sexual politics across and within cultures" (2000, p.xiv).

Yet Indigenous Australian women and men have participated in forms of resistance against racial, sexual, political and cultural oppression since colonisation (Moreton-Robinson, 2000; Huggins, 1998). Moreton-Robinson notes that Indigenous women have not been "passive victims" and that in the life writings of Indigenous women "there are numerous examples of overt acts of resistance on a daily basis. All these women break the rules of the mission or reserve and receive punishment, but that does not deter them" (2000, p.29). Moreton-Robinson provides examples of Indigenous women making use of white property, lying to white officials to protect others, stealing food, mimicking, and defying the restrictive rules of missions or reserves. Further, she highlights that Indigenous women's life writings illustrate "the resilience, creativity and strength of Indigenous women" (2000, p.31).

Just as song and dance has been used by Indigenous communities over long periods of time to musically document historical and social events, people, places, experiences, emotions and memories (see Bradley & Mackinlay, 2001), contemporary song is used by Indigenous Australian performers as a tool to respond to current and historical events. While there is some literature on the ways Indigenous Australian performers use contemporary music as a tool for Indigenous political concerns (e.g., Dunbar-Hall & Gibson, 2000; Dunbar-Hall, 1996; Reed, 2000) and how Indigenous Australian women use their music to fight against racism and sexism (Barney, 2008), there is little exploration of how Indigenous Australian women and men express resilience through song. Indigenous Australian women performers assert that contemporary song has the power to give sustenance and strength following adversity, and for many women "music is like a raft that ferries them through the hazards of the mainstream. For many, it has also been a lifesaver, keeping alive important knowledge and raising spirits" (Streit-Warburton, 1995, p.307).

The capacity to engage actively with traumatic events and cope with traumatic change is close to the current uses in psychology of the term "resilience." Resilience "refers to a dynamic process encompassing positive adaptation within the context of significant adversity" (Luthar, Cicchietti & Becker, 2000, p.543). Hawley and De Haan (1996) suggest that definitions of resilience interweave a number of themes. First, coping despite exposure to significant adversity. Second, it refers to the achievement of adaptation and third, resilience is described in terms of wellness rather than pathology (also see Garmezy, 1990; Rutter, 1990; Werner & Smith, 1992). Further Smith (2006, p.14) describes resilience as "the ability to rise above, move beyond or bounce back" and notes that specific "protective factors," or resources, play a role in assisting individuals in reaching adaptation despite adversity (2006, p.40). These resources that promote resilience are described by Friborg et al. (2003) as being classified into three categories: psychological attributes; family support and cohesion; and external support systems (see Bonanno & Galea, 2007; Masten et al., 2004 for other categories of resilience resources). Yet as Lemerle and Stewart assert there is "little understanding of culture-specific determinants of resilience unique to various cross-cultural groups" which "inevitably poses problems particularly for a society such as Australia" (Lemerle & Stewart, 2009).

The term "resilience" has also been used in relation to Aboriginal and Torres Strait Islander people. Goodall and Cadzow (2009, p.279) note that Aboriginal people "survived the expectations that they would disappear. They have explored different strategies to rebuild communities from fragments of early groups" which has been a "transformative process of resilience in conditions of stress, trauma and change." They also emphasise that Aboriginal and Torres Strait Islander people have many diverse stories of resilience and "now is a good time to start to tell those stories" (2009, p.25). This chapter offers a response to their call by telling three individual stories of resilience by Indigenous Australian women through song.

Context: Lexine

I am a Torres Strait Islander woman who was raised in North Queensland. I've released two albums (Solomon, 2002; 2006) and have performed nationally and internationally as a professional soloist, backing vocalist and choir director for over 20 years. I sing about a diverse range of themes in different styles and languages and an overarching theme in my songs is my identity as a Torres Strait Islander woman. During 2004 while working at the Central Australian Aboriginal Media Association (CAAMA), I was interviewed by PhD student Katelyn Barney for her research on Indigenous Australian women who perform contemporary music. I thoroughly enjoyed the experience of being interviewed by her, and from this I embraced an opportunity to become "the researcher."

In 2005 I relocated to Canberra and undertook my own research project, to produce a resource kit to empower Indigenous women across Australia. I interviewed 25 Indigenous women from my life—friends, family, and mentors—and then when finalising this project I got the idea of working with a qualified researcher. I thought of Katelyn and emailed her about possibly working together on a project. We talked about a lack of research and information regarding Torres Strait Islander women performers of contemporary music. We secured funding with the Australia Institute of Aboriginal and Torres Strait Islander Studies (AIATSIS) and we began the project "Performing on the Margins: Torres Strait Islander Women Performing Contemporary Music." We interviewed 20 of my fellow Torres Strait Islander women performers to find out their perspectives— these connections came from my family circles and from links Katelyn had developed through other research she had completed. During the project, I've listened to my sisters, cousins and friends tell their stories and share their hearts, minds and music.

Figure 1. Lexine and Katelyn in Canberra, October 2009 (Photo by M. Hade)

Many of our women have had very difficult and traumatic experiences and live hard lives. They have showed me how music can help heal the wounds of the past. I discovered some truths about myself. They have encouraged me to be a woman of peace and that I can lead, even if I happen to be at the end of the line. I think the greatest lesson has been that

I witnessed their passion despite difficult life experiences and how they answer their call in life through their love of music. While collaborating with Katelyn on our research project, I have also realised that I wear many hats. I have become the researcher, yet I am also a Torres Strait Islander, a woman, and a performer of contemporary music. I have a voice in the research and I must ensure that I reach the right outcome.

Context: Katelyn

I have been working with Indigenous Australian women performers since 2002 when I began my doctorate. I interviewed 20 Indigenous women across Australia, one of whom was Lexine. It was a rewarding, challenging and exciting experience from which I learnt much about the experiences of Indigenous Australian women and their contemporary music making. Since completing my PhD, my research with Indigenous Australian women performers has continued and research relationships have grown into long-lasting friendships. I continue to be guided by the performers I work with concerning how they wish to be represented and emphasise the diverse voices, performances, identities, and styles performed by Indigenous Australian women.

In 2006 Lexine asked me if I would like to work with her on a research project and we discussed ideas. I had been thinking about possibilities for new research and was excited about the prospect of a collaborative project with Lexine. After gaining funding from AIATSIS, we travelled together across Australia to Cairns, Thursday Island, Brisbane, Gold Coast, Canberra, Sydney and Melbourne, between September 2007 and December 2008, to undertake interviews with Torres Strait Islander women who perform contemporary music. During interviews, Lexine and I took turns asking open-ended semi-structured interview questions (Levesque-Lopman, 2000), which satisfied our agenda of allowing the performers to express their ideas, thoughts, and memories in their own voices and with their own language. With the permission of performers, the interviews were video and audio recorded and later we transcribed each one word for word. We then sent all quotations to the performers to obtain their approval and give them the opportunity to change, alter and edit their comments. We did this to allow the performers control over how they are represented in our writings. Over this time, our relationship has grown into a strong friendship that for me has been very rewarding both personally and professionally. It has reiterated how the power differentials between "researcher and researched" can be minimised through true collaborations between women (Dyck, Lynam & Anderson, 1995, p.622).

Many Indigenous Australian women have told me about their own personal experiences of adversity and those of their relatives. I have learnt much from working with Indigenous Australian women performers and I have attempted to listen carefully to their experiences or as Levesque-Lopman articulates to "listen in stereo" (2000, p.103). Indigenous Australian women musicians are multi-faceted and multi-talented performers who have diverse experiences and use contemporary music to express their emotions, identities, resist oppression and raise awareness about issues which they feel strongly about.

Luana Pitt and Lisa Maza: Who are they?

Luana Pitt is a Sydney based performer who has independently released two EPs and contributed to four compilation albums. She describes her identity in the following way:

> My name is Luana Pitt, my maiden name is Parsons. I am proud of my cultural identity, which is made up of Aboriginal and Torres Strait Islander heritage. My father's mother's people are the Yugerra people from the Ipswich area, and my mother's family come from the eastern Islands groups of the Torres Straits, Murray Island – language name "Uggar" (L. Pitt, 2008, pers. comm., 26 October).

Luana notes that because she identifies as both Aboriginal and Torres Strait Islander she's not always accepted by other Aboriginal and Torres Strait Islander people:

> There have been times in my life where I have experienced racism because of my cultural identity and most often the racism is from my own people, which I find very hurtful. There has also been times when I have been referred to as one over the other, but I will not choose one over the other, that is like denying one of my parents, and this I will do for no one. I have both of these strong cultural bloodlines that run through my veins, I am part of my communities and they know who I am – a strong Aboriginal and Torres Strait Islander woman (L. Pitt, 2008, pers. comm., 26 October).

Figure 2. Luana Pitt, Sydney, October 2008 (Photo by K. Barney)

Lisa Maza is a Melbourne based singer, actor and director. She performs with her sister, Rachael Maza Long as the duo the "Maza Sisters" and they wrote and directed their own show "Sisters of Gelam," which premiered in Melbourne in November 2009. Like Luana, she identifies as both Aboriginal and Torres Strait Islander:

> The most relevant thing about being an Australian to me is being Indigenous. I'm Yidinji, Murray Island and Dutch. Dad's father was born on Murray Island ... But Dad's mother is Yidinji, which is in Queensland, around and just below Cairns, that's where her country is. My Mum is Dutch. She came here when she was 7 years old. It's interesting, I'm a combination of people, of races, I'm white and I'm black, I'm both (L. Maza, 2008, pers. comm., 4 December).

Figure 3. Lisa Maza, Melbourne, December 2008 (Photo by K. Barney

She further notes in relation to her search for identity:

> I don't think this search for identity is everyone's journey. I think it may be
> a very Indigenous thing, this drive to find identity: who you are, and where
> you belong. I grew up in the city so I didn't go out hunting in the bush or
> on the islands. I don't speak [in] language or anything (L. Maza, 2008,
> pers. comm., 4 December).

Lexine's journal entry on identity: Who am I?

I can relate to Lisa Maza's comments about identity. My identity is really
important to me because I choose it to be, just as my mother's family is
really important too as South Sea Islanders from Vanuatu. Being raised by
her I was more exposed to her people than my father's. But when I use my
father's name and people say "you're that girl that belongs to" or "you're
that girl that recorded that song that belongs to Uncle Levi" that just links
me in so quickly. Luana Pitt is also an amazing woman and is like family
to me. I can relate to her pain of not feeling accepted. Being Indigenous
and accepted, it's a fight. Like many other Torres Strait Islander people, I
was raised on mainland Australia but I maintain ties to the Torres Strait
Islands. As I was not raised in the Islands I only have a kindergarten
understanding of language but my understanding of culture and custom,
and some of the traditions, make up who I am because of my father.
There's lots of cultural ties back to the Islands that I have and without
"living" parents, my connection is only as strong as I make it (Lexine
Solomon, journal entry, 15 October, 2008).

Luana Pitt's songs of resilience:
A narrative about healing the scars of abuse

Katelyn and Lexine parked in the small narrow car park at the block of
flats. Aboriginal children played in the street and eyed them wearily as
they got out of the car. Lexine called Luana on her mobile to let her know
they had arrived. They rode up together in the old rickety lift to the fifth
floor and followed the narrow dark corridor to the door. They heard the
door unlock and then Luana welcomed them warmly. The smell of
cooking on the stove wafted through the air.

"Oh my darlin' Lex, come in," Luana and Lexine embraced.

"This is Katelyn, the researcher who I'm working with," Lexine
introduced Katelyn to Luana,

"Nice to meet you" Luana said as she held out her arms to hug Katelyn.
"Come into the lounge. My girls are upstairs, you probably haven't seen
them in a while Lex," Luana smiled at Lexine and then glanced at Katelyn.

"I'm a single parent, I've raised two young girls. It's important for them to
also know their culture and have respect for their elders."

Katelyn smiled and nodded. They settled on the couches and while
Katelyn set up recording equipment Lexine and Luana talked about their
families. Luana noticed the video camera was set up. "I'd like to show you
my albums if that's alright," she said quietly.

"Yes definitely," Lexine and Katelyn both said at once, and smiled at each
other. They'd done at least 15 interviews together now and often found
themselves making the same comments at the same time.

"This is my 2004 CD single Mirror Child," Luana held up the CD for the
video camera.

Katelyn and Lexine both nodded at Luana to continue.

Luana cleared her throat. "I might just read the CD notes for you" and she
turned over the CD to read the back of the album:

The song title "Mirror Child" depicts my testimony of my childhood memories. As a child I was sexually, physically, mentally and spiritually abused, leaving me with painful and emotional wounds. These scars were reflected throughout my adolescent years and adult life. The lyrics in my song describe a mirror, reflecting my child like image weeping so endlessly. Hence the name Mirror Child. I am a proud Aboriginal and Torres Strait Islander woman and a survivor.

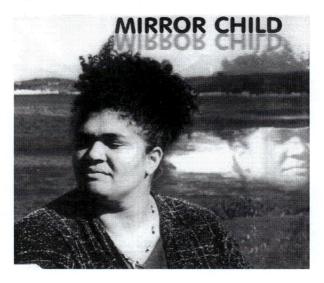

Figure 4. Luana Pitt, 2004. *Mirror Child*

Yes, Lexine thought to herself, Luana certainly was a survivor. She glanced at Katelyn but neither of them spoke as Luana continued.

"I often reflect on my own experiences and think that I am not the only one whose been through pain," Luana paused briefly, "and like my brother said there is always someone worse off than you, but it does not take away from your own experience, it just puts it into perspective."

"Does music play a role in helping you remain strong?" Katelyn asks.

"Oh definitely. In life I have experienced heartache and pain, and singing about these experiences always brings me through, and makes me feel alive. I told my mother that if I didn't sing life was not worth living, I would basically die. When I write the lyrics to a song and sing it, it comes from my heart and brings healing to me and gives me reason to live."

Lexine nodded, and thought about how her own music gave her reason to live.

"I've got a new song I'm working on too," Luana continued. "I could sing a little for you, it's a love song."

"Yes please," Lexine said, smiling.

"Yeah, that would be great." Katelyn joined in, as she checked to make sure the video was still recording.

Luana took a deep breath, closed her eyes and began to sing in a deep full voice, unaccompanied:

A big, black, beautiful lady
Looking for a man like you
With a silky tan and mysterious eyes
Can't wait for you to come true
Can't wait for you to come true

She finished the last note and Lexine and Katelyn cheered.

What an amazing woman, Katelyn thought, who has been through so much yet she finds strength and healing in performing her songs.

***

Luana is not alone in her experiences of abuse during her childhood. *The Health and Wellbeing of Aboriginal and Torres Strait Islander People* (2008) report found that Indigenous children were more likely to be the subject of a substantiation of neglect than other children. For example, in Western Australia 40% of Indigenous children were the subject of a substantiation of neglect, compared with 30% of other children. Other Indigenous Australian women performers such as Kerrianne Cox also sing about this issue (Barney, 2007). Luana asserts through her CD notes and album name choice that she has survived this trauma and uses her songs to give her strength and heal herself. She asserts that she is "a proud Aboriginal and Torres Strait Islander woman" (L. Pitt, 2008, pers. comm., 26 October) despite her traumatic childhood and singing her songs provides a platform to assert her survival, strength and identity despite adversity. Luana proclaims that she is a "big, black, beautiful lady" which resists the sexist and masculine framework of the music industry. She states, "this will not stop me from achieving my singing goals regardless of what the mainstream music industry does" (L. Pitt, 2008, pers. comm., 26 October).

Luana, like many other Indigenous Australian women performers (Barney, 2006), has independently released her recordings with the assistance of Government funding and her own finances. She notes, "it is hard being a single parent within the industry, as finances are hard to come by. That is why grants from the Commonwealth Government through the Australia Council for the Arts make it easier. I have also endeavoured to raise funds to support my music career as a professional singer" (L. Pitt, 2008, pers. comm., 26 October). While this could be read as an exclusion and marginalisation of Indigenous Australian women by the music industry, Luana emphasises that this allows her to maintain control and power over her artistic expression. Her songs also help make her "feel alive" and give her "reason to live" and have the power to resonate with emotions and healing. As Henderson suggests "music is effective because songs contain sensate memories of other songs, other selves, other moments" (Henderson, 1996, p.449), and certainly recording her contemporary music allows Luana to communicate her emotions and achieve a sense of relief and healing.

Lisa Maza's songs of resilience: A narrative about connecting with community and culture

Katelyn arrived at the hotel in Melbourne from the airport and Lexine was already having a cup of tea with performer Lisa Maza in the lounge. Katelyn hugged Lexine warmly and then shook Lisa's hand. Wow, she thought to herself, this is Lisa Maza.

"Maybe we could find a quiet spot for the interview," Katelyn suggested.

"Okay, whatever suits," Lisa responded.

They found some couches and settled facing each other.

"You've got family on Murray Island haven't you?" Lexine asked.

"Yeah but Dad wasn't actually born on Murray Island. He was born on Palm Island because of course they were all rounded up and put on Palm Island...I went up there for the first time about 10 years ago and it was fantastic to go there and set foot on your grandfather's country."

"Yeah, I know what you mean," Lexine responded. "I first went in 1992...I went up not sure where I was going...St Pauls, Moa Island – I just soaked it in. I just took it in, this is where my father was, he walked on this beach, he saw these coconut trees...it was worth it."

"I think due to the displacement and everything else that's happened to Indigenous people there is a real need to search, to find identity because so much has been taken away." Lisa kept her eyes down as she looked into her empty teacup. "I know who my parents are but there is a yearning to find who I am. I'm here, I grew up in Sydney so that's who I am as well, a city chick."

"Do you use your music to express your identity?" Kate asked and took a sip of water.

"The songs that I sing with my sister Rachael in the "Maza Sisters" are all about who we are; our experiences, stories and opinions. The show we're writing at the moment "Sisters of Gelam" is all about that as well. It's about who we are and what we want to say. So expressing identity through music, yeah absolutely, that's exactly what we're doing."

Lexine thought of her own song "I Belong" and how it expresses her own identity, heritage and a yearning to identify with people and culture.

"Our song 'I Remember' starts with part of a song our Dad taught us when we were young Zor Gob Ge," Lisa smiled, "and the second part was written by Rachael and we perform it together in harmonies with acoustic guitar. The words are *I remember when our land was a civilised nation, before artificial colourings invaded our shores, the people were the keepers and the carers of the land, keeping everything in balance, I try to understand.*"

***

Lisa's grandfather was part of approximately 1,630 Indigenous people from at least 57 different language speaking regions throughout Queensland who were forcibly removed from their homelands and relocated to Palm Island during the early 1900s (Watson, 2010). This greatly impacted on the identities of many Indigenous people. As Brady and Carey note, "the process of colonisation in Australia has brought with it the added burden of struggles for the survival of Indigenous Australians, not only of body, but in recognition of identity...for numerous Indigenous Australians, there was a sense of "unbelonging," that is, being not one or the other in their identity" (Brady & Carey, 2000, p.273). Atkinson points out that the government interventions into Indigenous Australian people's lives "have been multiple, protracted and many-layered, and at various levels have acted as traumatising agents, compounding the agony of already traumatised individuals and groups" (2002, p.68). She highlights that Aboriginal families continue to re-experience the trauma of colonisation and the impact continues to be felt by "individuals, families, and indeed whole communities" (2002, p.24).

Lisa is able to use her music to help her remain resilient despite the effects of this transgenerational trauma and strengthen and maintain her identity through her songs. While she has not yet had the opportunity to record her songs, Lisa performs her songs with her sister Rachael at festivals and in their own shows. The song "I Remember" reflects on the time before British invasion took place and allows Lisa and Rachael to document this colonial history and highlight the significance of land to Indigenous Australian people. Like many other mainland born Torres Strait Islander women performers, Lisa uses her songs to connect with family, culture and community, and make ties with the Torres Strait. She affirms for other mainland Torres Strait Islanders that constructing an Islander identity is possible and can be lived out through music. Her show with Rachael titled "Sisters of Gelam" (Figure 5) focuses on going back to Murray Island and connecting with a fractured family. They also draw on their mother's Dutch heritage in the play by using a puppet with long blonde plaits to acknowledge their mixed heritage and identities. Lisa illustrates how as an Indigenous Australian woman, whose family has been displaced and removed from their original homeland, she can still strongly express her identity and use her voice to sing back against the traumas of colonisation.

Figure 5. Promotional image for "Sisters of Gelam," November 2009

Lexine Solomon's songs of resilience: A conversation about song as sustenance to "raise up" family

Lexine and Katelyn stood in the front of the lecture room. The sea of 30 faces with green, blue, and brown eyes looked back at them. Katelyn glanced at Lexine and winked at her to begin.

"I acknowledge the traditional owners of the land on which we meet today. Thank you Katelyn for inviting me to your class." They smiled at each other. Katelyn was pleased Lexine was able to attend this class, which was part of a course that she was coordinating on Indigenous Australian women at The University of Queensland.

Lexine continued, "Kate and I thought we'd have a conversation about me and my music so you learn a little about me. Then we can do some singing."

They settled down on chairs, facing each other in front of the class. "So let's talk about your first album *This is Woman*," Katelyn began. "Can you talk a bit about it?"

"Well, I received some funding from the Australia Council to record the album and saved up my own finances. I wrote 11 of the tracks, there's three on there that I co-wrote with Aboriginal performer Warren H. Williams, then there's a song that belongs to Torres Strait Islander Miseron Levi called Baba Waiyar, and Amazing Grace, which has become a signature song for me."

"And there's lots of detailed CD notes," Katelyn said.

"Yes, there is," Lexine smiled. "The recording was specifically written for my siblings so that they could find answers in their lives. It was important that they got to remember, because by then my parents had died, my mother had been gone twenty years, so it was very important for my family, it was important that I could deliver it to them."

A few of the students leaned forward as they listened.

"I have been very candid and revealed some home truths," Lexine paused briefly. "My big brother had some problems with me doing this – but I let them input into the recording and revealing who we are – because of the women in our "past" – who are really in our lives," Lexine put her hands over her heart. "Ah you know, things like a dysfunctional family, like lots of people I suppose, but I decided that I could tackle some of the issues about what mothers expect of others..." Her voice trailed off.

Katelyn nodded. "So, it's really been an important way of documenting family history?"

"Oh definitely. The album really is a story for them because there's lots of history we don't have – it's gone with our parents and I've had my brothers and sisters ring me "oh Lex..." they remember something from their childhood and I've said "listen to that song and read what I wrote in the CD notes." Alright let's do some singing." Lexine announced. "My album *This is Woman* opens with a song called, "Cut to the Chase." This song is about me asking my mother who am I supposed to be, how can I be like you, how can I be you, am I strong enough to raise my brothers and sisters on my own?"

"I'll sing it through and then you can try it too." Lexine started the backing track and she confidently sang:

You died when I was 17
Did I turn my back on you?
To do my own thing
But how do I say the words?
Help me cut to the chase, to speak the words...

"Okay your turn now, repeat after me."

The students slowly began to sing the verses with Lexine.

"Any questions?" Lexine asked after they finished.

A student at the front, with short curly red hair raised her hand. "What does "cut to the chase" really mean?" she asked.

"Oh well I guess "cut to the chase" is a very "white" saying, meaning "get to the point." All the information about this song that I ever wanted to say is on the album cover but what I've found is that while I am ageing and maturing some of my concepts have aged and matured too. I remember in the early morning after my mother died feeling in my heart, Lord the sun has come up and my mother is dead. Does anyone know how I feel? How we feel? We are just children – please how can we endure this? My siblings didn't understand. That was the end of life as we know it. "Orphans" was what people called us, and still do."

***

Lexine's journal entry: Song as sustenance

Song is just sustenance. You don't believe how it can carry you past a really bad experience. It gives you hope, gives you purpose and it makes you find a drive you didn't have...I'm really protective of the album because it is a journey and a story. There are other factors which have really helped me remain resilient and continue to sustain me – my belief in God and also the support of my family. But music is definitely an important factor which really contributes to my strength and wellbeing. I've written a poem about my experiences and the role of song in helping me cope and it's called "Precious":

The heart has this secret
It knows when not to tell
I find that it's not easy
When I just want to yell

I haven't got a peace
I want to hide within
It's too hard to hide away
When all I see is sin

This life, is it a lie?
Who knows what from when?
I don't think I remember
If I spoke it or used the pen

I tell myself this little song
It churns inside with speed
That time is all we have
And love is all we need

Tell me your little secret
Heart of truth or lies
I see a field of flowers
Precious, in song, I will rise

Figure 6. Lexine Solomon, 2002. *This is Woman*

The first verse refers to a "secret" that's "not easy" which is that I am a
mainland based Torres Strait Islander. As Luana said, mainland based
Islanders are not always accepted in the community. But just because I am

on the mainland I should still be able to identify, it's my identity. The second verse is about rejection, because when interviewing Luana, Lisa and many other Torres Strait Islander women performers I was being a friend to them yet I was aware that Katelyn and I needed to get the information we needed as well for the project. This felt uneasy and not "at peace" with my relationships with them. The third verse is also about identity, my life, family issues sometimes I wonder is it all a lie? The fourth verse is about giving it time to be accepted and the importance of love and friendship to remain strong. The final verse is about how song is sustenance and healing. No matter what happens to me, despite whatever adversity I face and rejection I experience, I still have song. I will always have my music (Lexine Solomon, journal entry, 8 December, 2009).

Conclusion: Indigenous Australian women's songs of resilience

Aboriginal and Torres Strait Islander women have played, and continue to play, important roles in maintained communities despite the changes and trauma caused by colonisation. They assert their survival and strength through many different mediums including contemporary song. Lemerle and Stewart (2009) note, "there are various ways in which individuals may respond to adversity" and these three stories illustrate that Indigenous Australian women performers have had diverse life experiences and respond in contrasting ways. A common thread, however, is that they remain resilient despite these difficulties. Singing and writing contemporary songs provides them with strength to cope with adversity and assists them in defining their own identities. Their recordings also allow them to speak openly about issues that affect them and document this for others. Historically, Indigenous people had limited access to recording studios, yet Australian Government initiatives such as the Australia Council for the Arts provide an important economic resource to enable Indigenous Australian women and men to have their voices heard in recorded form. Jackson notes, "without stories, without listening to one another's stories, there can be no recovery" (Jackson, 2002, p.104-105). Indigenous Australian women performers like Luana, Lisa and Lexine tell their stories through song to connect with family, attempting to enact some recovery and healing within themselves and other Indigenous people. As Luana notes "a lot of our Aboriginal or Torres Strait Islander peoples are still hurting from past life experiences and I believe that we can use our voices as instruments to encourage healing" (L. Pitt, 2008, pers. comm., 26 October). Luana, Lisa and Lexine demonstrate how contemporary song can help them through traumatic experiences and the transgenerational trauma of colonisation, heal and connect community, and raise awareness of issues that continue to effect Indigenous people in Australia. They sing to strengthen their own wellbeing and proclaim Aboriginal and Torres Strait Islander women's resilience despite traumatic life events.

Certainly resilience is a multi-dimensional construct that refers not only to psychological capacities but also to the individual's ability to use family, social and external support systems to better cope with adversity (Friborg et al., 2003). These stories of Indigenous Australian women show that strong extended family support networks provide an important resource to assist them in remaining resilient. The effects of traumatic experiences continue to reverberate through Indigenous Australian families, communities and generations. Yet these women emphasise that no matter what adversities they face, they can still use their voices to proclaim their power and resistance. It is this physical act of using their singing voices that Indigenous Australian women assert helps them to stay strong and gives them a "reason to live." Contemporary song provides them with a powerful medium to speak out against the history of colonisation, empower themselves and encourage other Indigenous Australian women to tell their own stories of survival through song.

Acknowledgements

We wish to thank Lisa Maza and Luana Pitt for their continuing support and participation in our research. We are very grateful to AIATSIS for their generous funding support.

References

Atkinson, J. (2002). Trauma trails: Recreating song lines; The transgenerational effects of trauma in Indigenous Australia. Melbourne: Spinifex Press.

Barney, K. (2006). Women singing up big: The growth of contemporary music recordings by Indigenous Australian women artists. *Australian Aboriginal Studies,* 1, 44-57.

—. (2007). Sending a message: How Indigenous Australian women use contemporary music recording technologies to provide a space for agency, viewpoints and agendas. *World of Music*, 49(1), 105-123.

Barney, K. (2008). "We're women we fight for freedom": Intersections of race and gender in contemporary songs by Indigenous Australian women performers. *Womens' Studies Journal,* 22(1), 3-15.

Bonanno, G.A, & Galea, S. (2007). What predicts psychological resilience after disaster? The role of demographics, resources, and life stress. *Journal of Consulting and Clinical Psychology,* 75(5), 671-682.

Bradley, J., & Mackinlay, E. (2001). Songs from a plastic water rat: An introduction to the musical traditions of the Yanyuwa Community of the Southwest Gulf of Carpentaria. *Ngulaig,* 17. Brisbane: Aboriginal and Torres Strait Islander Studies Unit, University of Queensland.

Brady, W., & Carey, M. (2000). "Talkin' up whiteness": A black and white dialogue. In J. Docker and G. Fischer (Ed.), *Race, colour and identity in Australia and New Zealand* (pp. 270-282). Sydney: University of Sydney Press.

Beherndt, L. (1993). Aboriginal women and the white lies of the feminist movement: Implications for Aboriginal women in rights discourse. *The Australian Feminist Law Journal,* 1, 27-44.

Dunbar-Hall, P., & Gibson, C. (2000). Singing about nations within nations: Geopolitics and identity in Australian Indigenous rock music. *Popular Music and Society,* 24(2), 45-73.

Dunbar-Hall, P. (1996). Rock songs as messages: Issues of health and lifestyle in Central Australian Aboriginal communities. *Popular Music and Society,* 20(2), 43-68.

Dyck, I. J., Lynham, M., & Anderson, J. M. (1995). Women talking: Creating knowledge through difference in cross-cultural research. *Women's Studies International Forum,* 18, 611-626.

Friborg, O., Hjemdal, O., Rosenvinge, J. H., & Martinussen, M. (2003). A new rating scale for adult resilience: What are the central protective resources behind healthy adjustment. *International Journal of Methods in Psychiatric Research,* 12(2), 65-76.

Garmezy, N. (1990). A closing note: Reflections on the future. In J. Rolf, A. Masten, D. Cicchiettti, K. Nuechterlein, & S. Weintraub (ed.), *Risk and protective factors in the development of psychopathology* (pp. 527-534). New York: Cambridge University Press.

Goodall, H., & Cadzow, A. (2009). Rivers and resilience: Aboriginal people on Sydney's Georges River. Sydney: UNSW Press.

Hawley, D. R., & De Haan, L. (1996). Towards a definition of family resilience: Integrating life span and family perspectives. *Family Process,* 35(3), 283-298.

Henderson, D. (1996). Emotion, devotion, lingering and longing in some Nepali songs. *Ethnomusicology,* 40(3), 440-468.

Huggins, J. (1998). Sister girl: The writings of Aboriginal activist and historian Jackie Huggins. St Lucia: University of Queensland Press.

Jackson, M. (2002). The politics of storytelling: Violence, transgression, and intersubjectivity. Copenhagen: Museum Tusculanum Press.

Lemerle, K., & Stewart, D. (2009). A new conceptual framework for understanding resilience, October 10, 2009.
http://songsofresilience.wikispaces.com/A+theoretical+framework+for+the+concept+of+resilience.

Levesque-Lopman, L. (2000). Listen and you will hear: Reflections on interviewing from a feminist phenomenological perspective. In L. Fisher and L. Embree (ed.), *Feminist phenomenology* (pp. 103-132). Dordrecht: Kluwer Academic Publishers.

Luthar, S., Cicchietti, D., & Becker, B. (2000). The construct of resilience: A critical evaluation and guidelines for future work. Child Development 71(3), 543-562.

Masten, A. S., Burt, K. B., Roisman, K. B., Obradovic, J., Long, J. D., & Tellegen, A. (2004). Resources and resilience in the transition to adulthood: Continuity and change. *Development and Psychopathology,* 16, 1071-1094.

Moreton-Robinson, A. (2000). *Talkin' up to the white woman: Aboriginal women and feminism.* St Lucia: University of Queensland Press.

Pitt, L. (2004). *Mirror child.* Luana Pitt, compact disc.

Reed, L. (2000). Red headband history: The complexities of performance and presence at the Olympics closing ceremony. *Arena,* 50, 16-17.

Reynolds, H. (1981). *The other side of the frontier.* Townsville: James Cook University Press.

Rutter, M. (1990). Psychosocial resilience and protective mechanisms. In J. Rolf, A. S. Masten, D. Cicchetti, K. H. Nuechterlein & S. Weintraub (ed.), *Risk and protective factors in the development of psychopathology* (pp. 181-214). New York: Cambridge University Press.

Smith, P. N. (2006). Resilience in Xhosa families. Unpublished doctoral dissertation, November 20, 2009.
https://etd.sun.ac.za/jspui/handle/10019/127.

Streit-Warburton, J. (1995). Craft, raft and lifesaver: Aboriginal women musicians in the contemporary music industry in Australia. In R. Salolsky & F. Ho (ed.), *Sounding off: Music as subversion/resistance /revolution* (pp. 307-319). New York: Autonomedia.

Solomon, L. (2002). *This is woman,* Lexine Solomon, LS1000, compact disc.

—. (2006). *Strike a pose,* Lexine Solomon, compact disc.

The Health and Wellbeing of Aboriginal and Torres Strait Islander People.
    (2008). *The Health and Wellbeing of Aboriginal and Torres Strait
    Islander people*. Canberra: Australian Bureau of Statistics.
Watson, J. (2010). *Palm Island: Through a long lens*. Canberra: Aboriginal
    Studies Press.
Werner, E. E., & Smith, R. S. (Eds). (1992). *Overcoming the odds: High
    risk children from birth to adulthood*. Ithaca: Cornell University Press.

CHAPTER FOUR

STREET DANCE AND ADOLESCENT WELLBEING: USING HIP-HOP TO PROMOTE RESILIENCE IN YOUTH

N. HARRIS, L. WILKS, D. STEWART, V. GOPINATH AND S. MACCUBBIN

Introduction

In recent years television shows such as *So you think you can dance* and *Dancing with the stars* have raised the profile of dancing and created significant community awareness and interest in different dance styles. While most consider dance as an opportunity for fun and relaxation, it also offers opportunities for significant physical activity, improved mental health and social connectedness (Graham, 2002; Hanna, 2006). This chapter introduces street dance, more specifically a dance style within hip-hop culture known as "breaking," as a means to build resilience within adolescents from predominantly disadvantaged backgrounds. Aged between 10 and 17 years, adolescents are traditionally a difficult population to engage (Lerner & Galambos, 1998; Bergman, 2001). However, the popularity of dance with adolescents has been well documented (Fensham & Gardner, 2005) and, as such, presents a medium to work collaboratively on adolescent health needs surrounding physical activity, such as obesity. The potential for a dance based physical activity intervention to support future health outcomes by building resilience within an adolescent population is an exciting and innovative health promotion practice.

This chapter presents research on an innovative physical activity intervention called *HYPE: Hip-hop = Healthy* as an example of how breakdancing as a form of street dance can be used to positively impact youth health. The

HYPE program is a collaborative effort involving a university, private sector organisations including a dance studio, an event management company and various community organisations and government departments situated across the Logan area. The collaborators based the HYPE program on principles of contemporary health promotion, most particularly the notion of "starting from where the community is at" to facilitate engagement, empowerment and resilience through participatory practices. This was achieved by adopting a partnership approach to make an appealing form of physical activity, breakdancing, available either within the school day or as part of extra-curricular activities.

To evaluate the impact of the HYPE program on participants' physical, social and mental health, researchers at the School of Public Health, Griffith University collected data via participant surveys and feedback from teachers and principals involved in the program. Together, this information indicated that the HYPE program was successful in engaging the adolescents and that the participants perceived a range of health benefits as a result of the program. Of particular note is a central theme of social connectedness that emerged through the data collected and represents participants' increased awareness of, and access to, supportive social networks. This theme relates closely with the concept of individual and community resilience where individuals are provided access to, and actively build, health promoting social capital to increase control over their health. The potential of hip-hop breakdancing in building resilience and promoting wellbeing among adolescents is recognised as a critical area for further health promotion research and evaluation.

Dance, wellbeing and resilience

A growing body of literature suggests the usefulness of expressive arts in promoting health and wellbeing (Hamilton, Hinks, & Petticrew, 2003; Sanderson, 1996). Just as music has been integrated within health promotion interventions (Ruud, 2008), and associated with positive health outcomes (Draper, 2009), dance has also been used in this way (Karkou & Sanderson, 2006). Dancing, generally defined as rhythmical movement usually to music, is largely viewed as a fun and enjoyable activity (Sanderson, 1996; Stinson, 1997). Dancing can also represent a valuable form of physical activity that offers benefits associated with mental health and social interaction. As a general form of physical activity, regular participation in dance enhances fitness and could delay onset of chronic diseases, improve mental performance and concentration levels, help regulate mood, sleep and energy levels and decrease feelings of anxiety and depression (US Department of Health and Human Services, 1996). However, the majority of research investigating specific health benefits connected with dance is limited to dance therapy or remedial treatment (Cohen & Walco, 1999; Ritter & Low, 1996). Although limited, this research does suggest that dance can reduce the effects of injury, disease and stress (Hanna, 1995), and has been used to assist recovery from chronic illnesses (Byers et al., 2002).

As the dance health literature has developed, research has expanded to focus on the interaction between dance and adolescent wellbeing. Research findings indicate that dance, when coupled with popular contemporary hip-hop music, becomes an appealing form of physical activity for adolescents, over and above other forms of exercise (Flores, 1995). This means that adolescents are likely to experience the benefits of physical activity as a function of their engagement in dance. This is significant because physical activity levels have been shown to decline for many children as they move into adolescence. Yet, as some styles of dance also provide opportunity for social engagement and skill mastery, it has the potential to provide health benefits beyond those commonly associated with regular physical activity (Ritter & Low, 1996; Sanderson, 1996, 2008). Overall, dance may provide adolescents access to potential physical, social, and psychological health benefits, which together work to build resilience within this population (Blum, 1998). While anecdotal evidence exists to attest to this claim, there is a lack of evidence-based research that links dance and broad health outcomes, such as resilience, in adolescents (Quin, Frazer, & Redding, 2007).

Adolescent health and wellbeing

Adolescence is commonly recognised as a period of dramatic change during which a multitude of health needs arise (Lerner & Galambos, 1998; Love et al., 2007). In recent times, being overweight and/or obese has been highlighted as a major health concern for adolescents (O'Dea, 2008). Globally, it is estimated that 155 million children of school age are overweight (World Health Organization, 2000). In Australia, the prevalence of obesity in children and adolescents has jumped markedly in all age groups and for both boys and girls (Booth et al., 2001). The National Health Survey (2004–05) showed that 27 per cent of males and 20 per cent of females aged 15 to 24 years were overweight or obese. At a basic level, becoming overweight and obese is caused by an imbalance in energy consumed and energy expended by the individual. The types and amount of food eaten, and amount of physical activity or inactivity by the individual largely determine this equation.

Trends of physical inactivity during adolescence are commonly reported in the literature on adolescent health and are of concern for many reasons, not least of which is the relationship between health in adolescence and health outcomes over the lifespan (Banis et al., 1988; Flynn et al., 2006). For example, obesity is well established in the literature as a health risk that spans adolescence and adulthood with evidence that adult overweight and obesity status is largely predicated by health behaviours initiated during adolescence (Flynn et al., 2006; Glenmark, Hedberg, & Jansson, 1994; Kemper, Vente, & Twisk, 2001). Specifically, physical inactivity and poor eating habits that develop during adolescence are likely to continue into adulthood (Byers et al., 2002; Malina, 2001). These findings indicate that adolescence is a crucial time in the lifespan where conditioned habits go on to shape important medium to long-term health outcomes.

The obesity epidemic is complex with multiple factors underpinning this global phenomenon. Obesity is of particular significance for adolescents from lower socio-economic areas who experience both limited access to facilities and resources that encourage physical activity as well as high consumption of foods with poor nutritional content (Burton, Turrell, & Oldenburg, 2003). The increasing public health concern surrounding overweight and obese adolescents reflects the need for multiple strategies to address this issue. Promotion of increased physical activity seems critical as a key factor in the energy consumption and energy expenditure equation that underpins the overweight and obesity epidemic. Yet, youths and specifically adolescents are often a difficult population to engage and work with on health related issues, particularly physical activity (Salmon, Booth, Phongsavan, Murphy, & Timperio, 2007). Accordingly, innovative age appropriate strategies that engage this population's interest and encourage participation represent an appropriate means to facilitate increased physical activity in youth. Dance, particularly contemporary dance styles including breakdancing, is of considerable appeal to adolescents and, as such, worthy of consideration as a health promotion strategy for this population.

Hip-hop, youth and physical activity

Some of the most popular dance styles enjoyed by adolescents, especially those from a lower socio-economic background, stem from hip-hop culture which originated from the lower and often marginalised working class African American youth (Clay, 2003; Forman & Neal, 2004; Sanderson, 2008). Hip-hop dancing commonly involves breaking, locking and popping styles (and more recently krumping), which can be performed in a range of different settings from neighbourhood streets to the school playground (Motley, 2007). It is this accessibility of breaking and hip-hop culture more generally that contributes to its popularity among adolescents from lower socio-economic areas, where family income is limited and community facilities are scarce. These features of hip-hop dance styles also work to support its suitability as a means of physical activity for this target population.

Encouraging greater physical activity by providing activities favoured by a particular target population, in this case break dancing and adolescents, is very much consistent with the ethos that underpins the practice of contemporary health promotion (Naidoo & Wills, 2000). A major focus of contemporary health promotion is the development of social capital, which is defined as the resources and benefits that empower individuals and communities to take a greater role in securing improved health (Putnam, 1995; Raeburn & Rootman, 1998). As a framework of action for health, contemporary health promotion recognises the importance of equity and uses participative strategies to understand and act upon the underlying multiple determinants of health (Naidoo & Wills, 2000; Wallerstein, 1992).

Consistent with a socio-ecological approach to health promotion are concepts of participation, empowerment, and resilience (Kirmayer, Simpson, & Cargo, 2003; McLeroy et al., 1988). Health promotion interventions that are designed to actively engage communities also work to build resilience that spans individual and community levels (Stewart et al., 2004). At the community level, resilience may be thought of as the accessible social capital within a community that enables an individual to make health promoting choices (Putnam, 1995; Lemerle & Stewart, 2004; Sun & Stewart, 2007). An individual's capacity to identify and draw upon resources that support coping is indicative of resilience at an individual level (Rutter, 1987). Conceptualised in this way resilience becomes both a process and a critical outcome of health promotion interventions.

The importance of health promotion interventions to build individual and community resilience is magnified when the target population is exposed to a range of adverse conditions such as those associated with low socio-economic status (SES). Several barriers to maintaining health promoting behaviours stem from lack of resources and opportunities within low SES populations. To be effective, health promotion interventions must match the capabilities, interests and needs of the target population or community and develop resources that can support health outcomes in the long term. This is true for programs aimed at increasing physical activity in adolescents, where the population must feel empowered to actively engage with the preferred form of physical activity. Street and hip-hop culture in particular, including associated dance styles, has evolved into a tool used within educational and health domains to encourage participatory practices that empower youth populations (Mitchell, 2003). An example of such a project is the *HYPE: Hip-hop= Healthy* project that has been conducted over four years from 2007 to 2010 in the City of Logan, Queensland, Australia.

An overview of HYPE: Hip-hop=Healthy

The *HYPE: Hip-hop=Healthy* project is an innovative physical activity intervention aimed at engaging youth, building social capacity and promoting resilience among the target population within the Logan community. The project has invited high school students to participate in a dance program that provides regular dance workshops, a signature HYPE event to showcase dance skills learnt throughout the project, and a talent identification program that provides students with ongoing opportunities to be involved in dance. The workshops provided the opportunity for participants to engage with various elements of hip-hop fusing dance, rap, popping and locking, breaking, krumping, dance hall and reggae styles. Figures 1 and 2 below present the HYPE logo and HYPE intervention flyer for 2009. These were specifically designed to appeal to the target population. The HYPE project has expanded from 2007 to 2010 with an increasing number of schools participating each year (5 in 2007, 9 in 2008, 15 in 2009, 25 in 2010).

A lack of age appropriate physical activity opportunities was identified in a health needs assessment for Logan City where there are more than 150 different cultures and a high proportion of youth. Street dance, specifically hip-hop, was highlighted as being popular and part of the culture that is embraced by Logan youth. As noted above, research suggests that styles of dance that stem from hip-hop activate young people's love of movement, music and creativity, fostering self expression and, in turn, can build academic learning skills which include memory retention, active listening, comprehension and critical thinking (Dickinson, McKean, & Oddleifson, 1997; Petchauer, 2009). However, unlike other physical activity interventions, the HYPE project did not aim to impart certain life skills to participants or educate participants on health risks associated with physical inactivity. Rather, the focus of the HYPE project was on fostering broad health benefits involving increased physical activity, social connectedness and enhanced self-confidence. This was achieved by incorporating a range of elements within the HYPE program, including a performance in a signature event. Although performing in public is widely recognised as a stressful experience, exposure to planned adversity within a supportive environment of students, family, community members and organisational representatives, provides opportunity for increased self-efficacy (McPherson & McCormick, 2006). Together, these opportunities and outcomes associated with the HYPE program aid the capacity of this population to build resilience that will support and maintain health promoting behaviours.

Hip-hop dance workshops were conducted once to twice weekly for a period of 45 minutes over 12 weeks of the school calendar. Participation in workshops was voluntary, took place after school, and involved tuition by skilled, specialist dance teachers and choreographers. The program culminated with a signature event held at Logan Campus of Griffith University where participants had the opportunity to showcase their dance routines. There was no fee for participation in the weekly classes or performance at the signature event. Funding for the HYPE project was sourced from state government authorities for education and health, local government, local businesses, family and youth organisations, and the local university.

The intervention brought together a range of agencies operating in the city of Logan that are interested in youth, building community and population health. As an example, in 2009 the HYPE steering committee included representatives from the local city council, the local University, a community development agency, a coalition of community organisations, the State Education and Health Departments with a street dance studio and an events management company. This array of partners in the project has, of itself, built vibrant relationships across the city for youth health.

Figure 1: The HYPE intervention logo

Figure 2: The HYPE 2009 Flyer

Street dance and youth wellbeing:
Examining the impact of HYPE

Evaluating health promotion interventions aimed at preventing obesity and physical inactivity are critical in building an evidence base and theory for the discipline of health promotion. However, to date there has been limited structured evaluation of innovative physical activity interventions using street dance, such as breaking, involving adolescents in Australia. Such evaluation work could bring a wider conceptualisation of the associations between innovative physical activity interventions, street dance in particular, the concept of resilience, and the importance of evaluation and its contribution to health promotion theory and practice. The evaluation of the HYPE intervention offers insight into how street dance can be used to engage youth in a program of physical activity.

A cross sectional study design was used to assess students' perceived health benefits associated with participation in the HYPE program. Qualitative and quantitative data were collected via a questionnaire administered to a random sample of participants on the day of the HYPE signature event. This instrument gathered participant perceptions of how HYPE had impacted on their physical, mental and social health. The 8-item questionnaire comprised 4 quantitative and 4 qualitative questions together with demographics questions. School principals and teachers involved in HYPE were also surveyed on their views on the program and weekly attendance numbers at the dance workshops were collected.

Descriptive statistics were calculated for the responses to the closed questions. The open-ended questions were transcribed and analysed by thematic analysis with broad categories determined by the quantitative questions. Participation in the research associated with the intervention was voluntary, with informed consent obtained prior to commencing each interview. Potential respondents were advised of the purpose of the research, their time commitment to the research and structures in place to ensure their rights regarding participation including confidentiality. Interviews were conducted with participants on the day of the signature event while participants were rehearsing prior to the commencement of performances. This approach enabled the researchers to capture participants' views and excitement about the project and event in their own words and thereby build a fuller understanding of the impact of the intervention from the participants' perspectives. This approach was very much consistent with the overarching health promotion framework of the project.

Attendance rates for all participants in the HYPE program are presented in Table 1 and show a high and stable pattern across the life of the program. The level and stability of attendance suggests the dance workshops were well received by the students and an accepted form of physical activity.

Table 1: Summary of student attendance at the 2009 HYPE dance workshops

| | Week | | | | | | | | | | | |
	2	3	4	5	6	7	8	9	10	11	12	Total
Flagstone	14	16	13	15	16	16	15	15	15	16	16	**16**
Beenleigh	13	14	15	15	15	14	13	15	14	14	15	**15**
Ormeau Woods	7	7	5	7	8	8	8	7	7	8	8	**8**
Marsden SHS	24	28	26	27	28	26	27	28	28	28	28	**28**
Mable Park SHS	14	14	16	14	16	16	16	16	13	15	15	**16**
Browns Plains	16	18	16	19	19	19	18	19	18	19	19	**19**
Loganlea	26	28	27	24	23	27	27	25	24	29	29	**29**
Shailer Park	15	17	19	19	17	18	18	18	17	19	19	**19**
Rochedale	26	34	26	38	30	22	34	38	33	34	38	**38**
Park Ridge	7	11	11	11	8	11	10	9	9	11	10	**11**
Kingston	19	28	28	27	25	28	26	26	24	26	28	**28**
Windaroo	10	11	10	9	8	11	11	11	10	9	11	**11**
Woodridge	18	20	23	23	23	23	23	23	23	23	23	**23**
Springwood	0	2	4	5	5	4	5	5	3	5	5	**5**
Total	209	248	239	253	241	243	251	255	238	256	264	266

In general, the quantitative and qualitative data reveal positive participant perceptions of the impact of the HYPE program with almost all (97%) acknowledging that participating in HYPE was a positive experience. A breakdown of responses to this question, and the three other closed questions on the student participant questionnaire, are presented in Table 2. When asked whether participating in HYPE had improved participants' physical fitness, quantitative data indicate the majority of HYPE participants who were surveyed (77%) felt their physical fitness had improved, with only 6% indicating no improvement in their physical fitness. These results suggest HYPE had a positive effect on physical activity levels of participants.

With regard to participants' perceptions of mental health and wellbeing, almost all (91%) respondents agreed HYPE made them feel good about themselves with the remaining 9% being neutral on this issue. Social health benefits of HYPE were expressed by 82% of participants, who indicated they had gotten to know more people through participating in the program. Together, the responses to these questions portray multiple and broad health benefits associated with participation in the HYPE program. The thematic analysis of the qualitative data that relate to each question provides further information about these benefits.

Table 2: 2008/2009 Samples – combined responses in percentage to quantitative questions

Question	SA	A	N	D	SD
Participating in HYPE has been a positive experience for me	69%	28%	3%	0%	0%
Participating in HYPE has improved my physical fitness	26%	51%	17%	5%	1%
Participating in HYPE has made me feel good about myself	48%	43%	9%	0%	0%
Through participating in HYPE I have gotten to know more people	46%	36%	10%	7%	1%

Response in percentage (n = 171)

SA = Strongly agree, A = Agree, N = neutral, D = disagree, SD = strongly disagree

Overall perceptions

When asked how HYPE had been a positive experience, participants revealed three themes of: i) sense of community, ii) self expression, and iii) positive life experience. Each of these themes relates strongly to health outcomes, and importantly, connect street dance with youth wellbeing. Specific comments that linked participation in HYPE with an increased sense of community include:

> [I feel] confident, good to see Logan people coming together.

> Getting to know all the students and teachers in my group and learning new and interesting choreographs has really made this experience wonderful and exciting.

> At our school we have many different cultures and we've brought it all together.

These comments indicate that HYPE increased participants' awareness of social networks within schools, across other local schools, and in the community that are available to them. This developing sense of community is significant as a primary correlate to adolescent wellbeing described in previous research (Pretty et al., 1996). Moreover, this increased sense of social connectedness is central to the concept of resilience at the community level that enables individuals to make healthy choices that support long term wellbeing (Love et al., 2007).

The second theme provided more details as to why HYPE was a positive experience and centred on opportunities for self-expression through street dance. Self-expression, or the ability to express personality and feelings, is an important aspect of adolescents' overall perceptions of health. Specific responses included:

> I met new people and discovered I have real passion for dancing

> Opportunity to dance, express myself

> Being able to perform in front of people, it's cool

These comments show that participants felt the HYPE signature event provided the opportunity to express who they are and what they enjoy publicly through street dance. In the context of the present study, the signature event showcased the break dancing routines, enabling the broader community to observe the students' hard work and commitment. The comments also indicate that participants' experienced and overcame the challenge of a public performance at the signature event as a safe form of planned adversity. In this way the project used the performance event to help build participants' capacity for resilience.

The third theme identified within overall perceptions of HYPE was positive life experience. This theme relates to engagement in activities that are enjoyable and positive. Some specific comments were:

It's a fun way to keep fit

Positive vibe, no negativity

Kept me out of bad stuff

Makes me feel happy

Many participants spoke of the enjoyment and fun they gained from their involvement in the dance program. The broad impact of HYPE on adolescent health is well illustrated by comments that participation provided a diversion away from negative or socially undesirable behaviour, which is consistent with previous research by Resnick, Harris, & Blum (1996). Together, the overall perceptions of HYPE connect street dance with youth wellbeing through increased sense of community, self-expression, and facilitation of positive, pro-social behaviour among youth.

Physical fitness

More specific health benefits connected with participation in the HYPE program related to improvements in physical fitness. A central theme of improved physical capabilities emerged when participants were asked how HYPE had improved physical fitness. Some specific comments were:

I don't normally do much in the afternoons but now I am

[I have] More energy, feel like doing more stuff

Moving quicker and faster. More awake during the day

Participants spoke of feeling fit and having increased stamina and energy as a result of the weekly physical activity program. This is consistent with the literature suggesting engagement in physical activity is related to lower levels of negative mood and fatigue and increased feelings of vigour and energy (Puetz, Flowers, & O'Connor, 2008). The minority of participants who reported no improvements in physical fitness mostly stated they were fit prior to commencing the dance program which is consistent with current understanding relating to required frequency of physical activity and physical fitness. The weekly dance sessions offered through HYPE were not likely to cause significant improvements for already active youth (Fletcher et al., 1996). However, comments indicate that participating in a weekly HYPE dance class increased feelings of vigour and energy, which as a first step to a more active lifestyle, highlight the value of engaging this population in age and culturally appropriate physical activity. In accordance with the student responses, staff feedback following the signature event also suggests the HYPE program was a successful method of engaging with the target population:

> Students were dancing twice a week for an hour at a time so this increased their physical activity here at school. Not only this but they were also rehearsing at home, again increasing physical activity. A great event for students to realise that physical activity does not mean your typical 'sports' as such.

> Some very big kids who may not usually participate in physical activity participated in HYPE and there was a lot of confidence developed within these kids.

These comments indicate that students began to engage with physical activity at school and in their own time, when previously this may not have been the case. The second comment indicates the HYPE program was also successful at engaging students who would not normally participate in physical activity.

Mental health and wellbeing

With regard to participants' perceptions of mental health and wellbeing, almost all respondents agreed HYPE made them feel good about themselves. The elaborative question revealed the two themes of: i) self-confidence, and ii) identity. Predominantly, the responses related to increased confidence, some specific quotations included:

> I'm pumped, confident and makes me feel great that I can dance

> Made me more confident about myself in front of people

> Makes me feel good after the show people come up and say good job

These comments indicate positive feelings of self and a sense of self-pride associated with competence and skill mastery. These positive feelings of self are key to mental wellbeing and physical health (Mann et al., 2004). While the HYPE program may help to meet short term mental and physical health needs, participants experienced the opportunity to integrate new abilities and increased self-confidence into their self-concept. In this way, the program may foster sustained capacity to respond positively to future challenges, thus developing individual resilience (Nettles, 1997).

The second theme recognised was identity. Identity formations can be challenging, particularly during adolescence. Specific responses included:

> I'm not useless I can be out there without being criticised. I can be myself

> Makes me feel positive that we can actually do something together as a group

> The teachers support has made me feel an important part of a great team as well as the students' enthusiasm

A sense of identity is important for individuality especially through adolescence, a period where young people begin to make sense of who they are within the context of the society in which they live (Heilman, 1998). In addition to the themes of self-confidence and identity, a focus on connectedness and school pride also emerged in feedback provided by teachers and school principals as an outcome of the HYPE program. Specific comments from teachers and principals that express these benefits include:

> Participating in HYPE has definitely helped with a sense of school pride for our students involved. We need to make the next step to build this within the community.

> Our school was very proud.

> Students were proud to perform their dance on stage for the whole school. This has not necessarily been the culture at this school. However they were very proud to demonstrate their skills to all.

These comments also suggest that the sense of contributing to a team or broader school community as a function of the HYPE program may have worked to improve the mental and social wellbeing of HYPE participants.

Social health

With respect to participants' perceptions of the social health benefits of HYPE, the majority of respondents agreed that they got to know more people through participation. Analysis of the information collected through the associated open-ended question that asked, "What has this meant to you, why?" revealed the three themes of: i) social support network, ii) diversity of friendships, and iii) social status. Social support network refers to the range of social relationships available to the individual, for example, specific quotations from respondents included:

> Know more people especially when needing to ask things and find things out

> Helped with interacting with other, different people

> Some of the people who do hype I never used to talk to but now we talk all the time

These comments align with overall perceptions of HYPE reported above, and indicate participation in HYPE enabled individuals to broaden their social networks. This consistent finding is important as it supports the connection between involvement in street dance, social connectedness and youth wellbeing (Hendry & Reid, 2000).

The second social health theme identified focused specifically on friendships. The program enabled students to form multiple friendships and connections within the same year level as well as vertically across different age groups. Specific responses included:

> Lots more friendships. I know people from different groups across years 8 – 12

> Better friends, more people, no fights

> Good experience, removed inter-school rivalry

These responses indicate that new friendships were formed within the positive context provided by the HYPE program where street dance classes were taught in a non-threatening setting. Facilitating social behaviour in a positive environment is important, as adolescent behaviour tends to mirror that of friends and peer groups (Laird et al., 1999). These social ties and diversity of friendships also provide greater sources of information, thereby increasing the likelihood of having access to appropriate information to foster relevant health behaviours or to minimise stressful or risky situations (Harpham, Grant, & Thomas, 2002).

The third theme identified as part of social health was social status. This theme relates to popularity or standing among peer groups. Some specific comments were:

> Now I have more friends and now I do not feel intimidated

> I feel so good, becoming popular

> More friends show people what I've got

Social status is particularly important to teenagers as it has been associated with feelings of acceptance and approval within a peer group (Allen, Porter, & McFarland, 2005). Feedback collected from teachers and principals involved in the HYPE program also referred to a sense of connectedness and acceptance within the HYPE teams and broader school community. Specific comments referenced increased confidence and support of HYPE participants and also reflected the sense of connection across year levels. Examples of such comments include:

> There was a real buzz around the school about HYPE, before and after the event. The competitors become a tight-knit group and other students who don't even dance were asking about the event. The students got lots of support and praise when they performed their HYPE routine on assembly. Many students are asking about next year already.

> Our school was very supportive of our team in the program. Students were proud to be a part of the team and some participating students' attendance improved. The team consisted of year 9 to 12 students so it helped the students connect across the grades and the younger students were able to learn from the senior students as well as be mentored.

> Some seem to act as though they belong more and are more confident moving amongst social groups.

The feedback provided by teachers who supervised students throughout the HYPE program suggests it was successful at improving the social connectedness and wellbeing of HYPE participants, and the broader school community. Indeed, although each question probed different elements of health and wellbeing, a central theme emerged across responses. This central theme was connectedness and increasing awareness of social networks, which identifies a broad yet distinctive impact of the HYPE street dance intervention on adolescent wellbeing.

Building resilience in youth:
imagining the potential of street dance

A central premise of the socio-ecological health promotion framework is the necessity of engaging the target population by "starting from where the population is at" (Naidoo & Wills, 2000; Wallerstein, 1992). Results indicate that the HYPE program fulfilled this requirement. In accordance with contemporary health promotion, health needs relating to increasing physical activity were met by developing an intervention based on participative strategies aligned with the target population's interest (Davies & MacDowall, 2006). In this case, it was the attraction to street culture (with both positive and negative aspects) among adolescents, harnessed and directed into breakdancing as an element of hip-hop culture, that encouraged physical activity and produced a range of additional health benefits. The attendance numbers in the program provided an objective measure of engagement and were supported by participant responses in the impact questionnaire. When given a chance to agree or disagree that the street dance program was a positive experience and facilitated positive feelings of self, none of the participants who were surveyed disagreed. This indicates a high level of acceptance and feelings of enthusiasm towards the program. Specifically, comments from the program evaluation point to a central theme of social connectedness that made the HYPE experience appealing and rewarding.

The consistent theme of social connectedness that emerged from the HYPE program evaluation points to the potential of street dance to empower individuals by increasing their awareness of and access to social networks. Through participation in dance workshops and a showcase event, relationships and friendships developed that spanned year levels, school communities, and inter-school communities. The depth and breadth of these social networks provides increased opportunities to access resources that will positively influence current and future health outcomes.

In this way, the program worked to increase the resilience of the target population by both increasing opportunities to access resources and facilitating skills that help support participants' ability to take greater control of their health.

While the social aspect of the HYPE program was highlighted as a central element that helped to engage the adolescent population and provide health benefits, the potential of street dance to build the capacity for resilience in youth requires further research. Although not as strong, research on the HYPE program also revealed a theme surrounding skill mastery and increased confidence. These too are critical health determinants and relate closely to resilience capacity. Further research may be needed into these elements to develop fully the potential of street dance in facilitating positive health outcomes for youth and the communities within which they interact.

Conclusion

Dance remains a largely untapped type of intervention within the health promotion field. This is particularly true for physical activity interventions involving adolescents. At the same time, adolescent health literature suggests that obesity and overweight will be the critical health risk for this population in the 21st century. Not only do adolescents experience a drop in physical activity levels, they are also setting up health habits that will endure throughout adulthood. The impact of this is evident in the increasing health risks associated with overweight and obesity during adolescence, and the associated poor health outcomes experienced during adulthood. To overcome these public health concerns, it is important that health promotion interventions use participatory practices, aim to empower, and build resilience within the adolescent population.

HYPE is an example of such an intervention that was based on these contemporary health promotion practices that aimed to engage adolescents in street dance as an appealing form of physical activity for this population. As a health promotion intervention that built on the current social capital within the population, and provided avenues for others to access that social capital, the HYPE program increased physical activity, social connectedness and self-confidence. The most significant finding that emerged from the HYPE intervention was a central theme of social connectedness defined by participants' increased awareness of, and access to, supportive social networks. These social networks spanned year levels, school communities, and inter-school communities. Given the range of support systems and information sources available through such social networks, the potential for improved health and wellbeing is considerable. While further research is required to strengthen links between street dance, adolescent health, resiliency, and health promoting social capacity, tentative associations have been established.

References

Allen, J. P., Porter, M. R., & McFarland, F. C. (2005). The two faces of adolescents' success with peers: Adolescent popularity, social adaptation, and deviant behavior. *Child Development, 76*(3), 747-760.

Banis, H. T., Varni, J. W., Wallander, J. L., Korsch, B. M., Jay, S. M., Adler, R., et al. (1988). Psychological and social adjustment of obese children and their families. *Care, Health and Development, 14*(3), 157-173.

Blum, R. W. M. (1998). Healthy youth development as a model for youth health promotion. *Journal of Adolescent Health, 22*(2), 368-375.

Booth, M. L., Wake, M., Armstrong, T., Chey, T., Hesketh, K., & Mathur, S. (2001). The epidemiology of overweight and obesity among Australian children and adolescents, 1995-97. *Australia New Zealand Journal of Public Health, 25*(2), 162-169.

Byers, T., Nestle, M., McTiernan, A., Doyle, C., Currie-Williams, A., Gansler, T., et al. (2002). Reducing the risk of cancer with healthy food choices and physical activity. *Cancer Journal for Clinicians, 52*, 92-119.

Burton, N. W., Turrell, G., & Oldenburg, B. (2003). Participation in recreational physical activity: Why do socioeconomic groups differ? *Health Education & Behavior, 30* (2), 225-244.

Clay, A. (2003). Keepin' it real. *American Behavioural Scientist, 46*(10), 1346-1359.

Cohen, S. O., & Walco, G. A. (1999). Dance/movement therapy for children and adolescents with cancer. *Cancer Practice, 7*, 34-42.

Davies, M., & MacDowall, W. (Eds.). (2006). *Health Promotion Theory*. New York: Open University Press.

Dickinson, D., McKean, B., & Oddleifson, E. (1997). *Learning through the arts*. Washington: Center for the Arts in the Basic Curriculum.

Draper, P. L. (2009). Social interaction within a series of dance/movement therapy modified Ce´ili´ dance sessions: A group case study. Drexel University, Philadelphia.

Fensham, R., & Gardner, S. (2005). Dance classes, youth cultures and public health. *Youth Studies Australia, 24*(4), 14-20.

Fletcher, G. F., Balady, G., Blair, S. N., Blumenthal, J., Caspersen, C., & Chaitman, B. (1996). Statement on exercise: Benefits and recommendations for physical activity programs for all Americans. *Circulation, 15*(94), 4.

Flores, R. (1995). Dance for health: improving fitness in African American and Hispanic adolescents. *Public Health Report, 110*(2), 189-193.

Flynn, M. A. T., McNeil, D. A., Maloff, B., Mutasingwa, D., Wu, M., Ford, C., et al. (2006). Reducing obesity and related chronic disease risk in children and youth: A synthesis of evidence with 'best practice' recommendations. *Obesity Review, 7*(1), 7-66.

Glenmark, B., Hedberg, G., & Jansson, E. (1994). Prediction of physical activity level in adulthood by physical characteristics, physical performance and physical activity in adolescence: An 11-year follow-up study. *European Journal of Applied Physiology, 69*(6), 530-538.

Graham, S. F. (2002). Dance: A transformative occupation. *Journal of Occupational Science, 9*(3), 128-134.

Hamilton, C., Hinks, S., & Petticrew, M. (2003). Arts for health: Still searching for the Holy Grail. *Journal of Epidemiology and Community Health 57*, 401-402.

Hanna, J. L. (1995). The power of dance: Health and healing. *The Journal of Alternative and Complementary Medicine, 1*(4), 323-331.

—. (2006). Dance for health: Conquering and preventing stress. Lanham: AltaMira Press.

Harpham, T., Grant, E., & Thomas, E. (2002). Measuring social capital within health surveys: key issues. *Health Policy Plan, 17*(1), 106-111.

Heilman, E. (1998). The Struggle for Self: Power and Identity in Adolescent Girls. *Youth and Society, 30*(2), 182-208.

Hendry, L., & Reid, M. (2000). Social relationships and health: The meaning of social ''connectedness'' and how it relates to health concerns for rural Scottish adolescents. *Journal of Adolescence, 23*(6), 705–719.

Karkou, V., & Sanderson, P. (2006). *Arts therapies: a research-based map of the field.* New York: Elsevier Health Sciences.

Kemper, H. C. G., Vente, W. D., & Twisk, J. W. R. (2001). Adolescent motor skill performance: Is physical activity in adolescence related to adult physical fitness? *American Journal of Human Biology, 13*(2), 180-189.

Kirmayer, L., Simpson, C., & Cargo, M. (2003). Healing traditions: Culture, community and mental health promotion with Canadian aboriginal peoples. *Australasian Psychiatry, 11*(s1), S15-S23.

Laird, R. D., Pettit, G. S., Dodge, K. A., & Bates, J. E. (1999). Best friendships, group relationships, and antisocial behavior in early adolescence. *Journal of Early Adolescence, 19*(4), 413-437.

Lemerle, K., & Stewart, D. (2004). *Health promoting schools: A proposed model for building school social capital and children's resilience.* Paper presented at the 18th World Conference on Health Promotion and Health Education Conference.

Lerner, R. M., & Galambos, N. L. (1998). Adolescent development: Challenges and opportunities for research, programs, and policies. *Annual Review of Psychology, 49*(2), 413-446.

Love, J. G., Sutton, P. W., Williams, H., Mayrhofer, A. M., Yuill, C., Love, A. P., et al. (2007). *The emotional wellbeing of young people: Final report of phase one of a 'Choose Life' research project in Aberdeenshire.* Aberdeen: The Robert Gordon University.

Malina, R. M. (2001). Physical activity and fitness: Pathways from childhood to adulthood. *American Journal of Human Biology, 13*(2), 162-172.

Mann, M., Hosman, C. M. H., Schaalma, H. P., & Vries, N. K. D. (2004). Self-esteem in a broad-spectrum approach for mental health promotion. *Health Education Research 19*(4), 357-372.

McLeroy, K. R., Bibeau, D., Steckler, A., & Glanz, K. (1988). An ecological perspective on health promotion programs. *Health Education, 15*(4), 351-377.

McPherson, G. E., & McCormick, J. (2006). Self-efficacy and music performance. *Psychology of Music, 34*(3), 322.

Mitchell, T. (2003). Australian hip-hop as a subculture. *Youth Studies Australia, 22*(2), 40-47.

Motley, C. M. (2007). The global hip-hop Diasporas: Understanding the culture. *Journal of Business Research, 61*(3), 243-253.

Naidoo, J., & Wills, J. (2000). *Health Promotion: Foundations for practice* (2nd ed.). Edinburgh: Harcourt Publisher Limited.

O'Dea, J. A. (2008). Gender, ethnicity, culture and social class influences on childhood obesity among Australian schoolchildren: Implications for treatment, prevention and community education. *Health and Social Care in the Community, 16*(3), 282-290.

Petchauer, E. (2009). Framing and reviewing hip-hop educational research. *Review of Educational Research 79*(2), 946-978.

Pretty, G., Conroy, C., Dugay, J., Fowler, K., & Williams, D. (1996). Sense of community and its relevance to adolescents of all ages. *American Journal of Community Psychology, 24*(4), 365-379.

Puetz, T. W., Flowers, S. S., & O'Connor, P. J. (2008). A randomized controlled trial of the effect of aerobic exercise training on feelings of energy and fatigue in sedentary young adults with persistent fatigue. *Psychotherapy Psychosomotor, 77*, 167-174.

Putnam, R. (1995). Bowling alone: The collapse and revival of American community. New York: Simon and Schuster.

Quin, E., Frazer, L., & Redding, E. (2007). The health benefits of creative dance: Improving children's physical and psychological wellbeing. *Education and Health, 25*(2), 31–33.

Raeburn, J., & Rootman, I. (1998). *People-centred Health Promotion.* England: John Wiley and Sons.

Resnick, M., Harris, L., & Blum, R. (1996). The impact of caring and connectedness on adolescent health and well-being. *Journal of Paediatrics and Child Health, 29*(1), 3-9.

Ritter, M., & Low, K. G. (1996). Effects of dance/movement therapy: A meta-analysis. *The Arts in Psychotherapy, 23*(3), 249-260.

Rutter, M. (1987). Psychosocial resilience and protective mechanisms. *American Journal of Orthopsychiatry, 57*(3), 316-331.

Ruud, E. (2008). Music in therapy: Increasing possibilities for action. *Music & Arts in Action, 1*(1), 46-60.

Salmon, J., Booth, M. L., Phongsavan, P., Murphy, N., & Timperio, A. (2007). Promoting physical activity participation among children and adolescents. *Epidemiologic Reviews, 29*(1), 144-159.

Sanderson, P. (1996). Dance within the national curriculum for physical education of England and Wales. *European Physical Education Review, 2*(1), 54-63.

—. (2008). The arts, social inclusion and social class: the case of dance. *British Educational Research Journal, 34*(4), 467-490.

Stewart, D. E., Sun, J., Patterson, C. M., Lemerle, K. A., & Hardie, M. W. (2004). Promoting and building resilience in primary school communities: Evidence from a comprehensive 'health promoting school' approach. *International Journal of Mental Health Promotion, 6*(3), 26-31.

Stinson, W. W. (1997). A question of fun: adolescent engagement in dance education. *Dance Research Journal, 29*(46-69).

Sun, J., & Stewart, D. (2007). How effective is the health-promoting school approach in building social capital in primary schools? *Health Education, 107*(6), 556 - 574.

Wallerstein, N. (1992). Powerless, empowerment and health: Implications for health promotion programs. *American Journal of Public Health,* 6(3), 197-205.

World Health Organization. (2000). Obesity: Preventing and managing the global epidemic. Geneva: WHO.

CHAPTER FIVE

DOVETAILING DISCOURSES OF EMERGENT RESILIENCE IN VANUATU

THOMAS DICK AND MARCEL MELTHERORONG

Introduction

In 2006 the New Economics Foundation (NEF) proclaimed Vanuatu the "happiest country in the world" (Marcs et al., 2006, p.35). NEF collects information from local and national datasets that inform metrics for fields of health, "a positive experience of life," and the use of natural resources – the end result of which is a measurement of "ecological efficiency with which happy and healthy lives are supported" (Abdallah et al., 2009, p.3). In Vanuatu's capital, Port Vila, this news created a flurry of media activity as it soon became a rationale and rallying point for everything from fighting crime (unattributed, 2008a), the state of the economy (unattributed, 2008b), curbing political corruption (unattributed, 2010), and producing good coffee (unattributed, 2007). But outside the capital, where the majority of the population live a subsistence lifestyle, people continued in their unaltered quotidian activities: tending their gardens, pigs, and chickens, raising their children, building their houses, and perhaps harvesting cash crops (copra, cocoa, kava) to raise funds for school fees and the like.

This somewhat idealized picture of life in the islands of Melanesia provides a background for this chapter. Both the authors have lived substantial parts of their lives in Melanesia. One of them (Meltherorong) is a ni-Vanuatu – the term given to the Indigenous people of what was once known as the New Hebrides. The other (Dick) is an Australian who lived and worked for nine years in Vanuatu. Vanuatu is a Y-shaped archipelago of islands to the northeast of Brisbane, Australia, in the southwest Pacific Ocean (see Map 1). It is made up of approximately 83 islands, 70 of which are inhabited. Vanuatu has a population of approximately 240,000. It is one of the most linguistically diverse places on Earth with over 110 distinct languages (Tryon, 1996), second only to its neighbour Papua New Guinea. Along with the Solomon Islands, Kanaky (New Caledonia), Fiji, West Papua, and some other islands currently a part of Indonesia, they make up the region of Melanesia (see Map 2).

Vanuatu, Papua New Guinea and the Solomon Islands, are among the last places in the world where a "subsistence economy" – or "traditional economy" – still outweighs the cash economy in terms of providing livelihoods for the population (Regenvanu, 2009, p.30). Even though people in the outer islands use cash to pay for soap, tea, sugar, kerosene, metal implements, transport, and school fees, the participation of the 80% of the population (who live outside of the capital) in the traditional economy is far more significant than their involvement with the cash economy (Regenvanu, 2009).

In this chapter the authors draw on their collaborative practice as a non-Indigenous producer (Dick) and an Indigenous performer (Meltherorong) working with musicians, festivals, and events in Vanuatu, New Caledonia, and Australia to consider how resilience is enmeshed in the synthesis of traditional and contemporary Melanesian life. Autoethnographic vignettes, song texts and excerpts from interviews are used to weave together a narrative about the salutary trajectory of Meltherorong's life, career and how music is a vehicle for expressing struggles, coping with adversity, and affecting change.

Context

There are three main issues facing contemporary Melanesians and their capacity to tell their own story: changing culture, land tenure, and identity (Naupa, 2005). "In Vanuatu, land is identity and identity is culture. But what happens when a culture is evolving? How does it modify identities?" (p.11). These issues and their attendant questions apply to individuals, to communities, and to the entire population.

How is Vanuatu culture changing? This year marks the 30th anniversary of Vanuatu achieving independence from the joint colonial rule of England and France in 1980 (see Table 1). Up to this point Vanuatu was known as the condominium of New Hebrides (a condominium refers to a country governed by two or more different countries with joint responsibility) – sometimes referred to as "condocolonialism" (Miles, 1998) or more disparagingly "Pandemonium" (Lini, 1980; Ambrose, 1997). Table 1: Independence in Melanesia

> The end of colonial rule - Getting Independence in Melanesia
> 1970 Fiji (ex-UK)
> 1975 Papua New Guinea (ex-Australian Trusteeship)
> 1978 Solomon Islands (ex-UK)
> 1980 Vanuatu (ex UK-France *condominium*)
> 1970 Fiji (ex-UK)
> 1975 Papua New Guinea (ex-Australian Trusteeship)
> 1978 Solomon Islands (ex-UK)
> 1980 Vanuatu (ex UK-France *condominium*)
> Melanesian Islands and territories not independent
> New Caledonia (France, since 1853, now a *Pays Outre Mer*)
> Loyalty Islands (France, included in New Caledonia since 1853)
> Norfolk Island (Australia, since 1788)
> Torres Strait (Australia since 1872)
> Rotuma (Fiji, annexed by Britain and made part of Fiji in 1881)
> West Papua (Indonesia, since 1963/referendum in 1969)
> Adapted from Quanchi (2004, p.11)

The enduring legacies of colonialism in Vanuatu are fundamental to its changing cultures. One of these legacies is language and its significance for personal and collective identity constructs. The divide between anglophone and francophone groups remains the defining line between contemporary political parties (Miles, 1998), where French and English, along with Bislama, the *lingua franca* – a creole of these two languages and Melanesian Pidgin – are the three official languages. In addition there are more than one hundred vernacular languages dispersed through the islands. This linguistic and cultural diversity makes it more difficult than usual to create a sense of national identity, as stated by the first Prime Minister, Fr Walter Lini:

> A combination of geographical, social and political factors has made the emergence of the New Hebrides as a nation-state a particularly difficult process: on top of the existing variety of Melanesian languages and customs have been added the divisive influences of competing French and English cultures (Lini, 1980 p.30).

Another manifestation of colonial legacies resides in contemporary Melanesian society, and is characterized by what appear to be dual systems of governance and economics, but what is in fact, a multiplicity of systems. The national system of government and the modern cash economy have been recently overlaid onto many complex traditional systems. In Melanesia, the disputed Bislama term *kastom* refers to the idea of a traditional system of law, religion, economics and/or governance. It incorporates all aspects of life including birth, death and marriage rituals, art, music, dance, kinship and the entire spectrum of human interaction and the sights, sounds and smells which signify "the spiritual presence in combination with the participation of the earth itself" (Huffman, 2000). In reality, there are as many *kastom* systems as there are languages. "Each of the 113 language groups currently found in Vanuatu represents people with different oral histories, cosmologies, customs and traditions" (Hickey, 2006, p.13). This implies that each of the linguistic groups represents a distinct cultural identity. The problematic overlaying and interacting of efficiency driven systems is a threat to the various *kastom* systems, as are the Western systems of government and economics (Moutu, 2000; Turner, 2004; Regenvanu, 2009).

At the same time this diversity is a critical factor in creating the social and cultural resources that are the basis of the resilience in the local communities – in terms of their health, food security, kinship, and their power to make decisions about their own lives...and their own land (Naupa, 2005; Turner et al., 2004; Miles, 1998; Sparks, 2006; Regenvanu, 2009; Bolton, 2003; Huffman, 2009).

Kastom is a fluid concept. Each village community in Vanuatu has a different perspective on *kastom* and a different level of engagement with the cash economy. In some islands whole communities are rejecting any pressure to compromise on traditional beliefs. In other communities, only some aspects of *kastom* remain strong. Naupa summarises what this means to the individual:

> As cultural change blurs the boundaries between the traditional and the modern, indigenous reference to *kastom* in contemporary Vanuatu is rather vague. Ni-Vanuatu remain aware of *kastom* ideals but can manipulate interpretations to suit changing needs ... the ambiguous nature of *kastom* therefore allows communities to address the changing social (and natural) environments, while always rooted in basic cultural values (Naupa, 2005, p.12).

So for contemporary ni-Vanuatu there are tensions between: the traditional and the modern; communities and economies; English and French cultural forces and the emergent nation of Vanuatu; and the multiple discourses of Vanuatu, which are created within each distinct cultural group. But the one issue that seems to subsume all others is land tenure.

As the source of food, shelter, currency and stability, the land provides Melanesians with an economy that is arguably more robust than that of the Western world (Regenvanu, 2009; Huffman, 2009). There is little doubt that it is more effective and efficient than the western economy at dealing with adversities and crises for the people of Melanesia. Sparks (2006, p.14) identifies "the strengths and benefits of the continued existence and resilience of customary communal systems of land tenure, from precluding landlessness to providing a range of social security."

Since independence, many ni-Vanuatu have transferred enormous tracts of customary land to long-term leases thereby eroding their control over their own future. Land tenure in Vanuatu threatens to become one of the most volatile issues of the region as more and more Australians make the sea change and contribute to the property boom in Vanuatu (Rawlings, 2007). Bonnemaison explained the ni-Vanuatu perspective on land in terms that leave no doubt of the profound relationship the people have with their island. It is "not only the site of production but it is the mainstay of a vision of the world. It represents life, materially and spiritually. The clan's land, its ancestors and its men are a single indissoluble reality – a fact which must be borne in mind when it is said that Melanesian land is not alienable" (Bonnemaison, 1981, pp.1-2). Is it possible to purchase land as a commodity and also maintain this ecological view of land?

Methodology

Stories exist within systems such as religion, law, or economics; a country depends on stories to create a sense of national identity. Story and voice are especially critical concepts in Melanesia where language and culture are transmitted largely through oral modes. The narratives of nationality and the stories that define a nation are also instructive about the nature of the society that has created them – law, economics, family and art. In this chapter we use a narrative of Marcel's life story as a reflective case study of resilience in action.

Map 1. Vanuatu.
Source: http://www.geographicguide.com/oceania-maps/vanuatu.htm)

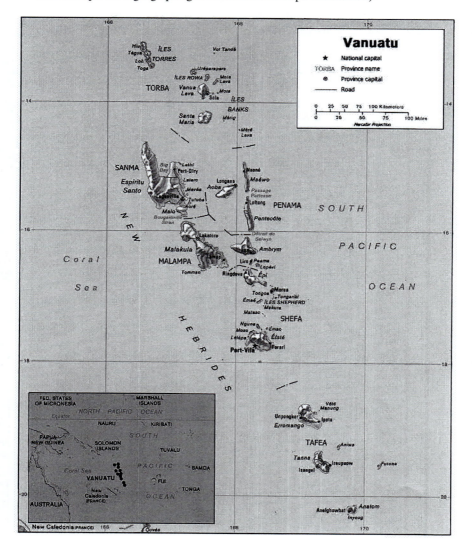

Map 2. Melanesia. Source: Wikipedia

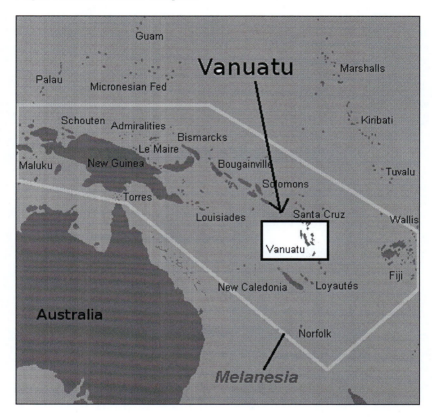

Rather than separating self from subject, the authors maintain a self-conscious awareness of the inseparability of theory, data, self and analysis in daily life (Allen and Walker, 2000). We employ a qualitative methodology: using the life writing technique (Jolly, 2001; Atkinson, 1998; Linde, 1993) we have created a narrative of Marcel's life in the context of the 30-year history of Vanuatu since it became an independent nation. Conscious that some view the western research tradition as a part of colonialism (Tuhiwai Smith, 1999), we have complemented this life-writing research method with the technique of overlay mapping. Stocker and Burke (2006) describe how overlay mapping can be used to bring together the ideas of a group of people.

> The method has a special validity because it can include empirical and
> experiential information in the same framework ... The identification of
> synergies and interactions among layers opens the space for further and
> deeper analysis, rather than being an endpoint in itself (2006, p.230).

To some extent this method enables Indigenous as well as non-Indigenous
cultural values to be made explicit. As Quanchi (2004) merged his own
voice with those of Indigenous thinkers, the authors of this chapter merge
their voices into an analysis of resilience in contemporary Melanesian life.
We draw conclusions from what we observe in contemporary music
interactions with the traditional economy – creating a cultural "edge
effect" (Turner et al., 2004), and how this interaction functions as a
contextual variable of resilience at the level of the individual through to
whole populations (see Lemerle and Stewart chapter two) and the cultural
life of a nation.

Our approach allows us to layer the theoretical understandings of the
authors with their artistic practices to exemplify each issue. Where does
Marcel's resilience come from? What resources does he use, and how does
he use them? To answer these questions we need to understand more about
the place from which Marcel grew and still resides. With this background
of a deep connection to place – where land, language, culture and identity
interplay – the authors have worked together for a decade, and have built
resilience amongst unemployed youth at music festivals, concerts, and on
tours. The life narrative of one of the authors is now overlaid onto this
complex background.

Early life and awakenings

Born and raised in the colonial war-zone of 1970-80's urban Noumea,
New Caledonia, Marcel and his family hail from the small island of Vao
off the north-east coast of Malekula in Vanuatu. During his childhood he
only visited Vanuatu once. He was moved by the strange place where
traditional life was celebrated – not vilified. He pondered the connections
between the stories of his uncles and grandfathers, and other old people in
the shantytown in Noumea whom were also from Vanuatu. It was all
foreign to him, but he now reflects that when they sang and told the stories
it was like they were experiencing an unbreakable solidarity, arms round
each other's shoulders, faces awash with tears in the gloaming.

As the tensions between the pro-independence Kanak movement and large
sections of the *Caldoche* community grew, many Indigenous young men

were targeted and punished as insurrectionists (Veracini, 2003). Marcel himself spent a year in prison (two weeks in solitary confinement). He was wandering the streets of Noumea with a group of young men. They happened to cross the path of a patrol of *gendarmes* who assessed them as matching the profile of insurrectionists and subsequently arrested them. This was perhaps the making and breaking of Marcel. The first time Marcel remembers referring to himself as being from Vanuatu is when he was eighteen and in prison. As he traces back his initial awakening to the value of the stories and solidarity that he had witnessed in the evenings with the old men, of the music and culture of resistance through the traditional songs, and through the songs of Bob Marley.

> Redemption Song: Rhythms of resilience
> Marcel: The music of Bob Marley matches the physical, social, and cultural environment of Vanuatu. We have the 'roots' that Bob sings about. Bob's music fits here in Vanuatu because it is a music of consciousness. It is an everyday music for everyday people. I feel our traditional rhythms share a similarity with the African rhythms. But reggae is a music born out of oppression and slavery and this is the main reason why we feel it matches with the cultural and social environments – connects Jamaica and Vanuatu.

In his book *Bass Culture*, Lloyd Bradley (2001, p.112) quotes Rupie Edwards who describes reggae as music that has "come down from slavery, through colonialism." He highlights the everyday nature of music in the way that "people sing. To get rid of their frustration and lift the spirits, people sing. It was also your form of entertainment at the weekend, whether in church or…just outside your house, you was going to sing. If you're cutting down a bush you're gonna sing, if you're digging some ground you're gonna sing…it's a way of life coming out of a people."

> Marcel: We feel like music is something that can pick you up and carry you out of the system

In his own song "Slava Land" Marcel refers to "the days of slavery" – the time when the *blackbirders* would come and "recruit" – sometimes violently – labourers for the sugar cane farms in the European colonies. It is a story that requires acknowledgment and reconciliation, and Marcel has gone some way towards achieving this through concerts in Bowen on the Central Coast of Queensland, home of one of the biggest communities of descendants of those labourers who never returned home.

> Marcel: We just came out from the bush and we see all the colonisation –
> the colonial system and the white people making us work in plantations
> and we get all the physical and verbal abuse – the 'rude talk' from the
> plantation bosses … they swear at us.

After a year in prison Marcel arrived in Vanuatu amazed at the power of
the local people. He felt an overwhelming sense of freedom and
independence – very much a touchstone – and he claims that the reggae
music of Bob Marley opened up something inside him. It was as though he
had been screaming at the walls until he had no voice, then one day he
woke up from this nightmare world and found himself in Vanuatu with a
new voice.

> Marcel: Bands like Herbs – they had a big effect. My father's generation
> and even his uncles were listening to this music, which must have affected
> the movement towards independence throughout the pacific.

The music of Bob Marley and its derivatives inspired Marcel's resilience,
measured by the aspiration to, and achievement of, independence for so
many of the Pacific Islands. This profoundly demonstrates the relationship
between music and resilience as it played out in the transition from
colonial to politically independent realities right across the Pacific
(Quanchi, 2004).

> *Wan Solwora* – One ocean, one people
> Marcel: Herbs are from the Pacific, from NZ – Maori – but we like to say
> in Vanuatu – we are wan solwora – and through this music people found a
> way to express their dissatisfaction with the way things were rather than
> resorting to violence. Wan Solwora - it means one ocean, one people.

Marcel's first novel is a semi-autobiographical narrative titled *Tôghàn*. In
December 2009, the second edition was released – this time with a
foreword by the winner of the Nobel Prize for Literature 2008, Jean-Marie
Gustave Le Clézio. Le Clezio writes of the "invisible continent"
(unattributed, 2008c) because from any number of perspectives and
rationales, it remains the least known or understood place on Earth. In the
dreamscape of Le Clezio's narrative he contours the myth and the reality
intertwining with imagination *"où le poème affleure"* (ibid).

> Marcel: Vanuatu is geographically in the middle of all this – in Vanuatu
> we have the bilingual colonial history. We have the big Melanesian
> countries of Solomon Islands and PNG to the north west and the French
> and Kanaky brothers to the South and Fiji and Polynesia to the east and

Australia right there on our doorstep to the south west. North of us is
Micronesia. We are like a crossroads of Pacific culture.

Huffman (2000) suggests that continental diaspora is a form of art and
Vanuatu is "at the juncture of undersea tectonic plates, with active
volcanoes on land and under the sea, the land itself moves: islands appear
and disappear, some are believed to be the handiwork of particular spirits
or spiritual powers, there are few larger 'artistic canvases' in the world!"
(2000, p.3).

For Marcel at least, it is a more practical but no less visceral concept of
continent:

> Marcel: When we see our neighbours suffering, even if it is another
> country, we cannot pass by and ignore them. We cannot pretend we are
> not concerned. We genuinely feel the pain of our brothers and sisters in
> West Papua. When we hear that they are being oppressed we feel that we
> are being oppressed. We know from our oral history and from the white
> man's history too that we came to be in Vanuatu by coming through the
> island of PNG/West Papua. That was the road. The canoe started in Asia
> and we came down through all of these islands. I feel a responsibility to
> speak up about independence for our brothers and sisters in West Papua
> and in Kanaky.

He is not the only one. At the most recent edition of Fest'Napuan – the
annual five-day music festival in Vanuatu – every local band sang their
own West Papuan freedom song. This was not an organized or
orchestrated gimmick. For Vanuatu people there is a serious and genuine
desire to see their Melanesian family independent, and all Indigenous
people free of imperialism. *Wan solwora* – a free and independent Pacific
continent.

Quanchi (2004) agrees that an Oceanic or pan-Pacific way, what he calls a
"regional epistemology," might develop as Pacific writers further
investigate "multicultural identities and pan-Pacific nationalities." But he
warns "regionalism is motivated by uncertain identity politics and alleged
commonalities of culture rather than actual distinctive, shared knowledge,
wisdom and learning processes" (2004, p.8).

> Marcel: In Vanuatu we feel like we have known the French version of
> colonisation and the English version too – we feel that this bilingual
> colonial system has one very important legacy for us – it has shown us that
> imperialism is not a universal principle. We have many languages and one

language equals one culture in our kastom so we have many cultures already. Then with colonization you add in Bislama and English and French and this western influence.

This idea that each language represents a unique culture is something both salutary and unifying, however Quanchi cautions us to be circumspect as "indigenous epistemologies are best thought of as location-specific rather than regional or Oceanic" (2004, p.8). Anthropologists and linguists support this idea (Huffman, 2000; Simo, 2005), and recent research by Biermann (2008) suggests that multilingualism and multiculturalism can have profound human rights implications in everyday life. Biermann writes about the age of translators, with hundreds of languages, multilingual inhabitants and autonomous but interrelated peoples. This suggests the idea of an ecology of resilience – a culture of multilingualism and translation, different cultures living together more or less harmoniously and a capacity for a socio-economic system to adapt and survive. An important human-rights related aspect of learning to speak another language is having to go outside of one's comfort zone, making oneself vulnerable and being open to different ways of seeing and thinking about life. Translation brings to light the peculiarity of the otherwise invisible elements of one's own language and ways of thinking. As such, it is as important a tool for self-reflection as it is for communication (Biermann, 2008).

Marcel: When we speak French we understand French and we understand their culture to some extent – same with English. And we even made up this creole, this Bislama. The children in the towns they only speak two languages Bislama and English or French – but in the islands they speak their father's language and their mother's language plus Bislama – at least three languages. So really we are multilingual. We are multilingual and multicultural. And the western life just reformats everything into one standard reality – the western perspective doesn't see the differences between each of the cultures we have in Vanuatu and for us these differences are the things which make us who we are. Because we had two oppressors we feel that we are well placed to convey a different reality – the reality of freedom and independence. In one of my songs I sing that you cannot give freedom to people who are already free. We take the view that our brothers are already free and that it is the would-be colonizers who are mistaken. And we want to promote this idea. We believe we are strong – our kastom makes us strong. And the ocean unites us as one Pacific and this unifying force is very strong. We are a very strong culture – we are water but we are a continent. We have these differences but there are also similarities between all of the cultures and this is what makes us so strong – we respect these differences.

'We just live our own lives here'

For 80% of Vanuatu people, and people across the Pacific, a referral to a traditional system of knowledge is not an academic exercise. Geua Dekure, a Papua New Guinean woman, notes "we just live our own lives here ... we recognise each others strengths and traditional knowledge. That is why we are still happy" (in Quanchi, 2004, p.7).

> Marcel: So a lot of us artists in Vanuatu we try and bring the things from the past into the present so that the future will be better for our children. But we are scared that one day we will lose this: sandrawing, bamboo flute, stories, dance. The meaning of the dance, how to cut the canoe. In Vanuatu we still have this knowledge this structure this kastom which is all about respect – respect of everything and respect of differences. So that's what I try to promote with my music – kastom is our root system connecting us to the water deep in the ground during those times of drought. Without our roots, our kastom, we will die.

The respect that Marcel talks about is one of the fundamentals of Melanesian society (Huffman, 2000; Biermann, 2008; Bolton, 2003). It is part of an organic system of human interaction, and *kastom* is an ecological system. It is alive, dynamic, changing, and grounded in the everyday; it also holds a multiplicity of meanings and realities (Regenvanu, 2009; Huffman, 2000, 2009; Bolton 2003; Naupa, 2005). It is an ecology of resilience.

In the same way that ecological peripheries are places of biodiversity, so to "cultural knowledge systems can intergrade producing a richness of knowledge and practices that enhances the resilience of local societies" (Turner et al., 2004 p.440). This "edge effect" has been prevalent in Vanuatu society for thousands of years and there has been a constant state of flux between various communities which "has probably been more responsible for its startling diversity through the admixture of various ideas, peoples, customs and traditions" (Hickey, 2006, p.118). The interplay between the legacies of colonialism: between traditional and contemporary expressions of identity (individual, communal, national); between communities and markets; between anglophones and francophones; between the desire for quick cashflow and the need to control one's own land ... these tensions create new cultural edges, increasing the diversity of ecological, social, and cultural capital upon which many people base their livelihoods in traditional economies.

Marcel: In Vanuatu we have a traditional system of governance but with the 'modern' democracy the politicians put this aside and focus on and promote this western economy rather than our traditional economy. And now it has come to the situation where I feel like we are forced to choose between the two things – between kastom and western ways of being.

Regenvanu (2009) outlines a compelling argument that the traditional economy is a type of reciprocal resilience resource for Melanesians, which has allowed them to cope with the vicissitudes of the global economy over past decades. He uses these characteristics of Melanesian resilience to argue that a shift in perspective is required (by policy makers, academics, think-tanks, donors, investors) to grasp the idea that the traditional economy is a powerful asset not a problem to be solved or a challenge to be endured.

Marcel: I see my music as a tool - a way of teaching my children and future generations about holding on to Vanuatu culture, our customs and our traditions at a time when western influence is changing our way of life. I remember an old bloke told me that if we can marry western knowledge with our traditional knowledge that would make our children 'twice wise.'

One of the more visible aspects of Marcel's cultural tool of music is the Fest'Napuan music festival.

Fest'Napuan – the Vanuatu music industry
Marcel: Fest'Napuan is combination of an English word 'festival' and a word from Tanna meaning dance and music 'napuan' – in Vanuatu we cannot separate these concepts.

Fest'Napuan is an annual 5-day contemporary music festival that is free to the public and attracts over 30,000 people each year. It is funded by a combination of corporate sponsorship, revenue-raising through the rental of stalls, and donations. It was established in 1996 to mark the anniversary of the opening of the new National Museum building. In the words of Ralph Regenvanu, President of the Fest'Napuan Association that organizes the event, "with the museum we're celebrating things from the past and so we wanted to celebrate our contemporary culture, to show that our culture is always evolving. It's really contributed to the development of life in Vanuatu - the cultural life of a nation" (Pacific Pulse, 2008).

Marcel: The first time I saw fest'Napuan I said to my friends next year I will be like those guys [on stage] – I will be up on stage. My friends, they laughed at me. My first band was Blak Maka. This band was made up of the guys who were laughing at me when I told them I would be on stage next year. They were in my band and we were all on stage the next year. I pretty much had to show them everything as none of us really knew how to play, but I loved it so much I think my passion was contagious. Some people in the audience were very rude to us. We were not very good musicians back then.

The idea of making a living from his creativity only occurred to Marcel many years after arriving in Vanuatu. He subsequently found work with Alliance Francaise in their satellite office based on one of the southern islands called Tanna. This was another critical step for Marcel. In this role as a kind of cultural liaison, responsible for organising events, managing a small office and resource centre, and promoting the French language, Marcel found that he had a gift for working with others and a talent within himself for writing poetry. He had been experimenting with poetry ever since his time in prison where he read anything and everything that he could access. When there was nothing left to read he wrote. At this stage he was writing as a cathartic process and as an act of resistance to oppression – arguably an early form of life writing as salutary resilience. And although he was essentially composing songs, writing lyrics, and (literally) finding his voice and range, the idea of being a professional musician had still not entered his mind.

> Marcel: After this I moved to Tanna one of the outer islands in the south of Vanuatu. These guys in the village had received a full set of equipment – PA, keyboards, guitars everything but they didn't even know how to connect it all let alone play music. So I taught them what I knew. Then we wrote some music, some songs - not notation just kind of jamming until the song comes out. We called the band Nauten and we went to Vila and recorded an album – a lot of the songs on that first album were songs I wrote with them. After the album was released they went back to Tanna but I stayed in Vila and started another band – XX Squad.

So much of the work Marcel has done and the life he has lived has demonstrated how he is autotelic or "internally driven, ... as an exclusive difference from being externally driven, where things such as comfort, money, power, or fame are the motivating force" (Csikszentmihalyi, 1997 p.210). In fact, this is true of most creative enterprise in Vanuatu. Hayward (2009) suggests that this Melanesian propensity for working without extrinsic reward may be because of a desire for "public expression and prestige." But for someone living in the Melanesian cosmology, the idea of working for the sake of it, or because it fulfils one's sense of purpose, is not an unusual one, nor is it necessarily about prestige. Hayward (2009) provides a useful insight into the necessity of reconceptualizing our ideas of what the creative industries means, so as to begin to understand the reality of Melanesian creative enterprise.

By 2003, Marcel had established himself as one of the most gifted songwriters in the country. XX Squad was one of the most recognisable bands in the region and their album *Children's Day* received much critical acclaim. It blends socio-political commentary, thoughtful poetry, clever wordplay, and Pacific roots/reggae/ska rhythms.

Marcel has a gift for the use of compositional techniques like word painting: deliberately manipulating the musical elements to imitate the emotion, action, or natural sounds as described in the lyrics of the song. For example in the song "Politician" from the *Children's Day* album, when he sings about using his voice "like a gun," he delivers the words in a staccato fashion imitating the sound of bullets being fired.

XX Squad was very much a band borne out of the Vanuatu Cultural Centre, a statutory institution established in 1960. When the band first started Ralph Regenvanu was playing the drums – at that time he was director of the Vanuatu Cultural Centre and is now a Member of Parliament in Vanuatu. The technical director of Vanuatu Broadcasting and Television Corporation was the guitarist, the director for Television Blong Vanuatu played bass, and on lead guitar was Maka Silona, the sound engineer for the Vanuatu Cultural Centre recording studio. This was a group of people who were very involved in the cultural life of the nation; they were committed to the cause of raising the profile of contemporary culture.

> Marcel: So we all worked for these government and quasi-government bodies – but we were very critical of these very same institutions – but more so of the politicians who were supposed to be responsible for them. When our first album came out we were vilified in the press, for the hypocrisy of taking our salaries on the one hand and criticising them with the other. Now in my new band Kalja Riddim Klan I try to bring together all the musical influences that we have in Vanuatu: reggae, R'n'B, traditional, stringband.

KRK – Kalja Riddim Klan

KRK is where Marcel now expresses the full range of his musical gifts. In a low register his voice is very earthy and resonant. When he is singing in his full voice it is nasal and edgy – gravelly, with imperfections, but deliberate in his use of colour and shape. The way he phrases and inflects certain notes with an edgy quality creates a sense of urgency and import – it seems clear that he has a message he is trying to get across: strident, insistent, and urgent. He contrasts this with sensitivity and softness – a very mellow gentle airy tone that is capable of blending with the sound of the flute, the wind, the ocean – like the haunting overtones of a conch shell. Many Pacific vocalists have this tone – they are able to match the tone of those airy instruments and convey sensitivity and care about the content of the lyrics. Marcel's delivery never sounds contrived, and one gets the impression that each time he sings a particular song it will be different.

KRK has involved a lot of teaching and mentoring of the younger members. In 2006, Marcel formalised this mentoring approach to music. He established the Tura Nambe Musik Senta – an association which aims to promote the development of traditional music by: i) creating a media library; ii) providing lessons for various musical instruments; and iii) organizing musical concerts and workshops to provide opportunities for young people. Tura Nambe has become the nursery ground for the young musical talent of Port Vila, providing a meeting place, a full set of instruments for bands to practice, and resources for young people to access further information on a range of topics.

> Marcel: Musicians in Vanuatu are not making money from their work – it's more like a mission or a vocation and so it's very important to us. The content reflects this. The content of the contemporary music, stringband music, even the traditional chants – in all of our music we sing about real things, the things which affect us in our daily life. Like for my first album, *Children's Day*, we were on the front page of the newspaper because we were criticizing the politicians of the day for breaking their promises and lying to the people. There is a big gap between the authorities and the people. Recently I wrote a song about a guy who escaped from prison and went and visited his wife and child. The authorities came after him, caught him and beat him up until he died. We asked the authorities who did this? and that someone had to be held responsible for it, but to this day we still don't know who did it. I use my music in this way as a tool – like a gun – but not to shoot people – but to open people's minds so that these things don't happen again so that my children and their children will live in a better world.

Resilience in action – Marcel Meltherorong

Author, poet, storyteller, playwright, producer, musician, songwriter and sand-artist, Marcel Meltherorong, is now one of Vanuatu's most prolific creatives. In an SBS Radio program (2008) he was described as part of the "renewal movement in politics and music" – a key driver of resilience in Melanesian life and art. He is one of Vanuatu's most accomplished storytellers. He was instrumental in the establishment of the *Kastom Stori* Association (formerly *Titamol*), and is the Director of *Tura Nambe*, which is a resource centre, library, and studio in Port Vila. Marcel remains the only ni-Vanuatu to have published a novel: his semi-autobiographical work of fiction titled *Toghan* was selected for the *Prix RFO du Livre 2007*.

As a *kastom* storyteller Marcel is also able to practice the fleeting beauty of the rich and complex tradition of sand drawing. Using one finger he traces a continuous, graceful pattern usually via a circuitous and opaque route. This practice often results in a delightful moment of awareness for the viewer when s/he finally recognizes the figurative element of the drawing (see http://songsofresilience.wikispaces.com/Marcel+Meto).

A sand drawing is a mnemonic device used to record and transmit rituals, mythological lore and a wealth of oral information about local histories, cosmologies, kinship systems, song cycles, farming techniques, and architectural and craft design. Traditionally, sand drawings possess several functions and layers of meaning: they can be "read" as a simple message or set of directions, maps and family trees, repositories of information, artistic works, illustration for stories, signatures, and objects of contemplation (UNESCO, 2003). For the uninitiated, these delightful designs speak of wisdom unpossessed, existing on the periphery of concept, in the interstices of dreams, in that dark empty space of our mind. It is a tradition so profoundly different to the Western notion of classical art, framed and hung and preserved, as it is, that the idea of it shimmers fleetingly while the tide rises and washes away the patterns, leaving new ones and old ones merging into the hungry wet sand. And it leaves a strange new pattern merging in the viewers mind – a pattern which also shimmers and casts a chimera of doubt over what exactly art means. Sand drawing brings us close to the core of this chapter. A person tells a story and creates a figurative representation of that story using the ground as both palette and paint. The act itself connects people with the story, the language in a timeless pattern that grounds it firmly in sense of place.

Conclusion

Like his sand drawings, Marcel's story of resilience dovetails with the story of sovereign nations like Vanuatu and others in the Pacific Islands. Yet narrow projections of colonized individuals resonate with the reified overtones of *kastom,* and the boundaries blur between yesterday and tomorrow, adding to the sense of remoteness from western material reality. In a distinctively non-western way this chapter has sought to show how an individual lends resilience to the community and the collective culture of kinship provides further resources for resilience in return. In a sand drawing, the land is both palette and paint. The act connects people with the story and language in a timeless pattern and grounds it firmly in a specific place. We have explored the contextual background of one of the most linguistically and culturally diverse regions on the planet, and investigated the possibilities this diversity brings with it: something consciously constructed as a way to increase the resilience of a population. We have explored the way contemporary music interacts with the traditional economy creating a cultural "edge effect" and how this interaction functions as a contextual variable of resilience at the level of the individual through to whole populations and hence, the cultural life of a nation.

The autotelic behaviour that Marcel has demonstrated since moving to Vanuatu is reflected in how he teaches (kinaesthetically and aurally), informs, and nurtures young people in local communities. He is actively engaged in music therapy, capacity building, music for wellbeing, and the generation of sustainable resources in his communities. Marcel's contemporary version of *kastom* offers non-Melanesian countries a model for resilience (if not a Pacific epistemology), as outlined by Regenvanu (2009). For most people in Oceania the topics of "resilience" and "indigenous epistemologies" remain a distant intellectualising of what, on a daily basis, is accepted as a normal procedure underpinning local decisions about food, respect, genealogy, ceremony, schooling and development (Moutu, 2000; Quanchi, 2004).

> Marcel: We don't have lots of money or income but we are very rich in terms of culture. We are still here. We still exist... You see, when I first discovered music I loved it and I wanted to share it with everyone around me.

These ideas require a substantial shift in thinking from the dominant discourse of the west still coming to terms with the process of reconciliation.

But for Marcel, he is simply telling stories from a storytelling tradition with a long oral history. He does this because he can and because it affirms his sense of purpose.

References

Abdallah, S., Thompson, S., Michaelson, J., Marks, N., and Steuer, N. (2009). *The Happy Planet Index 2.0: Why good lives don't have to cost the Earth*, New Economics Foundation, London.

Allen, K., and Walker, A (2000). Qualitative Research, in Hendricks, D. and Hendricks S.S., eds *Close Relationships. A Sourcebook.* Sage Publications, London.

Ambrose, D., (1997). 'Vanuatu politics—two into one won't go', *Pacific Economic Bulletin*, 12(2):115–22.

Atkinson, R. (1998). *The Life Story Interview* Thousand Oaks, Ca. Sage.

Bazeley, P. and Mullen, B. (2006). *Vanuatu: Economic Opportunities Fact-Finding Mission*, On Behalf of AusAID and NZAID, July.

Biermann, S. (2008). Found in Translation: Differences, Tolerance and Enriching Diversity in Activating Human Rights and Peace: Universal Responsibility Conference 2008 Conference Proceedings Published by Southern Cross University, Centre for Peace and Social Justice, accessed online on 4/5/09.

Bolton, L. (2003). *Unfolding the Moon. Enacting Women's Kastom in Vanuatu* Honolulu, University of Hawai'i Press.

—. (1998). 'Praying for the revival of kastom: Women and Christianity in the Vanuatu Cultural Centre' Source: *Women, Christians, Citizens: Being Female in Melanesia Today*, Oceanic-Whitehall Guesthouse, Sorrento, Victoria 11-13 November 1998 http://rspas.anu.edu.au/melanesia/lissant2.htm.

Bonnemasion, J. (1984). 'Social and Cultural Aspects of Land Tenure' in P Larmour (ed) *Land Tenure in Vanuatu* (Institute of Pacific Studies of the University of the South Pacific, Suva, 1984) 1.

Bradley, L. (2001). Bass Culture: When Reggae Was King; Penguin.

Csikszentmihalyi, M. (1997). Finding Flow: The Psychology of Engagement with Everyday Life; Basic Books.

Feeny, S. (2010). The impact of the global economic crisis on the Pacific region, Oxfam Australia, Melbourne.

Hayward, P. (2009). Local Interpretation: music video, heritage and community in contemporary Vanuatu, *Perfect Beat*, vol. 9, no. 2.

Hickey, F. R. (2006). Traditional Marine Resource Management in Vanuatu: Acknowledging, Supporting and Strengthening Indigenous

Management Systems. *SPC Traditional Marine Resource Management and Knowledge Information Bulletin* 20: 11–23.

Huffman, K. (2000). *Traditional 'Arts' in Vanuatu.* Published online October 17 www.vanuatuculture.org accessed online on 4/5/09.

—. (2009). A Palmy Balm for the Financial Crisis, The Sydney Morning Herald, February 9, 2009, www.smh.com.au accessed online on 4/5/09.

Jolly, M. (2001) Encyclopedia of life writing. Autobiographical and Biographical Forms. Fitzroy Dearborn Publishers, London, Chicago.

Lemerle, K. & Stewart, D. (2009). A New Conceptual Framework For Understanding Resilience unpublished paper accessed online at http://songsofresilience.wikispaces.com/A+theoretical+framework+for +the+concept+of+resilience on 9/11/09.

Linde, C. (1993). *Life Stories: The creation of coherence.* Oxford University Press.

Lini, W. (1980). Beyond pandemonium : from the New Hebrides to Vanuatu, Asia Pacific Books, Wellington.

Marcs, N., Simms, A., Thompson, S. and Abdallah, S. (2006). *The Happy Planet Index: An index of human well-being and environmental impact*, New Economics Foundation, London.

Miles, W. F. S. (1998) Bridging mental boundaries in a postcolonial microcosm: identity and development in Vanuatu, University of Hawaii Press.

Moutu, A. (2000). Rhetorics: a blurred image of reality - navigating the waters of Melanesian thought, Papua New Guinea National Museum & Art Gallery, accessed online at http://www.pngbuai.com/600technology/information/waigani/w97-moutu.html on 6/6/09.

Naupa, A. (2005). 'Rooted in the land: evolving culture, land tenure and identity in Vanuatu', paper presented at Pacific Islands Workshop, Australian National university, Canberra, 31 January – 4 February.

Pacific Pulse (2008). Celebrating Contemporary Music, Australia Network, Australian Broadcasting Corporation.

Quanchi, M. (2004). Indigenous epistemology, wisdom and tradition; changing and challenging dominant paradigms in Oceania. In: Social Change in the 21st Century Conference, Centre for Social Change Research, 29th October.

Rawlings, G. (2007). Tax havens, expats and sea-changing property developers: current patterns of land use in Vanuatu, paper presented to State, Society and Governance in Melanesia Seminar, Australian National university, Canberra, 28 February.

Regenvanu, R (2009) The traditional economy as the source of resilience in Melanesia. Paper presented at the Lowy Institute conference 'The Pacific Islands and the World: The Global Economic Crisis', Brisbane, Australia, 3rd August 2009.

SBS French program (2008). SBS Radio, November 22.

Sidebotham, N. (2009). The White Man Never Wanna Hear Nothin About What's Different From Him: Representations of law's 'other' in Australian Literature, paper presented for Doctoral thesis at Murdoch University.

Simo, J. (2005). Report of the national review of the Customary Land Tribunal Program in Vanuatu, Vanuatu National Cultural Council, Port Vila.

Smith, P.N. (2006). Resilience in Xhosa families. Doctoral Dissertations. Available online at https://etd.sun.ac.za/jspui/handle/10019/127 [Accessed 17/09/2009].

Sparks, C. (2006). Rural women and everyday resistance to structural adjustment in Melanesia. U Victoria (Canada) Masters Thesis.

Stocker, L. and Burke, G. (2006). Overlay Mapping – A Methodology for Place-Based Sustainability Education in Wooltorton, S. and Marinova, D. (Eds) *Sharing wisdom for our future. Environmental education in action: Proceedings of the 2006 Conference of the Australian Association of Environmental Education.*

The 730 Report (2009, April 20). Foreign investors exploit cheap Vanuatu land, Australian Broadcasting Corporation.

Tryon, D. (1996). Dialect Chaining and the Use of Geographical Space. In Bonnemaison, J., Kaufmann, C., Huffman, K., and Tryon, D., editors, *Arts of Vanuatu*, pp 170-181, Bathhurst, Australia. Crawford House Publishing.

Tuhiwai Smith, L. (1999). Decolonising methodologies; research and indigenous peoples, Auckland, Zed Books, 34.

Unattributed (2010). Coroner's report on Bule's death – a real test of the Government's resolve, Vanuatu Daily Post, March 12.

Unattributed (2008a). VIPA pushes for Forum Against Crime, Vanuatu Daily Post, January 11.

Unattributed (2008b). Vanuatu economy in peril, Vanuatu Daily Post, December 13.

Unattributed (2008c). [Book review of Raga: Approche du continent invisible, Le Clézio, J-M. G. Paris: Éditions du Seuil] Oceania Newsletter 49, March.

Unattributed (2007). Winners are grinners in the happiest country on earth, Vanuatu Daily Post, October 29.

UNESCO (2003). Proclamation 2003: 'Vanuatu Sand Drawings'
http://www.unesco.org/culture/ich/index.php?lg=EN&topic=mp&cp=
VU#TOC1

Veracini, L. (2003). The 'Shadows of the colonial period' to 'Times of
sharing': history writing in and about New Caledonia/Kanaky, 1969-
1998.

CHAPTER SIX

SINGING FOR MENTAL HEALTH AND WELLBEING: COMMUNITY INITIATIVES IN ENGLAND

STEPHEN CLIFT, IAN MORRISON, TRISH VELLA-BURROWS
AND GRENVILLE HANCOX[1]

ELLE CALDON AND UDI PERRY[2]

PENNY HOLDEN, CHRISSIE PARSONS-WEST
AND KATE HESKETH MOORE[3]

CHRISTINA ROWLAND-JONES AND SAM HAYES[4]

Introduction

The potential contributions of the arts to health care and health promotion have attracted a growing interest in the United Kingdom (UK) over the last 25 years (Clift et al., 2009). Across the country, a wide range of innovative arts and health projects utilise different forms of creative arts activity that include visual arts, dance, literature and crafts of all kinds. Many projects draw upon the power of music and capitalise on the social and psychological benefits which self-evidently follow from active engagement in music-making. Foremost among musical activities, in terms of accessibility, is singing. Although many people may say, "I can't sing!", the fact is that virtually everyone can sing given a supportive context and good facilitation. Undoubtedly, the human capacity to sing is rooted in our

[1] Sidney De Haan Research Centre for Arts and Health, Folkestone
[2] Mustard Seed Singers, Canterbury
[3] Sing Your Heart Out, Norwich
[4] Michaelhouse Chorale, Arts and Minds, Cambridge

evolutionary history (Mithen, 2005; Pinker, 2002), and draws upon cognitive and social capacities, which must have had adaptive significance in the survival of our species over the last hundred thousand years. Group singing is fundamentally possible because we all have an innate capacity to synchronise our actions with others, and this is turn has demonstrable physiological, mental and social effects (Wiltermuth & Heath, 2009). Singing interactions between babies and caregivers, especially mothers, are also culturally universal from the earliest moments of life, and clearly form the basis for early associations between the singing voice and bonding and a deep sense of security and comfort (Malloch & Trevarthen, 2009). It is a matter of huge consequence, and real damage, when children at an early age are told that they cannot or should not sing, and many people carry this notion of being unable to sing throughout their lives even though they may feel a deep desire to sing.

There is increasing international interest among health professionals and researchers in the idea that group singing is beneficial in promoting and maintaining health for people who are otherwise free from health problems, and for those whose physical and mental health is compromised in some way (see Clift, Hancox, Staricoff and Whitmore, 2008; Clift, Nichol, Raisbeck and Morrison, under review). In the UK, singing groups have been established, for example, for people affected by chronic obstructive pulmonary disease (COPD)[5], to help improve breath control and to combat social isolation and increased risks of depression which follow from chronic illness. Similarly, singing groups for people with Parkinson's disease[6] serve the same social and psychological functions for their members, but in addition help to maintain vocal functions such as speech volume and clarity, which are often compromised by the disease. In this chapter, an account is given of the development of three singing for mental health groups and the benefits that mental health service users, with

---

[5] Two groups are running in Brighton and Hove, facilitated by Udita Everett, see: http://www.uditamusic.co.uk/voice_coaching.html
Singing groups and a small experimental trial are also running at the Royal Brompton and Harefield Hospital in London, See:
http://www.rbht.nhs.uk/about/fundraising/arts/whats-on/workshops/
[6] Sing for Joy has been running in London for six years, see:
http://www.carolgrimes.com/pages/workshops/sing_for_joy.html
Q2, Quivers and Quavers, a singing for speech therapy group has been running in Hereford for a similar period of time, see report in the European Parkinson's Nurses Network journal, issue 14, 2008:
http://www.epda.eu.com/pdfs/epnnJournal/issue14.pdf

a history of severe and enduring mental health difficulties, have gained from being part of a small choir. The groups are: Sing Your Heart Out, Norwich, the Michaelhouse Chorale, Cambridge and the Mustard Seed Singers, Canterbury. The focus of this chapter is not on singing as a form of music therapy, but on singing as a distinctively human activity that brings its own intrinsic rewards and benefits.

In the context of health services and public health, the case for the value of group singing for wellbeing and health needs to be made empirical given that a strong emphasis is placed on demonstrating that interventions are evidence-based and cost-effective. The challenge of theorising the connections between singing and health may carry less weight in the struggle for securing funding for projects and services yet is central to the scientific task of understanding "how" and "why" singing together can impact on subjective wellbeing and physical health. In this respect, the title of this book *Songs of Resilience* helps to focus attention on a potentially key theoretical mechanism, namely the musical character and lyrical content of what is being sung. When people sing, they sing songs, and the songs themselves, in some contexts, may be central to the impact that singing can have for wellbeing and health. This is an idea explored further in the case studies presented below.

From a social science perspective, Lemerle and Stewart (chapter two) offer a general framework for understanding resilience, which can be applied to the specific case of group singing. Building on a socio-ecological as opposed to bio-medical paradigm for health, they argue that health is influenced "by the combined effects of accrued risks to which one is exposed (both innate and contextual), and those protective factors to which one has access and which may buffer those risks" (p.40). On a social level, they place emphasis on the resources or "capital," which social systems make available to individuals, and on a personal level, the extent to which individuals have the capacity to access them. Indeed, Lemerle and Stewart suggest that "social systems expose individuals to varying levels of resources or capital that determine the availability of protective factors to which the individual has access, from the macro level … through the meso level … and finally micro level" (p.29). Organised health services are an important social resource provided to support people with health problems, but in reality the availability and quality of such services, and the ability or willingness of individuals to access them, are important determinants of health and health inequalities in all societies. But beyond the obvious issue of health services as a form of social system capital available to address ill-health, Lemerle and Stewart argue for a broader conception of resilience to include personal resources (human capital), social inter-connectedness (social capital) and tangible and intangible resources supporting "a sense of group identity" (community capital). All of these processes are seen to be significant in determining how individuals and communities respond in the face of challenges to wellbeing.

In the context of this book and chapter, therefore, the activity of singing together in groups can be seen as a form of social and community capital, and participation may well contribute to the strengthening of human capital on an individual level. Group singing brings people together in a common pursuit that can build a sense of group identity. The existence of singing groups for individuals to join, and particularly groups which are welcoming to people with existing health issues, is a function of the wider social system, and the extent to which commitment and enthusiasm, as well as finance, resources, venues and personnel, are available to make such activity happen. Equally, individual engagement with the potential benefits afforded by singing groups depends on personal issues of value, self-belief, awareness and accessibility (i.e., Do I want to sing? Do I believe I can sing? Do I know about singing groups locally? Is there a singing group I would feel comfortable to join? Does it meet at a convenient time? Can I actually get to it?).

The challenges of establishing singing for health groups and of keeping groups going is an important theme running through the experience of singing for health groups in the UK. The fact that these groups exist, and have continued to exist in the face of these challenges, is testimony to the tangible benefits participants gain for their wellbeing as people would hardly continue to attend week by week if they did not experience benefits on some level. Such groups also provide a model in miniature of the socio-ecological paradigm of health and the processes involved in developing and maintaining resilience in the face of serious challenges to health and wellbeing.

This chapter is the outcome of a collaborative effort between researchers within the Sidney De Haan Research Centre for Arts and Health and musicians and mental health service users involved in the three singing for health projects noted above. The research team provide an account of the research context in the next section of the introduction. This is followed in the second part of this chapter by accounts from key service users, managers of services and musicians who set up these singing for health groups. The contributors to these case studies were asked to explain how the groups were established, to describe some the benefits observed among group members, and to identify particular songs which have emerged as having special significance for the groups. No attempt has been made to standardize the style in which these accounts are written.

Review of research on singing, wellbeing and health

Recent systematic reviews of research on singing and wellbeing (Clift et al., 2008; Clift et al., under review) have revealed a relatively small corpus of research which varies considerably in terms of focus, method, sample characteristics, sample size, nature of the singing investigated, data gathered and approach to analysis. In fact, the studies are so diverse that a coherent synthesis of the evidence on the value of singing for wellbeing is not possible. Rather, studies were categorised according to their design and the nature of data gathered, and the evidence they provided critically evaluated.

A number of qualitative studies on the benefits of community singing have been undertaken with diverse samples of singers, and these provide evidence from subjective reports on a range of social, psychological, and health benefits associated with singing. Bailey and Davidson (2002, 2005) for example, interviewed choir singers from a range of social backgrounds in Canada; Silber (2005) explored the impact of a singing group established in a women's prison in Israel, and Watanabe (2005) explored the experience of individual engagement with Karaoke lessons and performance in Japan.

The work of Bailey and Davidson is of particular relevance to the focus of this chapter as many of their participants experienced mental health problems together with difficulties arising from substance dependencies. In their first study (2002), they interviewed members of a small choir for homeless men set up in Montreal. Four themes emerged repeatedly in the men's accounts:

> Group singing alleviated depression and enhanced emotional and physical well being;
>
> Performing to an audience encouraged a sense of personal worth and provided a means of re-engaging with wider social networks;

The choir provided a supportive context for the men in which they could develop their social skills and achieve collective goals;

Singing is mentally demanding, and required the men to concentrate and learn new material in order to perform. Such concentration also directed their attention away from internal preoccupation with their problems.

In further work, Bailey and Davidson (2005) interviewed members of a singing group in an economically disadvantaged area, together with more socially advantaged and affluent choral singers. The themes identified in the 2002 paper are considered to be broadly applicable to singers irrespective of social context and the character of the repertoire being sung, but some differences of emphasis did emerge. Both disadvantaged and more privileged singers, for example, highlighted the broadly "therapeutic" value of participation in singing, particularly in relation to creating energy, positive emotional experience and relaxation. For other themes, some important differences emerged, particularly in relation to the cognitive dimensions and the impact of singing in a group. For the more marginalised participants, singing provided a stimulating activity which helped to promote concentration and an ordering of their inner mental space. For the middle class singers, in contrast, a greater stress was placed on developing musical knowledge and skill which enabled them to meet the challenges of classical repertoire and gain a sense of achievement.

The idea that singing can be beneficial for wellbeing and health is also supported by surveys in which choral singers have been asked to respond to a range of statements about the effects of singing. Beck et al. (2000) report that 67 per cent of semi-professional choral singers in their survey agreed or strongly agreed that "Singing has contributed to my personal well-being," and Clift and Hancox (2001) report that 71 per cent of singers in a university choral society agreed or strongly agreed that singing was beneficial for their "mental wellbeing." Clift and Hancox identified six dimensions of benefits associated with choral singing from a Principal Components Analysis of their questionnaire. These were labelled (in order) as: "benefits for well-being and relaxation," "benefits for breathing and posture," "social benefits," "spiritual benefits," "emotional benefits" and "benefits for the heart and immune system." There is also a clear link between the set of components emerging from this analysis and the model of positive benefits of group singing emerging from the work of Bailey and Davidson (2002, 2005). For the first and most important factor of "wellbeing and relaxation," Clift and Hancox found that women had higher scores than men, which suggests that women experience or perceive greater wellbeing benefits from singing.

Clift et al. (2008) report the largest study on choral singing and wellbeing undertaken to date. Their cross-national survey took the World Health Organisation's (WHO) definition of health[7] as a starting point and utilised the short form of the WHO Quality of Life questionnaire (WHOQOL-BREF)[8] to gather data on 1124 choral singers drawn from choirs in Australia, England and Germany. In addition, singers completed a specially constructed 12-item "effects of choral singing scale" and gave written accounts of the effects of choral singing on wellbeing and health in response to open questions.

Clift et al. (2010) and Clift and Hancox (2010) have analysed written accounts of the effects of choral singing on wellbeing given by participants with relatively low psychological wellbeing as assessed by the WHOQOL-BREF, and high scores on the singing scale indicating a strong perceived impact of singing on a sense of personal well-being. Four categories of significant personal and health challenges were disclosed by members of this group: enduring mental health problems; family/relationship problems; physical health challenges and recent bereavement. The following quotations point to the value of singing in supporting resilience in the face of with such challenges:

> I have had to stop working due to an on-going medical condition (bi-polar disorder). I have had several episodes of this. Requiring varying lengths of time spent in hospital, followed by months of time needing support for depression and lack of self-confidence. Being a member of this particular choir has lifted my self-esteem again and restored self-belief. English Female 54

> I had a full time panic attack last week. Tried some swimming exercises which made it worse – then sang in the car for half an hour. By the end my heart rate and breathing had returned to normal, neck and shoulders relaxed, stomach unknotted. Generally find it unwinds and relaxes me. Always feel "looser" after rehearsals. Australian Male, 38

---

[7] "Health is a state of complete physical, mental and social well-being and not merely the absence of disease or infirmity" (WHO, 1946).

[8] The WHOQOL-BREF is the short form of a quality of life questionnaire constructed by the World Health Organization Quality of Life project on the basis of a large-scale international collaborative project. See:
http://www.who.int/substance_abuse/research_tools/whoqolbref/en/

As a carer of two relatives stricken with schizophrenia, I have suffered from reactive depression. (…) Having a pleasant start to the day knowing I shall meet like-minded people and enjoy music making, hopefully having a laugh along the way. Hearing the harmonies helps me forget family worries. English Female 70

It plays a significant part in my emotional health and wellbeing. I find music uplifting. When recovering from a major stroke, singing was one of the ways of lifting my spirits out of depression. English Male, 65

My husband died 3 months ago so all the questions about negative feelings etc. are distorted by this fact. One of the greatest supports in my life at this difficult time is the [choir I belong to]. I think choral singing is fantastic for emotional health. English Female, 6

In addition to qualitative studies and questionnaire surveys, more objective, experimental research has also assessed the impact of singing on physiological variables assumed to have wellbeing and health implications. Several studies, for example, have assayed levels of immunoglobulin A in saliva taken from participants before and after singing, and reported significant increases, which points to enhanced immune system activity (e.g., Beck et al., 2000; Kuhn, 2002; Kreutz, et al., 2004). Two quasi-experimental studies have also reported positive health impacts from group singing for elderly people using standardised measures and objective indicators of wellbeing and health. Houston et al. (1998) report improvements in levels of anxiety and depression in nursing home residents following a four-week programme of singing, and Cohen et al. (2006) found improvements in both mental and physical health in a group of elderly people participating in a community choir for one year. Recent studies have also suggested benefits of singing for people with chronic lung conditions (e.g., Engen, 2005, Bonilha et al., 2008), Parkinson's disease (e.g., Di Benedetto et al., 2009) and dementias (e.g., Myskja & Nord, 2008).

THREE UK SINGING FOR MENTAL HEALTH GROUPS

Sing Your Heart Out, Norwich/Norfolk

Sing Your Heart Out (SYHO) was started in 2004 by Tracy Morefield, a psychotherapist in Norfolk working for the local mental health Trust.[9] There is a story behind this. In 1988, St Andrew's Mental Hospital in Norwich (the old Victorian Lunatic Asylum) was closed down. When clearing the site for redevelopment, a large quantity of sheet music was found in a cupboard. It was later discovered that the music had been written and arranged for the hospital orchestra which had consisted of both staff and patients, and played for concerts and dances from the 1820s to the 1920s. Luckily this was saved from the skip and sent to auction. It ended up in the possession of David Juritz, violinist and leader of the London Mozart Players (LMP). Juritz then got in touch with Dr Steve Cherry at the University of East Anglia who had written a book on the history of mental health in Norfolk[10] to find out more about the history of the music. This request came to Maggie Wheeler, Chair of the Trust, who put an article in the Trust's magazine, *Insight*, asking if anyone had any memories of this or would anyone care to form a tribute band. Tracy, a keen choral singer herself, thought that this would be the ideal opportunity to launch a project she had been mulling over for a while.

Tracy Morefield had two excellent ideas which have since formed basic principles for SYHO. The first was that the voice coach should be a professional with suitable skills and experience to work with all sorts of people. And the second that the workshops should not be just for patients, but for staff, carers, family, and anyone who was interested in joining in.

Initially, funding for the workshops came from various small charities within the Trust, and from Staff Development money, and a room was found within Norwich's mental hospital at Hellesdon. The first SYHO workshop was held in October 2004 at Hellesdon Hospital. The first two terms were led by Sian Croose. When other commitments prevented her

---

[9] Norfolk and Waveney Mental Health NHS Foundation Trust.
[10] *Mental Health Care in Modern England: The Norfolk Lunatic Asylum, St. Andrew's Hospital 1810-1988*

from continuing, Chrissy Parsons-West[11] stepped in and brought with her a sense of fun and laughter, an important feature of the sessions ever since. SYHO ran for a total five terms in various rooms in the hospital to the end of March 2006.

Around this time, a radio producer, Margaret Renn, had heard about David Juritz's acquisition of the asylum's sheet music and she was interested to hear about SYHO and came to interview us and to record us singing. This programme, "The Asylum Band," narrated by Juritz, was transmitted on Radio 4 in June 2006. It looked at the history of the old asylum, and incorporated interviews with people who remembered the Band and had worked at the old institution. Included were interviews with Morefield and a service user about how it started and the benefits to be gained. The programme finished with a recording of a special "Sing Your Heart Out" session featuring Juritz on violin and a pianist from the LMP.

A way had to be found of keeping SYHO alive. Penny Holden, a service user and Perry Marshall from Social Services joined with Morefield, Renn and Parsons-West to form the first steering group. Our first success in fund-raising was a grant from The Lilly Reintegration Award.[12] Following the publicity which this generated, the idea of a joint project with David Juritz and his colleagues suddenly blossomed into fruition and we were invited to perform with the prestigious London Mozart Players at the Norfolk & Norwich Festival in 2007! Workshops restarted in January with this aim, and we commissioned composer Fraser Trainer[13] to develop a new piece in workshops with us. Trainer's approach was in complete empathy with the SYHO ethos of building complex music from a basis of simple building blocks. This resulted in a piece which incorporated the participants' ideas and improvisations that gave them a great sense of ownership and pride. Parsons-West's community choir "Hearts and Voices"[14] joined us for this project and new relationships were formed. The concert was a great success and led to many other things including a Channel 5 TV programme in their series "Mad for Music,"[15] which

---

[11] http://syho.org/Chrissy.aspx
[12] Established in 1996 by Eli Lilly & Co., the awards specifically honour treatment teams, programs and services, as well as individuals with bipolar disorder or schizophrenia who provide hope and support to their peers, for stellar contributions and services. See:http://www.lilly.co.uk
[13] See:http://www.frasertrainer.com/
[14] See: http://www.heartsandvoices.co.uk/
[15] See: http://www.communitychannel.org/content/blogcategory/142/132/

featured Christopher Bridgeman and included SYHO & Hearts and Voices singing "Stand by Me" (Ben E King).

In 2008 we were awarded funding[16] which enabled us to move away from the hospital into the community and start satellite SYHO groups in other parts of Norfolk. One of these venues featured in a recent BBC film about SYHO which can be viewed on our website.[17]

So what happens at a SYHO session? Each workshop starts with stretching, wriggling and groaning exercises, gently leading into hums until people are singing. The songs are taught by ear, and while there are words supplied for those who feel the need, they are seldom necessary as the lyrics can be picked up easily as in traditional folk-singing culture. We always sing in harmony, using rounds, part-songs and simple arrangements from as many styles as possible in order to appeal to a wide range of tastes in music. The songs which seem to meet the broadest approval are easy African songs, spirituals, traditional rounds and arrangements of pop classics.

At first sight, SYHO sessions may look just like any other singing workshops. However there are some subtle differences which are important for the success of the project. The inclusion of staff, carers, friends, family and interested people from the local community, alongside mental service users, is one of the key factors in the project's value in combating stigma and facilitating re-integration into ordinary life, especially for service users who have spent time in institutional care. With no badges and everyone on first names basis, encounters are person-to-person, rather than, for example, staff to service-user or mentally-ill to "healthy." One unexpected outcome of this merged community has been the gradual acknowledgement amongst the supposedly mentally "well" of their own struggles with mental health at various times in their lives. This has opened the door to more honest relationships and a breakdown in the barriers put up by fear.

Commitment is something which develops on an individual basis. While some people attend very regularly, for others, having to make an ongoing commitment would be a deterrent. For this reason every group is run as an open session and everyone is welcome to drop-in and out as suits them.

---

[16] Norfolk Community Foundation Mental Health Fund from the Goldsmiths Livery Company.
[17] See:http://syho.org/

This provides challenges for the voice coach in terms of providing a sense
of progress for regular attendees whilst creating an inclusive atmosphere to
enable a new person on any week to join in with ease. Choosing repertoire
with many potential layers is very helpful; each time a song is revisited
there is the chance to teach the best-known parts to newcomers while
offering new variations to those who have already sung the song many
times. The repertoire is circulated so that a simple piece learned (and
forgotten) two terms ago can be revived to be totally fresh for a newcomer
and still hold some fond memories for a long-term member. Overall we
need to have a large stock of songs that are quick and easy to learn,
alongside more complex pieces with parts of varying difficulty.

Members of Sing Your Heart Out

While we have enjoyed some very special performance opportunities and
continue to welcome them as a part of the project, the core of the SYHO
experience is being part of the ongoing week-by-week inclusive singing
community. The group works in the moment toward an instant
performance at whatever level is appropriate and achievable for a
particular song on that day with the group in the room. Everyone
contributes whatever they can to the sound and mood, and what emerges
can be tender, joyful, touching, raucous and powerful, leading sometimes

to moments of breathtaking beauty and at other times to uncontrollable giggles!

One of our special songs, which we sang at are Norfolk & Norwich Festival is "Stand by me" (based on the Sharon/Raugh arrangement). The first time the group managed the complex chorus section, and heard what an amazing sound they were making, the pride was evident in the ear-to-ear smiles around the room. This song has become something akin to an anthem for us, expressing as it does the need we all have for support in times of difficulty:

> When the night has come
> And the land is dark
> And the moon is the only light we'll see
> No I won't be afraid, no I won't be afraid
> Just as long as you stand, stand by me

In contrast is "Zuarende," a deceptively simple African lullaby based on only two words and with gratifyingly sumptuous harmonies. The words describe a child unable to sleep in the dark as the sun has gone away. The mother reassures him that the sun will again come back. This song seems to bestow an instant sense of calmness and well-being to those singing it. For this reason it is often requested within the group by any participants who are feeling over-agitated.

Our repertoire continues to develop and new songs come to the fore as favourites. While these first two have been long-term classics, the surprise hit more recently has been "Praise You"[18] made famous by Norman Cook. It has given rise to great fun and high energy in the group, and the men have appreciated being the lead singers while the female singers provide the backing.

Michaelhouse Chorale, Arts and Minds, Cambridge

"Arts and Minds"[19] is a charity established in 2005 to promote and support access to all art forms for mental health service users, learning disabled people and offenders, across the Cambridgeshire & Peterborough Mental Health Foundation Trust, in both the hospitals and the related community. The Michaelhouse Centre, also a charity, is situated in the ancient St

---

[18] Composed by Cook/Yarborough arranged by Kirsty Martin
[19] See: http://www.artsandminds.org.uk/

Michael's chapel in the centre of Cambridge. It re-opened for worship in 2002 with a community centre, meeting rooms and a very popular café.

In 2007 the Friends of Michaelhouse sought advice from Arts and Minds about a possible collaboration to offer friendship and support to people with a mental health condition. A choir for mental health service users of any age, their informal and professional carers and friends was proposed and agreed to. Michaelhouse offered the venue at no cost, and charitable funding was secured for a conductor and music. The "Michaelhouse Chorale"[20] was launched in November 2007, run by Sam Hayes, director of music at the nearby University church.[21]

The Chorale has met weekly for two years. As well as mental health service users and carers, anybody is welcome to participate – even the occasional tourist. Run with enthusiasm and humour, the purpose is enjoyment and no ability or experience is required. Sessions start with physical and vocal exercises to aid relaxation, and an element of movement and drama is encouraged in some pieces. Percussion is used where appropriate. The songs reflect the taste and capabilities of the participants; some have considerable musical ability and are able to read music; others have never sung before, or not since schooldays.

The repertoire ranges from the classical tradition of the mediaeval period – secular and sacred – through to the present day popular music. The standard of singing is high, and many pieces feature the elements of singing in harmony, or antiphonally. The Chorale runs as a "drop-in," so the number of participants varies from week to week, but can reach 20. The core membership of 14 mental health service users, their carers and others, ranges in age from the early 20s to early 80s. Illnesses include panic attacks, mild and severe clinical depression, bi-polar, schizophrenia, dementia and learning disability.

After eighteen months an informal evaluation was carried out. Members with a mental health condition, and carers, provided verbal and written views of their experience of singing with the Chorale. The key findings were:

> Participation in a meaningful, joyful activity, which provides excited anticipation, motivation and purpose;

---

[20] See: http://www.artsandminds.org.uk/projects/2008/michaelhouse.html
[21] See:http://www.gsm.cam.ac.uk/Music_and_the_Arts/Music/body_music.html

The learning of a new skill, or a return to an activity previously enjoyed, in a welcoming, relaxed environment;

Alleviation of stress levels;

Improved concentration and memory;

Increased self-worth; an opportunity to be in control – as a person, not a patient;

Increased self-confidence, buoyancy and general well-being, which help in coping with mental illness;

A marked improvement in mental well-being;

Better physical health, through improved breathing and posture;

Social inclusion, camaraderie, laughter;

Increased concern for others;

A reported reduction in medication.

These benefits were reported by both male and female members of the Chorale, and continue to manifest themselves. Singing involves the whole body, not just the voice, and the Chorale members clearly relish the physicality of singing together. The original intention was not to sing in public, but they are now confident enough to do so, and enthusiastically share their enjoyment with others.

A 70-year old Chorale member, being treated for panic attacks, had not sung since schooldays. He enjoys singing so much that he decided to learn to read music. Lessons were arranged with a volunteer music therapist, and such good progress was made that he recently gained a distinction in Grade 3 theory. He lives alone and music is now the highlight of his life; much better than crosswords, he says. Outside the Chorale he regularly meets up with an 82-year old member, a professional composer, and together they study music, which is proving beneficial for them both.

The composer himself joined the Chorale in a state of anxiety and profound depression following an accident. He was withdrawn, unsmiling, no longer playing the piano he so much enjoys. After 18 months singing he is a changed man; smiling, chatty and, accompanied by his wife, he always arrives early enough to play the piano beforehand. She describes the miraculous change in him, and the gradual reduction in his medication to the lowest level.   As his carer she says she has also benefited from participating with her husband in an activity they can enjoy together.   It gives her enormous pleasure to see her husband once again enjoying his day-to-day activities as well as his music, and they have made new friends.

Members of the Michaelhouse Chorale

A dementia sufferer in her mid-70's had previously sung in choirs, and the weekly Chorale sessions are never long enough for her.   She has very limited recall of daily activities, but experiences no problems remembering the music and words of pieces, totally new to her, which the Chorale had not sung again for some weeks.   As well as remembering songs from many decades before, she retains the ability to sight-read, follow a score, and uses quite abstruse music terminology.   She says it is important and a joy to her that coming from a musical background, she is able to help other members and feel useful instead of constantly needing help herself.

Since the Chorale's foundation members have tackled an ever-increasing range of music and the second year has been one of consolidation.   We are now confident in the attendance of a dedicated, talented group of participants, which places the group in a position for expansion and growth.   The members were recently asked to choose which of the many pieces they have sung they most enjoy, and what they mean to them.   This presented quite a challenge because they all said how much they enjoy everything they sing, whether sacred or secular.   They described singing as now very important to them; a coming together, bringing a sense of fellowship and community which is especially helpful and supportive for some members who said they had previously been hiding themselves away as a result of their mental illness

Their first choice was unanimous; a simple setting of "The Lord's Prayer," by the composer member of the Chorale.   This was written before he became unwell and joined the choir.   It has special significance for the members because it was written by one of them, and they know how much pleasure it gives him to have it sung.   But personally they find it extremely beautiful; reflective yet uplifting.

Second, they chose a setting of "The Gospel Train," a folk spiritual which is part of an African American song tradition developed during the period of slavery.   The chorus is a constant repetition of words; an element of African music and one of the ways through which the slaves reinforced their religion and experience of slavery.   It includes train noises and whistles and has an exuberant, toe-tapping piano accompaniment:

> The Gospel train's a-comin'
> I hear it just at hand,
> I hear the car wheels rumblin'
> And rollin' thro the land.
>
> Get on board children,
> Get on board children,
> Get on board children,
> There's room for many a-more

The members said how much they love singing this because it is great fun, makes them feel very happy, and carries a strong message of inclusiveness: "The fare is cheap and all can go, the rich and poor are there.   No second class aboard the train, no difference in the fare."   It also provides members with physical exercise because it is sung with tremendous vigour.

Their third choice was "An Irish Blessing" (Bob Chilcott).   This is a very beautiful and expressive setting of a traditional Irish benediction:

May the road rise to meet you,
May the wind be always at your back.
May the sun shine warm upon your face
And the rains fall soft upon your fields.
And until we meet again
May God hold you in the palm of his hand.

Chorale members find this song very moving, and like The Lord's Prayer, uplifting; they feel it sends a message that comes from the heart.   Both words and music clearly generate a strong emotional response.   It is sung in harmony and is not particularly easy; a wonderful example of the tremendous progress made by the choir.

Writing about the Chorale, one member described the friendship and companionship that develops between people who meet as strangers and sing together.   They become at ease with one another, not through the sharing of an illness but through a shared interest in song.   Performance is not the goal, he says, but mental wellbeing and happiness through the fellowship of song.

Members of the Mustard Seed Singers

In a choir made up of mental health service users and professional workers gives a particularly powerful message in the context of mental health care. People facing challenges to their mental health are looking first and foremost for personal and professional friends they can rely upon to help get them through their difficulties, and this can be as true for professionals in health services as anyone else.

The third song, which is perhaps the signature tune of the choir, is "The Rose" (Bette Midler) – a song with harmonies almost certain to create chill experiences in performers and listeners alike, and which can readily bring tears to the eyes. The song speaks of "love" and how the complications of love in its many forms, including addictions and dependencies, can be damaging in our lives. But essentially the song is about hope and self-belief. Belief that all of us can find within ourselves the resources and sense of self-worth central to a capacity for resilience in the face of life's challenges:

> When the night has been too lonely
> And the road has been too long
> And you think that love is only
> For the lucky and the strong
>
> Just remember, in the winter
> Far beneath the bitter snows
> Lies the seed that with the sun's love
> In the spring, becomes the rose

During one meeting of the choir, a member arrived a little late looking distressed. In the interval another member listened to her share details of her day. She said "I almost didn't come, but I'm glad now I made the effort." He replied, "I'm glad you made it. Singing is the best anti-depressant I've ever had!"

Discussion

Given the fundamental human nature of music, our universal capacity to sing, and the clear implications singing can have for our deepest sense of wellbeing, it is surprising that so little research attention has been given to the value of singing for health, both physical and mental. From the late 1990s however, this idea has attracted growing interest from researchers, and a leading role in promoting research in this area is being provided by the Sidney De Haan Research Centre for Arts and Health. The evidence clearly shows, not only that people who sing in choirs and choral societies can experience considerable benefits in helping them cope with existing challenges to their health, but also that establishing singing groups for people with specific health issues can make a substantial and measureable difference to their sense of wellbeing and quality of life. With the accumulation of such research, it is to be hoped that health and social care services will increasingly recognize the value of singing groups for wellbeing and health, and support such initiatives financially, given that community singing is a relatively inexpensive activity to fund.

The findings from well-designed and rigorous research projects clearly have a central place in building the evidence-base to support public sector funding, but there is also a key role for reflective case studies of on-going groups for the concrete insights they can provide regarding the challenges, processes, outcomes and impacts of community singing groups for health. We need to demonstrate effectiveness and cost-effectiveness using validated and widely recognised measures, but also to understand theoretically how engagement with singing can make a difference to people recovering from periods of acute ill-health or coping more effectively with on-going chronic health conditions. The application of existing theoretical frameworks in the field of health and wellbeing to guide qualitative investigations has a key role to play here. Such perspectives as Antonovky's (1978) salutogenic approach to health, Csíkszentmihályi's (1990) theory of "flow," the psycho-neuro-immunology perspective, and socio-ecological models of social determinants of health, all have particular relevance. Lemerle and Stewart (chapter two), provide a valuable account of "resilience" to provide a context for contributions to this volume, and the phrase "songs of resilience" is especially redolent in pointing first and foremost to the resources available in music itself, and particularly songs, in helping to support and promote resilience in the face of life's challenges.

In the case studies of singing for mental health groups described in this chapter, we have narratives which highlight common challenges and shared experiences. Each of the projects has emerged in different ways in different contexts, but each has needed not only the vision and determination of a key individual or small group of individuals, but also a supportive organisational infrastructure with people in positions of management with access to resources and who are willing and able to offer support. Importantly, such people have gone ahead, not on the basis of clear research evidence of effectiveness, but on the basis of personal, lived experience of the value of singing for wellbeing. In considering organisational support and the availability of even limited amounts of funding to make groups possible, we are concerned with the contribution the social system can make to resources for resilience that are available to communities and individuals.

In terms of individuals, a key role is clearly played by the facilitator of singing groups, and in each of the case studies, groups have been fortunate in finding skilled and committed musicians to lead them in singing, able to be both adaptive to the group's needs and provide suitable challenges through new repertoire and opportunities for performance, which keep the experience of singing alive and fresh. Each of the groups has also worked from a philosophy of inclusiveness and normalisation. The groups are open not only to people in the mental health system, but also family, friends, supporters, and most importantly, professional staff in health and social care services. People are coming together not to engage in "music therapy," but simply to sing together as a group without regard to any distinctions of health or social position. The sense of being part of a team, and of having a group identity – one that is substantially reinforced through performance events – is another level through which singing groups offer resources for resilience in building confidence, self-esteem, a sense of purpose and of achievement.

Finally, when people come together to sing, they sing songs. This is so obvious that it might seem unnecessary to state it, but in fact both the musical character of the songs, their melodies, harmonies and lyrics, are central to the process through which group singing builds a sense of comradeship, camaraderie, identity and belonging, and supports a strong sense of self-confidence and esteem. In each group particular songs have assumed special significance – they have become "anthems" for the group – and in a real sense their own "songs of resilience."

References

Antonovsky, A. (1987) Unraveling The Mystery of Health: How people manage stress and stay well, San Francisco: Jossey-Bass Publishers.

Bailey, B.A. & Davidson, J.W. (2002) Adaptive characteristics of group singing: perceptions from members of a choir for homeless men, *Musicae Scientiae*, *VI*(2), 221-256.

Bailey, B.A. & Davidson, J.W. (2005). Effects of group singing and performance for marginalized and middle-class singers, *Psychology of Music*, *33*(3), 269-303.

Beck, R.J., Cesario, T.C., Yousefi, A. & Enamoto, H. (2000). Choral singing, performance perception, and immune system changes in salivary immunoglobulin A and cortisol, *Music Perception*, *18*(1), 87-106.

Bonilha, A.G., Onofre, F., Vieira, L. M., Prado, M. Y. A., & Martinez, J. A. B. (2008) Effects of singing classes on pulmonary function and quality of life of COPD patients *International Journal of COPD, 4*, (1), 1-8.

Clift, S., Camic, P.M., Chapman, B., Clayton, G., Daykin, N., Eades, G., Parkinson, C., Secker, J., Stickley, T. & White, M. (2009) The state of arts and health in England, Arts & Health: An international journal for research, policy and practice, *1*(1)6-35.

Clift, S.M. & Hancox, G. (2001). The perceived benefits of singing: findings from preliminary surveys of a university college choral society, *Journal of the Royal Society for the Promotion of Health, 121*(4), 248-256.

Clift, S. & Hancox, G. (2010) The significance of choral singing for sustaining psychological wellbeing: Findings from a survey of choristers in England, Australia and Germany, *Music Performance Research*, (in press)

Clift, S., Hancox, G., Staricoff, R. & Whitmore, C. (2008). *Singing and Health: A Systematic Mapping and Review of Non-clinical Research*, Canterbury: Canterbury Christ Church University. Available from: http://www.canterbury.ac.uk/centres/sidney-de-haan-research/ Accessed 20 May 2010.

Clift, S., Hancox, G., Morrison, I., Hess, B., Stewart, D. & Kreutz, G. (2008). *Choral Singing, Wellbeing and Health: Findings from a Cross-national Survey*, Canterbury: Canterbury Christ Church University. Available from: http://www.canterbury.ac.uk/centres/sidney-de-haan-research/ Accessed 20 May 2010.

Clift, S., Hancox, G., Morrison, I., Hess, B., Stewart, D. & Kreutz, G. (2009). What do singers say about the effects on choral singing on physical health? Paper presented at the *7th Triennial Conference of European Society for the Cognitive Sciences of Music,* University of Jyväskylä, Finland, August 12-16, 2009.

Clift, S., Hancox, G., Morrison, I., Hess, B., Kreutz, G. & Stewart, D. (2010) Choral singing and psychological wellbeing: Quantitative and qualitative findings from English choirs in a cross-national survey, *Journal of Applied Arts and Health*, 1, 1, 19-34.

Clift, S., Nicol, J.A.J., Raisbeck, M. & Morrison, I. (under review) Group singing, wellbeing and health: A systematic review, *UNESCO Journal.*

Cohen, G.D., Perlstein, S., Chapline, J., Kelly, J., Firth, K.M. & Simmens, S. (2006). The impact of professionally conducted cultural programs on the physical health, mental health, and social functioning of older adults, *The Gerontologist*, *46*(6), 726-734.

Csikszentmihalyi, M. (1990) *Flow: The psychology of optimal experience.* New York: Harper and Row.

Di Benedetto, P., Cavazzon, M., Mondolo, F., Rugiu, G., Peratoner, A. & Biasutti, E. (2009). Voice and choral singing treatment: A new approach for speech and voice disorders in Parkinson's disease, European Journal of Physical and Rehabilitation Medicine, *45*(1), 13-19.

Engen RL. (2005) The singer's breath: Implications for treatment of persons with emphysema. *Journal of Music Therapy, 42*(1), 20-48.

Houston, D.M., McKee, K.J., Carroll, L. & Marsh, H. (1998). Using humour to promote psychological wellbeing in residential homes for older people, *Aging and Mental Health*, *2*(4), 328-332.

Kreutz, G., Bongard, S., Rohrmann, S., Grebe, D., Bastian, H.G. & Hodapp, V. (2004). Effects of choir singing or listening on secretory immunoglobulin A, cortisol and emotional state, *Journal of Behavioral Medicine*, *27*(6), 623-635.

Kuhn, D. (2002). The effects of active and passive participation in musical activity on the immune system as measured by salivary immunoglobulin A (SigA), *Journal of Music Therapy*, *39*(1), 30-39.

Lemerle, K. & Stewart, D. (this volume). Resilience: Thriving Beyond Adversity in Brader, A. (Ed) *Songs of Resilience*. Newcastle: Cambridge Scholars Publishing.

Mithen, S. (2005) *The Singing Neaderthals*, London: Weidenfeld and Nicolson.

Malloch, S. & Trevarthen, C. (eds.)(2009) *Communicative Musicality: Exploring the basis of human companionship.* Oxford: Oxford University Press.

Myskja, A. & Nord, P.G. (2008). "The day the music died": A pilot study on music and depression in a nursing home, Nordic Journal of Music Therapy, *17*(1), 30-40.

Pinker, S. (2002) *The Blank Slate*, London: Penguin Books.

Silber, L. (2005). Bars behind bars: the impact of a women's prison choir on social harmony, *Music Education Research*, *7*(2), 251-271.

Watanabe, H. (2005). Changing adult learning in Japan: the shift from traditional singing to karaoke, *International Journal of Lifelong Education*, *24*(3), 257-267.

Wiltermuth, S. S. & Heath, C. (2009) Synchrony and cooperation, *Psychological Science*, *20*(1), 59-65.

WHO (1946), The WHO definition of health is to be found in the: Preamble to the Constitution of the World Health Organization as adopted by the International Health Conference, New York, 19-22 June, 1946; signed on 22 July 1946 by the representatives of 61 States (*Official Records of the World Health Organization*, 2, 100) and entered into force on 7 April 1948.

CHAPTER SEVEN

RESOURCING RESILIENCE THROUGH RECREATIONAL MUSIC PROGRAMS

BEN FARR-WHARTON, ANDY BRADER, GREG DODGE AND TOM DICK

Introduction

Several music programs in Australia deliver a United States (US) model created by the *Recreational Music-Making Movement,* founded by Karl Bruhn and Barry Bittman. This quasi-formal group of music makers, academics and practitioners uses the logic of decentralised global networks to connect with local musicians, offering them benefits associated with their "Recreational Music Program" (RMP). These RMPs encapsulate the broad goals of the movement, developed in the US during the 1980s, and now available as a package, endorsed by the National Association of Music Merchants (NAMM), for music retailers and community organisations to deliver locally (Bittman et al., 2003). High participation rates in RMPs have been historically documented amongst baby boomers with disposable income. Yet the Australian programs increasingly target marginalised groups and associated funding sources, which in turn has lowered the costs of participation.

This chapter documents how Australian manifestations of RMPs presently report on the benefits of participation to attract cross-sector funding. It seeks to show the diversity of participants who claim to have developed and accessed resources that improve their capacity for resilience through recreational music performance events. We identify funding issues pertaining to partnerships between local agencies and state governments that have begun to commission such music programs. Our assessment of eight Australian RMPs includes all additional music groups implemented since the first program, their purposes and costs, the skills and coping strategies that participants developed, how organisers have reported on resources, outcomes and attracted funding. We represent these features through a summary table, standard descriptive statistics and commentaries from participants and organisers.

This study contributes to the research literature by advocating an ecological view of resilience, which aims to better understand the allocation and use of health, education, recreation, cultural and economic resources across contexts. Our case study research has collated historical and current data from participants, organisers and instigators central to the emergence, adaptation and expansion of the US package of RMPs in Australia. We examine the adaptive qualities and key features of these music programs as sustainable resources, which have assisted participants to access, develop and bring into use significant transferable skills.

For most participants the pre-defined, explicit goal of RMPs – to produce a musical performance – is a short-lived challenging situation to which they are exposed. The skills and resources that participants use and develop through these performances relate directly to Ungar's (2008, p.23) definition of resilience, which notes three capacities for individuals and groups 1) to navigate their way to resources that sustain well being; 2) the ability of their physical and social ecologies to provide these resources; and 3) the ability to negotiate culturally meaningful ways for resources to be shared. Our analysis indicates that these music programs improve individual and group capacities to access, create and use resources that foster resilience, but do not manage to report effectively on the significance of live musical performances that support and motivate participants through challenging situations.

Context

The Webster dictionary indicates that the term *recreation* derives from the Latin root, "recreatio," which means restoration to health. Whereas the Oxford dictionary defines the same noun – an enjoyable leisure activity – with Latin origin from "recreare," which means create again, renew. US academics aligned with Recreational Music-Making have published a substantial scientific literature using these constructs of recreation to document a wealth of medical benefits (e.g., Bittman, 2001; Bittman et al., 2001; 2003; Hull, 1998; Burt, 1995). This and subsequent literature has become significant enough to warrant a large-scale global review, which reports on five outcomes related to the power of music (Hallam, 2001, p.4).

1) Physiological functioning
2) Motor Effects
3) Mood, arousal and emotion
4) Behaviour
5) Intellectual stimulation

These medical accounts of music's ability to affect an individual's cognition have left a gap in the literature on the "other" outcomes (or benefits) of recreational music programs. A gap that has been filled by practitioners and action research teams coalescing around arts, culture and community based activities, typically drawing attention to "wellbeing" indicators and "non-academic" outcomes from respective fields of health and education. Howard and Johnson's (2004) study of resilient teachers who resist stress and burnout through music performance, and chapter four (Harris et al.) of this book are good examples of research into the musical interventions that cut across "other" outcomes in health and education, using sector appropriate language.

In Australia, the health debate surrounding arts funding has been well documented by Wreford (2010), who depicts an instrumentality discourse of measurement and evaluation conflicting with the intrinsic qualities of health promotion through the arts.   Most arts-based practitioners in education and community development would echo Wreford's concern that all arts workers should incorporate the language and outcomes that health partners are seeking (Madden & Bloom, 2004), but view them as "secondary instrumental benefits to reflect the interest of various non-arts portfolios (2010, p.18)." In the case of RMPs, enjoyable and recreational elements of music activity are a primary concern of participants and organisers. Yet to be considered authentic applicants for funding, administrators require these RMPs to report on secondary outcomes of their music making activities, and as Barleet et al. (2009) remind us, community music organisers in Australia have learned to become increasingly pragmatic about changing their aims and objectives over time.

All the Australian RMPs derived from the Recreational Music Making Movement are projects aligned with Wreford's notion – non-arts outcomes are "secondary instrumental benefits." Applicable music projects include drumming circles, rock 'n roll bands and choir groups to name just a few. Regardless of musical purpose or genre, these projects are not commercially driven, and many RMPs have introduced the self-management of the group to ensure its sustainability. The RMP organisers we contacted were aware of the myriad of secondary benefits their recreational activities produce. The main distinction we highlight in this chapter is that since 2001, most Australian RMPs have attempted, with varying degrees of success, to shift away from the "user pays" model towards joint funded programs; this move requires event organisers to pay more attention to instrumental "secondary" or "other" benefits. Although we have gathered compelling reflective evidence of the effects of these RMPs on participants, it is the organisers' need to report on secondary benefits that is paramount if they are to maintain these public, private and commercial funding arrangements and reduce user costs.

Method

Our case study research and associated tools help us answer the question – Can we identify resources that foster resilience in participants and organisers of Australian RMPs?

A growing body of literature demonstrates substantial benefits for qualitative researchers who complement their observation field notes and interviews with data obtained from participants' online public communication in the form of emails, social networking activity, blog commentaries and promotion materials (Bruns, 2007). This smart use of information allows researchers performing content analysis to triangulate their data sources. A typical research schedule employing these methods would gather online information about the target population's communication trends to complement their observations, interviews and surveys (Burgess & Green, 2009). The research team first decides whether it is important to gather and analyse additional public data sequentially or simultaneously, and proceeds to use; 1) descriptive statistical methods to identify patterns of frequency and dependency in activities and communication processes; 2) network analysis to identify patterns in the structure and grouping of online communicative activity and; 3) textual analysis to determine correlations between them.

In accordance with the three stages of content analysis outlined above, our research team gathered primary and secondary data sources to inform what Glaser & Strauss (1967) call a "grounded" investigation into Australian RMPs. Several applications are available to researchers to assist their organisation and analyses of these varied information sources. NVivo and

Detextive were the specific tools that provided our team with audio/visual timelines, geotagging, tagclouds and thematic clusters that grounded our explanations in the data we collected.

For ten months during 2009, the research team observed and interviewed former and current organisers and participants of officially recognised RMPs in Australia. With the assistance of staff who organised the first RMP in Queensland, we identified eight currently active and proceeded to collect their media releases, audio-visual artefacts, blogs, public announcements, pamphlets, surveys, testimonials and published accounts of participants, mentors and organisers (several examples of which are located on our Songs of Resilience WIKI page http://songsofresilience .wikispaces.com/Agents+of+Change). Our research team had unlimited access to a co-author of this chapter, Greg Dodge, who instigated the first Australian RMP and contributed to many others. Researchers from the Queensland University of Technology guided the team's efforts in collecting and collating feedback and testimonial data that RMP organisers had collected from the 1,782 program participants.

Having gained appropriate ethical clearance, we also analysed RMP mailing lists, communications and post participation surveys to evaluate the skills gained as well as the resources accessed and created through participation. We supplemented this data with several in-depth interviews with lead organisers of three of the most active RMPs in Queensland – *Weekend Warriors, Come Together* and *CreActive Kids*.

Our analyses centred on the meanings that participants, mentors and organisers associate with their RMP experiences. We organised our data according to five question areas for all meaning making systems proposed by Cope and Kalantzis (2009, p. 176).

Representational: To what do the meanings refer?

Social: How do the meanings connect the persons they involve?

Structural: How are meanings organised?

Intertextual: How do the meanings fit into the larger world of meaning?

Ideological: Whose interest are the meanings skewed to serve?

To analyse our text based and digital artefacts we reviewed the modalities of meaning outlined first by the New London Group (1996) and developed by Cope and Kalantiz (2003, 2009). We narrowed our focus to five modes of meaning most evident in our datasets: *written* and *oral* languages, *visual, audio,* and *spatial* representations. We organised analytic themes according to these five modalities of meaning and subjected each to the five questions above.

We also present a chronological summary of these RMPs evolution supported by a summary table (see Table 2) to show the diversity of participants who claim to have developed and accessed resources that improve their capacity for resilience through recreational music performance events.

Early use of the RMP model in Australia

The Weekend Warriors program (hereafter referred to as WW) was one of the first documented applications of the RMP framework in the US. WW specifically targets men from the baby boomer generation and engages them in developmental music lessons. These lessons take place over a month and are geared towards performances. Typically fifteen to thirty participants enrol in the program and the facilitators help them organise into appropriate band structures. A team of mentors (usually active community musicians) achieve this process through a "show-and-tell" workshop, which filters individuals into ability groups and instrument/band-ensemble groupings. Early in our investigation the instigator of the first WW program in Australia told us:

> It is important in the first phase to create a supportive environment where new members feel nurtured enough to be willing to participate. Part of my attraction to the WW program is to draw back musicians who have long since parted with any form (amateur or other) of musicianship.

Over four weeks participants meet and practice with their respective bands, and under the direction of their mentor, forge a performable set list of Rock 'n Roll classics. The official program ends once all the bands come together at a venue and perform their set list in a live concert. The audience is typically made up of family, friends, mentors, and members of the general public.

Table 1. Summary of datasets

Instrument	Data Set	Mode of Meaning	Analysis
Observation	Observations about participants & mentors (all recorded online)	Oral	Textual
Interview	Face to face, in-depth interviews with organisers (n – 3)	Oral	Textual
Archives	Anonymous database exports Attendance Demographics Set lists Equipment and Venue lists	Written Spatial Visual	Textual Standard Descriptive Statistics Geo-tagging
Post-Participation Survey	4 multiple choice questions 2 closed questions 3 open-ended questions (n. 37)	Written	Textual Standard Descriptive Statistics
Promotions material & audiovisual artefacts	Movies, Photos, Presentations, Music, Press releases and reports	Written, Oral, Visual, Audio, Spatial	Multi-modal Textual & Standard Descriptive Statistics, Geo-tagging
Online Communication Tools	Websites, Social Networking Groups, Mail lists, Blogs, email exchanges with former participants (n. 4)	Written, Spatial	Tag Clouds Textual Standard Descriptive Statistics

The evolution

Ten RMPs in Australia have drawn heavily upon the WW format. Some have been active in a particular geographical location but are no longer current. For the sake of coherence, we use the term "derivatives" to identify all the RMPs that have adapted the WW model in Australia.

The evolution is as follows: *Weekend Warriors* (original; initiated in 2001), *Amp'd Up* (2003), *Swing Cats* (2003), *Boardroom Blitz* (2003), *Come Together* (2004), *CreActive Kids* (2005), *The Band Thing* (2007), and *Rhythm City* (2008).

Weekend Warriors - In a model largely unchanged since 2001, WW delivered twenty programs per annum around Australia at the height of its popularity (some simultaneously). In all instances the WW program did not primarily aim to make a profit, though small surpluses did occur in some instances. Greg Dodge secured the license from NAMM to deliver the US package in Australia adopting the user-pays model that focused on marketing and customer relation outcomes rather than sales; the 2001 cost was $250 (AUS) per entrant. Ellaways Music (Kedron, Queensland) provided the program's physical and human resources, which secured equipment, venues, marketing and the management of a participant database, in return for potential increases in their sales and customer base. In an interview, Dodge reflected on the dominant marketing pitch used by music retailers at that time.

> I had heard somewhere that the baby boomer generation held 80% of the western world's wealth. However, up until that point (2001) music retailers were only marketing to under-25 year olds.

The positive, medium-term economic impact of the first WW programs prompted the Australian Music Association (AMA), the national music industry body, to promote WW to its clients as a mechanism to boost sales to over-25 year olds. Subsequently, AMA commissioned Greg to train retailers around Australia to deliver the program locally. Working with AMA, he trained more than forty personnel over three years (2003-2005), only twenty of which acted on this opportunity to run the program in partnership with their local retail outlet.

During school holidays in 2003, Dodge adapted the first of many Weekend Warriors styled programs for high-school students. The derivative titled Amp'd Up evolved through a series of multi-agency collaborations in north Brisbane, between four local Schools, Brisbane City Council, Jabiru/Respec Community and Children's Services, Black Star Media and Ellaways Music. Now a successful annual program, it creates opportunities for young people aged 10-17 years to showcase their work at the Zillmere Multicultural Festival. Senior participants work in partnership with a youth worker and music teacher before the performance to design and facilitate the junior Amp'd Up program, thus receiving academic accreditation for their High School Senior Certificate. This certification is a good example of an instrumental secondary benefit, which is measurable and has recurrent value for the participant after the initial RMP experience.

Swing Cats also emerged in 2003 as a WW derivative with a musical theme of swing music. This participant-initiated program had no designated target demographic, and the bands that formed consisted of participants from a variety of age groups. The program was effective in catering for people that had associations with brass and woodwind bands as well as school instrumental programs. Yamaha Music supplied instruments at reduced hire and purchase rates for this program. This RMP acts as a good example of what Bartleet et al. (2009, p.159) recommend in their recent review of Australian community music, as public (schools), private (music businesses) and community sectors (swing musicians) all received appropriate secondary benefits.

Boardroom Blitz is an interesting derivative of the WW program as it adopted the mentoring and performance structure, but acted as a one-off corporate-charity and team-building event. Businesses donated $10,000 to charity in exchange for "professional development" for selected employees. These employees formed bands and received mentoring to reach a performance standard. Obvious secondary benefits are evident here for charities, employers and employees.

Come Together was the first derivative of the Weekend Warrior program to have a predetermined social benefit, and was the first to receive significant government funding. In the years leading up to 2004, one of Brisbane City Council's (BCC) Events Officers noted the situation facing the suburban, middle-aged males living in and around Brisbane. When interviewed, Athol Young revealed that council perceived this specific demographic as "isolated" and the local government saw this as a situation of concern. Subsequently, BCC commissioned a WW styled program that directly aimed to increase social interaction amongst this cohort.

Young collected key statistical indicators from the Australian Bureau of Statistics to identify Brisbane's outer suburbs, which had a high representation of the isolated demographic (see Collis, Felton & Graham 2010, a recent review of Brisbane's outer suburban creative workers for more details). This lead up work for the RMP focused on the following indicators: dog ownership, utility-car ownership, single person dwelling, and income level. Determined to reach this demographic, Young was aware of the inability of typical advertising strategies to target this cohort. He used posters and flyers as the only form of RMP advertising, displayed in specific locations in the identified suburbs – veterinary practices, hot bread shops, and mechanic's garages.

The expected number of attendees for the introductory meeting of Come Together was between twenty and thirty participants. On the first day ninety participants attended, only two of whom were outside the target demographic. The culminating first performance of Come Together occurred at the Algester Sports and Recreational Club and drew a crowd of approximately 300 people. It was reported that the club had never sold as much food and beverages as it did during that event. Further, Young described the makeup of the audience.

> It was great! Participants were bringing their ex-partners, and their kids. Some even brought their parents along with them. The focus was not on the music, the focus was on the pride gained by participants.

After the event a flow of positive anecdotal benefits and testimonials from participants prompted BCC to facilitate and partially fund the program in similar suburbs for another three years. By 2005 Come Together was active in four suburbs: Algester, Jindalee, Albany Creek and Zillmere.

CreActive Kids emerged in 2005 as part of a partnership funding agreement with the Brisbane Powerhouse – Centre for Live Arts, Brisbane City Council, Ellaways Music, and Greg Dodge. *CreActive Kids* targeted young children (ages four to eight, and nine to twelve) in a "Rock School" styled program. The official outcome of this RMP is increased creative activity for kids, and like Amp'd Up, it is currently active. In school holidays a week of intensive music/band mentorship focuses on the musical theme of rock and pop. This RMP provides skills like songwriting, performance, instrumentation, improvisation, singing, music/visual technology, recording processes, copyright issues, production and music business. In CreActive Kids, coaches empower young participants to unleash their creative expression in much the same way that Webb (2007, p.68) outlines in his assessment of the Rock School phenomena – "to offer a model for the 'teaching' of 'non-learned' music like rock." Secondary benefits are once again linked to education, alongside an expectation that "creative activity" is a desirable and transferable skill for young people to acquire

The Band Thing was another successful *WW-derivative* that formed part of an Education Queensland initiative in Inala State High School in 2007. Inala is an identified low-socio economic region of South East Queensland, and the RMP organiser reported that local high schools wanted to capitalise on the huge success of the Stylin-Up festival, which had been consistently growing in audience and reputation (Bartleet et al., 2009). Engaging youth groups within the high school student cohort, the musical theme of this derivate was Hip-hop, and it specifically targeted Pacific Islander, Indigenous and other ethnic minorities present in the local schools. *The Band Thing* was fully subsidised for the participants by funding contributed by Education Queensland, the Australian Music Academy and Brisbane City Council. Secondary benefits here are both educative and social.

Rhythm City is the final WW-derivative this chapter documents. *Rhythm City* was significant as it formed part of another popular, council organised, multicultural festival. Subsidised by the BCC and combined with the user-pays model ($90 per person), adult participants from different cultural backgrounds had the opportunity to perform in front of a large audience at the Brisbane Multicultural Festival in 2008.

Post-participation survey

We now present selected results from adult respondents who completed a post-participation RMP survey. Organisers designed the survey to produce descriptive statistics and qualitative responses that aimed to corroborate many of the participants' testimonials. Admittedly, this non-scientific data from a small sample cannot provide any conclusive findings, but it does contribute noteworthy data to assist in the identification of resources that foster resilience in participants Australian RMPs since 2001.

Did the music-making program make you a stronger person?

Yes   81%
No   19%

Did you learn any of the following skills during your involvement with a music-making program? (participants could opt for any combination)

Skills	Total
Music	30
Social	21
Literacy/Numeracy/Language	3
Organising	12
Negotiation	15
Other	4

Did you develop any coping strategies through your participation in the music-making program? (participants could opt for any combination)

Coping Strategy	Total
Health related	7
Learning related	15
Work related (paid or voluntary]	8
Social life related	28
Other	4

The following comments exemplify a dominant theme of "transferable skills" in participants' qualitative responses.

> Weekend Warriors takes you out of your comfort zone and challenges you to face your fears and triumph. You also learn to be considerate of your band mates and your partner and think from other people's perspectives. This experience translates positively into the rest of your life.

> It gave me the ability to grow within myself; gain the self confidence I now have; the ability to understand, negotiate and remain level-headed; to understand constructive criticism (and not take it personally); to challenge myself and push myself right outside my comfort zone.

Both comments and the survey responses highlight participants' perceived ability to react better to challenging situations in everyday life, which relate to Ungar's three capacities for individuals and groups. Albeit limited and tentative, our synopsis shows that the majority of RMPs participants have navigated their way towards musical activities, strategies and skills that sustain well being; consolidated their physical and social ecologies to provide these resources through the self-management of music groups and; negotiated culturally meaningful ways for resources to be shared through new funding arrangements.

Analysis of findings

The first Weekend Warriors RMP in Australia and each of its derivatives engaged participants in an intensive music program culminating in a live performance. The organisers, volunteers and participants we investigated concur that mentoring, group interactions and performance were integral to their program's success. A comparative analysis of the programs reveals subtle differences between the derivatives and the initial Weekend Warriors RMP, which we summarise in Table 2 as: 1) the *geographical location*; 2) the *funding profile*; 3) the *musical theme* and; 4) the *target demographic*.

Our most significant finding was that although each RMP provided us with detailed documentary evidence of participation in performances, their funding partners have not requested any detailed evaluations or even suggested areas in which to report the program's secondary benefits. This finding is significant because it implies the next time an Australian RMP organiser completes a funding application s/he will have no hard evidence base from which to argue a case other than reproducing testimonial statements and promotion materials. Our analysis shows that each derivative collected qualitative information through testimonials, but not enough to warrant detailed textual analysis; the same was true for the survey data. This confirms Dillon's (2006) assessment of the Band Thing and Amp'd Up RMPs, which reported it was only when a participant observer combined survey data with audiovisual content that the effects on the participants were more noticeable.

As a result of this finding, we turned to focus on the funding issues we had identified for each RMP since the initial 2001 WW program. We managed to document a move away from a focus on sales towards joint-funding arrangements that reduced the user cost in return for a focus on "secondary instrumental benefits" of non-arts portfolios. We expected to easily locate some hard evidence related to these funders' requirements, but found that most of them were satisfied by softer measures such as overall numbers of participants, media reports and testimonial accounts. As we had access to RMP groups that remained active long after the user-pays program had ended, we further examined their online and face-to-face participation activities and strategies. We found that these self-organised groups have mobilised using resources across online networks and applied for appropriate funding sources in a pragmatic manner. In turn, distinctive cross-sector music partnerships have raised the profile of the Australian RMP model to the extent that government agencies now approach the organisers we have mentioned, and the WW derivative self-organised groups to deliver programs for those they deem in need of additional recreational services. In order to understand how organisers might sustain the songs of resilience produced by these RMPs we now discuss this summary of findings with reference to two types of resources we have identified that foster resilience in participants and organisers of Australian RMPs since 2001; those that participants developed personally and funding sources required to curate performance events.

Personal resources

The data presented above suggests that RMP participants are able to identify skills (notably music, social, negotiation and organising) and coping strategies (notably learning and social) as "personal resources," which assisted them to build resilience across contexts. Several chapters in this book refer to the ways individuals respond to adversity; of course this depends on many contextual factors, but none provide overviews, which aggregate and analyse successful music programs that report on secondary benefits. The generic feature of the RMPs we examined exposes participants to confronting and emotionally challenging situations: group interactions, rehearsal pressure and public performance. Like many community music activities the RMP model anticipates and aims to reduce the effects of these stressors on participant through nurturing engagement with the group's mentors. Further, it is significant to note that in the majority of documented accounts listed in Table 1, RMP participants purposefully seek out new music performance opportunities after their first experience. A detailed classification of RMP personal resources acquired across contexts would improve our understanding of culture-specific resilience towards a performance situation. We believe that resilience is realised in RMPs through people's responses to performances and whether they are frequent experiences or not; the RMP model creates a relatively safe form of adversity as a personal challenge for participants every time it curates a public performance. The personal resources that participants develop though RMPs are clearly transferable and as such they foster resilience according to Ungar's definition.

Funding

The lack of an adaptive taxonomy of secondary benefits has compounded organisers' attempts to reduce the cost for participants. Many RMPs have been successful in reducing the cost of participation, yet all organisers we spoke to reported that funding their program has been problematic. If RMP organisers can learn to report more accurately on what Wreford calls "secondary instrument benefits," they will surely increase the number of potential funding opportunities available across sectors and reduce the cost to users even further.

Performance can be an emotional, destabilising activity as McPherson and McCormick (2006, p.1) note: "the specific attributes that artists develop must be resilient enough to breakthrough the stress of public performance." In this context, participants, organisers, researchers and funding administrators all want to view examples of successful programs that can articulate and document their outcomes and benefits effectively. The significance of the performance event as a form of socially engineered adversity is a useful starting point for researchers to explore and use in the development of evidence based theory. The ability of RMPs to attract funding and sustain affordable programs requires more focus on the challenging situation they create and the personal resources participants develop in response. Although they do not articulate it as such, RMPs intentionally orchestrate a performance situation that builds participants' resilience towards adversity across contexts. RMP providers can attract the attention of funders and researchers by clearly identifying the personal and physical resources that participants accessed, and how they manage to translate them into benefits that assist them with everyday adverse situations. The post-participation survey present in chapter four (Harris et al.) provides a compelling example to which RMP organisers should aspire.

Discussion

In chapter two Lemerle and Stewart argue that we lack evidence-based, universally recognised techniques or resources for promoting and evaluating resilience. We agree with this assertion and confirm that the RMPs we investigated could have benefitted significantly from the use of universal techniques that evaluated each project's outcomes. The adapted RMP model in use in Australia currently lacks a systematic, adaptive taxonomy of benefits and outcomes associated with sustained participation. This small-scale case study identifies a sub-group of Australian RMPs, each of which has performed numerous songs of resilience. The US RMP format, with its social, medical and commercial aims, has been successfully adapted in Australia to focus on populations of baby boomers, isolated middle-aged males, children, cultural minorities and disengaged youth. The generic performance feature of these adapted RMPs provides individuals and groups opportunities to create and use skills and coping strategies that increase their capacity for resilience.

Over time, these RMPs show a reduction in participant costs through an increased number of funding sources. We have outlined Australian derivatives of the WW model to plot RMP features, but failed to compare several context specific outcomes. There is no doubt that these music programs have a positive influence on individuals and groups, but our findings highlight the shortcomings of RMPs evidence base to support "secondary instrumental benefits of non-arts portfolios."

Many members of the Recreational Music Makers Movement would of course renounce attempts to over analyse and package RMPs as competency based training packages, and so they should. However, a pragmatic middle ground would allow these RMPs to develop context specific derivatives of the model and report effectively on the resources participants develop. A culture has certainly developed amongst participants and those who espouse the benefits of RMPs, which this research team endeavours to explore further. Having reviewed eight we now have a enough information to conduct a more rigorous assessment of the direct and perceived outcomes from engagement with RMPs on the part of participants, mentors, as well as expand on the role organisers play in identifying the type of resources developed.

If more countries are to adapt and sustain this US model in their locales, they have to be sensitive to the populations they serve and the outcomes they require.   This chapter attends to specific Australian conventions, constraints and opportunities to encourage more academics and practitioners to adapt this model for recreational music programs so that they are fit for purpose across context.

By analysing written, oral, audio, visual and spatial meanings, we have managed to identify but not quantify secondary benefits pertaining to the personal and economic resources that foster resilience in participants and organisers of Australian RMPs since 2001.   The skills and coping strategies that participants and organisers attribute to their participation are subjective, but when we aggregate these voices they produce significant songs of resilience that strengthen individuals' ability to respond to adverse situations, whilst spreading the economic cost required to deliver RMPs to groups.

Table 1. Summary table of RMPs in Australia since 2001

	Geographical Location	Start date	Funding source(s)	Musical Theme	Targeted Demographic
Weekend Warriors	Kedron (1ˢᵗ), Capalaba (2ⁿᵈ), Adelaide, Sydney Melbourne, Perth, others	2001	User pays (original cost $250per person)	Rock'n'roll	Baby Boomer Generations
Boardroom Blitz	Brisbane area	2003	Enterprises paid, profits to charity ($10000 per band)	Rock music	Mixed
Swing Cats	Brisbane area	2003	Music Suppliers (Yamaha) supplied hire equipment, user pays (-$250per person)	Swing Music	Mixed – musicians looking to play swing / Jazz music as opposed to Rock music
Amp'd Up	Kedron	2003 –in school holidays	Ellaways subsidised equipment cost, user pays ($180per person)	Rock and Pop music, and song writing	High School students
Come Together	Algester, Jindalee, Inala, Zillmere	2004	Council Funded, with user pays (original cost $90per person)	Music from the 70s	Disengaged 40-50 year old men
CreActive Kids	Brisbane	2005	Subsidised by a number of sources; both state and private, and user pays ($90per person)	Rock Music	Children 4-8 and 9-12
The Band Thing	Glenala State High School	2007	Fully subsidised; Education Queensland, the Australian Music Academy, and Brisbane City Council	Reggae, Roots and Rhyme	Disengaged indigenous and Pacific Islander students at Inala Secondary High School
Rhythm City	Zillmere, Tarragindi	2008	Council Funded, with user pays ($90per person)	Cross cultural – Reggae, Roots and Rhyme	Cultural minorities

References

Bittman, B. (2001) Music-making: an integrative strategy for managing chronic pain. *The Pain Practitioner*. 11(1). pp 2-11.

—. et al. (2001) Composite effects of group drumming music therapy on modulation of neuroendocrine-immune parameters in normal subjects. *Alternative Therapies Health Medicine*. 7(1). pp 38-47.

—. et al. (2003) Recreational Music-Making: A Cost-Effective Group. Advances. *Mind-Body Medicine*. 19 (3/4)

Burgess, J. & Green. J. (2009). YouTube: Online Video and Participatory Culture. London: Polity Press.

Bruns, A. (2007). Methodologies for mapping the political blogosphere: An exploration using the IssueCrawler research tool. *First Monday*, 12 (5).

Dillon, S. (2006) Assessing the positive influence of music activities in community development programs. *Music Education Research* 8, (2), 267 -280

Howard, S., & Johnson, B. (2004). Resilient teachers: Resisting stress and burnout. *Social Psychology of Education, 7*(4), pp 399-420.

Burt J.W. (1995) Distant thunder: drumming with Vietnam veterans. *Music Therapy Perspectives*. 13. (61) pp 110-112

Castells, M. (1997) *The power of identity*. Oxford: Blackwell

Glaser, B. & A. Strauss (1967) *The discovery of grounded theory, Strategies for qualitative research*. New York: Aldine.

Hallam, S. (2001). *The Power of Music. The strength of music's influence on our lives*. The Performing Right Society: MCPS-PRS Alliance.

Hull A. (1998) *Drum Circle Spirit: Facilitating Human Potential Through Rhythm*. Reno: White Cliffs Media.

McPherson, G. E., & McCormick, J. (2006). Self-efficacy and music performance. *Psychology of Music, 34* (3), p322.

Sacks, O. (2006). The power of music. *Brain*, 129 (10), p.2528.

Suter, E. (2000) Focus Groups in Ethnography of Communication: Expanding Topics of Inquiry Beyond Participant Observation. *The qualitative report*. 5 (1/2).

Webb, M. (2007). Rock Goes to School on Screen: A Model for Teaching Non- Learned Music Derived from the Films 'School of Rock'(2003) and 'Rock School' (2005). *Action, Criticism, and Theory for Music Education*, 6 (3), p 23.

CHAPTER EIGHT

VOICES OF THE UNHEARD

BRIAN PROCOPIS AND STEVE DILLON

Introduction

Adversity has the effect of eliciting talents, which, in prosperous circumstances, would have lain dormant. —Horace - Roman lyric poet and satirist 65BC – 8 BC

This quotation from Horace could well be the chorus to a medley of songs sung by people who face extraordinary adversity and have gained emotional resilience through music making. In this chapter we present three composition ventures that are stories or verses in a new song and whose chorus summarises the nature of the resilience factors present in the narratives. We are aware that words on a page like this can have the effect of filtering out the engaging nature of musical experience and reduce music to a critique or an evaluation of its aesthetic value. This disjuncture between language and the ephemeral, embodied experience is a problem for those who use these creative processes in therapeutic and salutogenic ways (Antonovsky, 1996) for public health. The notion of salutogenic health, put simply, delineates it from therapy in that the processes focus upon wellness rather than therapy. Whilst we include evidence from the fields of community music therapy (Pavlicevic, 2004; Leitschuh et al., 1991), neuroscience (Bittman et al., 2001) and community music (Bartleet et al., 2009) the framework for a salutogenic health outcome in community music is one which seeks to employ music practices and the qualities of music making that provide positive health benefit to communities – to enhance health and well being rather than the "treatment" of disorders. It is essentially a holistic and interdisciplinary study. Therapy and salutogenic health are not mutually exclusive as both depend upon the qualities of music experience to affect change. Collecting, analysing and presenting evidence of change in human behaviour that can be directly attributed to creative music making is a problem of evaluation.

Evaluations that show evidence beyond a placebo or Hawthorne effect, where any attention to the problem produces a result (Dillon, 2006) is difficult to distinguish. The goal of evaluating these kinds of projects starts by identifying a "most significant change" (MSC) (Davies & Dart, 2005) that is agreed upon by all the stakeholders to represent a form of democratic evaluation, which considers the often compelling nature of the creative product and an effect perceived by all stakeholders to be "significant." The following projects, whilst not evaluated using the MSC technique, do satisfy the criteria for outcomes of that approach which includes democratic evaluation and clear and replicable public outcomes. What we present here are not model examples of salutogenic health programs involving music making to affect social change, but examples of the continuous struggle with all of the factors discussed above. We seek to highlight the successes while drawing out the ethical and evaluative problems that arise in these contexts.

Music making with people who are experiencing marginalization (and subsequently suffering adversity) has become a regular activity for Lifeline Social Inclusion and Community Connection (a non government aid agency) who are in partnership with social justice record label, Sweet Freedom Inc. We encourage readers to take a few minutes and listen to the performances online because we know that the song and video will say in a few moments what we will struggle to describe in words: http://songsofresilience.wikispaces.com/Sweet+freedom.

The approach for this song of resilience we like to call a choral autoethnography. Using autoethnography as a way of presenting research data enables musicians to examine, understand and communicate the personal ideas behind their creative experiences (Bartleet & Ellis, 2009). Brian Procopis is the co-founder of Sweet Freedom Inc and a community development activist who works with Lifeline Community Care Queensland (LCCQ) – an organization that exists to strengthen the lives of individuals, families and communities through wide-ranging community services.

Procopis has been the community musician present in all of the following vignettes and his story comes from the perspective of social psychology, community development principles, and music. He works in the field making music in communities. Steve Dillon is an academic music educator active in researching and documenting innovation in sound communities (http://www.savetodisc.net/). Dillon has taken an active role in developing the ethical and evaluative aspects of Sweet Freedom as co-chair; he has participated in several projects as a co-worker and researcher/observer endeavoring to use Web 2.0 technology as a means to promote and document Sweet Freedom's work in ways that capture it effectively.

The choral autoethnographic approach has been used successfully in cases where multiple voices need to remain in the "I" so we can maintain an ethnographic and personal tone (Dillon et al., 2010). Bartleet et al (2009) report examples of autoethnography in music that maintain this relationship to the music itself. Our intention is to allow both Procopis and Dillon to speak in the first person. Procopis will simply tell the stories of each verse and Dillon will provide an academic chorus that deconstructs each experience into the identifiable aspects of resilience. We hope the dialogue between us will unfold as a "choir of voices" where solo voices emerge whilst others intertwine in consort to support or contrast them in a chiasmatic dialogue. Chiasmus in musical terms refers to how musical voices rise to the foreground or recede to the background. We hope that issues will rise and recede in a similar manner through this approach.

Verse 1: My Life My Voice DVD

http://www.youtube.com/watch?v=yB02EYNRSII&feature=channel/

"My Life My Voice" – the song and music video is unique in that the song has been co-written by people with Down syndrome to give others a window into their world. The project was triggered by a conversation between Procopis and parents at the Down syndrome Association of Queensland. The organisation wanted to provide an opportunity for those with Down syndrome to showcase and positively affect their public image. Procopis has a son with Down syndrome and decided to apply the processes he had used in community development and music making with Lifeline. According to Procopis,

> The resultant song…is not one that asks for pity or assistance. It has not been composed to engage tears from its listeners. The song is up-tempo, centre-stage and proud. Why wouldn't it be? The performers are lovers of life who are singing of what they value – the lyrics are theirs.

The request for the children to have their own song came from Kerry, mother of Olivia – a sparkling 7yr old with Down syndrome: Olivia is amazingly articulate and self-assured – she's pretty, sings and dances and is featured on magazine covers as an ambassador of the Down syndrome Association. Procopis' son, Alexander, who also has Down syndrome as well as some autistic characteristics, is non-verbal, shies away from gatherings of people, and finds his own safe place in the corner or at the back of the room. Procopis continues:

> I wasn't sure how this would work, how we could construct a song project that would be inclusive, collaborative and be of benefit to all of the participants. Down syndrome is not a "one size fits all" category. These children have different capacities, different strengths.

A decision was made to begin the project and involve the children in every step. A date was set, the children and their parents gathered – familiar faces, kindred spirits, fellow travelers. Through many workshops run by Procopis together with parents and friends of DSAQ members, sing-a-longs and discussions, a style of music "bubbled up" out of the participants. Quotes, favourite expressions, "na na nas" (for those in the group who were non-verbal) as well as some extremely poignant and insightful comments, were structured by Procopis into the lyrics. Acoustic guitars set the scene "If you're happy and you know it, clap your hands ..." The children were excited – parents sang along. Alexander sat at the back of the room.

Parents talked about their desire for this venture to enable the broader public to see their children as they saw them – as productive members of society with their own unique gifts to offer, not as victims to be cared for by others. The question was put to the children "what do you love about your life?" The responses came through – active kids with their own passions and interests.

It was the first of five meetings during which the song "My Life My Voice" took shape. The developing lyrics were brought back each time and submitted to the group for checking. Changes were made when the songwriter (Procopis) didn't quite get it right or it didn't seem to fit the needs of the people involved. There were lines for individuals and a chorus for everyone. There was a "na na na" section for those with limited language capacity. Procopis recalls:

> We practised and practised...repetition is comfortable territory for the participants with Down syndrome – it meets their need for familiarity and security. We parents who felt the stirrings of exasperation when one or

another of the participants called out excitedly "again" just had to get over it. It was not about us.

The department of Music and Sound within the Creative Industries Faculty of Queensland University of Technology (QUT) responded with enthusiasm to Procopis' request for assistance with a commitment to provide a producer/recording engineer and studio facilities. Dillon organised for postgraduate and undergraduate students to participate in the production and enlisted the assistance of technical officers to enable studio use. The music department has a long history of commitment to community service and the involvement was classified as a community engagement project. The recording weekend provided groups of five children, their siblings and parents with a recording session time. The whole experience of young people with Down syndrome was un-chartered territory for the QUT team of musicians and producers – they were entranced by the younger ones who freely dispensed their hugs while the older ones tried their very best to comply with the producer's directions.

Vocal capacities were limited – low muscle tone or hypnotonia (http://www.cdadc.com/ds/hypotonia.htm) is very common amongst those with Down syndrome as are hearing difficulties and speech problems. Discussions took place between Dillon, Procopis and the producer who asked, "Should we use auto-tune?" The decision was made quickly. "No let's keep it authentic," said Russell the producer with conviction, "in saying that though, let's offer the singers the opportunity to sing their lines as many times as they need – we'll use their best effort." It was an agreed-upon position – more work for Russell with 177 tracks - no studio magic.

Siblings featured on the instrumental tracks. A guitarist friend and a friend-of-a-friend drummer rose to the occasion who said, "I'll do it for these kids," confirming the recognition that those with complex needs tend to summon what is most substantial from others. "It's their gift to us," Kerry, mother of Olivia, reflects. Everyone loved the result. The children were ecstatic. The song is not a chart-buster. It was never meant to be. It is accessible by a unique group of children and young adults. They own it and are proud of it. The DVD is given as a gift to bewildered and distressed parents whose child has just been born with Down syndrome. It is given to primary, secondary and special schools to support their efforts to create an inclusive culture.

Procopis' son, Alexander, was learning the keyboards in a one to one arrangement at school. In spite of the urgings of his teacher, he refused to touch the keys. He would laugh and jig around as she played familiar nursery rhymes. Music teacher Maria could barely contain herself on the phone nearing the end of the school year, as the "My Life My Voice" project was well under way - "You won't believe it but Alexander approached the piano this morning and actually pressed down one of the keys." Excitement all around. A Casio keyboard mysteriously appeared under the Christmas tree. Santa must have heard the story. Yet in an inexplicable anti-climax, Alexander refused to play his newly received Christmas present.

The master recording of "My Life My Voice" became available in February. Procopis continues, "I brought it home, sat down and watched it with Alexander and he was mesmerised. When it finished he tapped his chest with his open hand – the Makaton sign language's visual gesture (Reid, 2005) for "more please." We played it again. More chest tappings. We played the song five times after which Alexander went downstairs to the rumpus room, turned on the key boards and began jamming with the notes. It made no musical sense. It didn't have to – for us parents, it was already beautiful."

Chorus: Na na -nanana na - Na na -nanana na

When I look at the credits to the "my life my voice" video," I try to count the number of people involved. The community that was identified and strengthened by this project is present in the number and diversity of participants represented in the credits. As a researcher I was conscious of identifying both the meaning for the participants and the ethical dimensions of how the project was enacted. I was searching for ways of evaluating it that were respectful to the community of participants while also ensuring the required level of rigour also figured highly in the grounded theory (Strauss, 1990) themes and codes that emerged from my experiences. What I surmised from these observations was that the ethical underpinnings of the process and the meanings created through participation were deeply entwined. The quantity and diversity of the eighty participants in this project were observable and measurable. Participants were linked in many ways but principally via family relationships. Music making processes served as both common ground and common purpose.

The inclusiveness of the approach was amplified by critical moments. Firstly the "na na na" chorus acknowledged that spoken language is not necessary to sing and participate; this utterance became a powerful expressive force that allowed access for non-speaking participants. Procopis' son did not participate at all in the recording process but when he saw young people like him singing and playing music via the repeated playback of the video, his response was to ask for it to be repeated so that he could "play" his keyboards. The joyfulness of the video is compelling and has been a great advocacy statement for the Down syndrome Association who has attracted responses from across the globe from parents, friends and relatives. What emerged from this experience was an inclusive approach to making music that traversed the ethical dimensions of enabling the voices to be heard in ways that created a refined sense of social meaning and cultural pride.

For a community music researcher the issue of quality versus a "feel good outcome" is always a concern especially when the work becomes public. The producer's approach to the notion of quality was insightful. Whilst correct pitch and timing is conventionally important for recorded performance, what he applied skillfully was a pedagogy that sought to capture the character of each performer's voice through its timbrel qualities. The multiple "takes" enabled him to select the most compelling and characteristic performance.

The "potential opportunities to acquire and sustain the capacity for recovery and growth following adversity" (see Lemerle & Stewart chapter two) is observable here at three levels. First, the social relationships existent within families were enhanced by the songwriting and recording process and provided a basis for deeper understanding between participants. Second, the linking of those with Down syndrome, their families, friends and advocates to a wider "mainstream" audience reinforced awareness of networks of support for families while at the same time stimulating social capital. Finally, there was recognition that music making serves as a vehicle for a communion and expressive experience without the need for words. It provides a framework that is both procedural and ethical for encouraging resilience amongst participants. In this case resilience is as much a part of the development of resistance factors for those with Down syndrome as it is for their parents and friends. It provides a means of amplifying the voices of the unheard while encouraging identity development and expanding networks of supportive relationships.

Verse 2: Scattered people

http://www.safecom.org.au/scattered.htm

At a gathering in August 1998 of the Management committee, around the table in the backroom of the Asylum Seeker Centre, Brisbane, Queensland Program of Assistance for Survivors of Torture and Trauma (QPASTT) was represented as was the Red Cross and the South Brisbane Immigration and Legal Service. Anglican Refugee and Migrant Services (ARMS) and Benarrawa Community Development Association fielded their social workers. Mercedes Sepulveda (originally from Chile), coordinator of the Centre, chaired the meeting while I (Procopis - representing Lifeline) took the minutes.

It was an ordeal for all of us. We were impatiently reading the correspondence from the Federal Immigration Minister's Department in Canberra to our letters of advocacy for the asylum seekers who attended the Centre. Many were languishing without access to social security, housing, Medicare, work permits, education etc., while Departmental representatives considered their applications for a protection visa, which was a lengthy process – years in most cases.

Dates and names were different but the content of the letters was the same: "We refer to your recent correspondence in relation to your client and wish to acknowledge your comments and advise that they will be taken into consideration at the appropriate time." We were exasperated. "What else can we do to counter the seemingly wide-spread perception that asylum seekers are queue jumpers, terrorists in disguise, opportunists seeking a more comfortable lifestyle?" Our commitment was to portray, to a hopefully compassionate public, the reality that these people are just like us – only they have had to leave their volatile environments any way they could and apply for protection for themselves and their children in countries that are signatories to the Universal Declaration of Human Rights which says "everyone has the right to seek and to enjoy in other countries asylum from persecution"

(http://www.un.org/en/documents/udhr/index.shtml. Article 14).

It was then that we heard the music. Wafting down the corridor like the aromatic percolations of an espresso machine, the gentle tinkling of an acoustic guitar accompanied by rich and melodic humming. These sounds found a welcoming resonance within each of us. We pushed back our chairs and tiptoed to the source of our entrancement. Here they were, Chilean asylum seekers taking refuge from the murderous regime of Augusto Pinochet while strumming a battered no-named nylon stringed instrument. It was soothing in itself but the fact that asylum seekers from Ethiopia, Bosnia, China and Sri Lanka – all swaying quietly to what was probably unfamiliar music from the strumming Chileans, gave this moment substance and significance.

Amongst the management committee, the collective realisation was palpable.

> Here we are sitting in another room devising strategies and writing letters to politicians with minimal benefit while the raison d'être of this place – the asylum seekers themselves - are using music to connect with and bring comfort to, one another.

From this moment onwards the process of using music to express these unheard voices accelerated. A meeting was arranged by the coordinator and her support team – asylum seekers and supporters were present. Those of us with musical inclinations tentatively described the proposal.

> How would it be for music to be used to introduce yourselves to the Australian public and saying what in your hearts needs to be said – your thoughts not ours, your voices not ours?

Bewilderment gave way to enthusiasm as some said, "I can't sing." The response followed swiftly "None of us are divas - maybe you can't sing, maybe you can, especially when others are singing around you. In any case there will be a place for you in this project."

The song writing process began with some strategic questions: "what are you thinking of whilst awake at three o'clock in the morning?" One of the asylum seekers who had escaped the Tiannamen Square massacre replied, "I think of lotus plants and buffalos." Others stumbled over words, assisted by other participants to describe what it was about their home towns, their loved ones and their fading history that they missed. The song "Hometown" began taking shape.

> We belong – never lonely we belong
> Safe and warm this is our hometown ... we belong
> My hometown how I love the summer lotus plants and buffalo
> We are fishing, swimming - this is life in my hometown

My hometown working with my hands and I feel proud of what I do
I support my family this is life in my hometown
My hometown work the land 'til harvest feel the sweat then celebrate
Let the seasons turn for this is life in my hometown
My hometown how I yearn to be there lotus plants and buffalo
Lay me down there someday let me sleep in my hometown

Funding was secured from the Brisbane City Council by the consortium of participants at Lifeline and from the Sidney Myer Foundation as part of community projects grant schemes that sought to address issues of public significance in communities. A kindred-spirited music producer who guaranteed quality at an affordable price was sourced via the local musician's grapevine. Production on the *Scattered People* album commenced in May 1999. Age-old production dilemmas surfaced. How do we authentically represent and involve the participants considering that many have had minimal singing experience, many can't speak English well and most don't play instruments? We spoke of our uneasiness and came up with a plan:

Let's invite musicians with a multi-ethnic background (preferably those with refugee experience) and let's open the collaboration to other kindred spirits – vocalists with a sense of justice who share the outrage relating to the trauma that asylum seekers experienced in their own countries as well as in ours.

All associated with the production became involved in an educative process – to this extent we all had "a refugee experience" through listening to the participant's stories and working collaboratively to express them through music. Verity Clisby of partnering organisation Brisbane Multicultural Arts Centre (BEMAC) suggested the name "Scattered People" and it became the title of the opening monologue. It had relevance for all of us and symbolised the feelings of being uprooted and scattered.

We are from El Salvador, Chile and Columbia.
Some of us have escaped from Eritrea, Ethiopia and Sudan
We have come seeking safety from Bosnia, Iran, Sri Lanka and East Timor.
Many of our families and friends have escaped to other countries.
We have no hometown to return to.
Yet in countries that could offer safety and a future for our children and ourselves we are told we cannot stay.
We are refugee claimants, asylum seekers.
We are the scattered people...

Asylum seekers who couldn't sing were invited to "say something that needed to be said in their own language, something that was burning a hole inside." These emotion-fuelled comments were then included in the songs during the spaces between verses with music beneath them. The relationship of the participants to the project was sensitively monitored by the musicians, community development and refugee claimant support workers. Their comments were regularly invited.

> It is all the people feeling together.

> It is easier to sing about some things than to speak about them.

> I like the choir, I like what we sing about. It belongs to us. The words belong to us. They are our words.

The album that resulted surprised us all – not in the familiar content but in the quality of its production. Participants hearing it for the first time nodded silently to one another. They had been honoured by the collective endeavor that delivered a quality outcome. A vehicle had been constructed for their voices to be heard.

Chorus: Singing in the dark

Anthropologists suggest that human beings began to sing communally before they could speak, and that this played a significant role in social cohesion (Mithven, 2005, p.205). Singing and making music together have qualities that confirm our humanity and affirm our connections with one another. Horace's words could not be more aptly applied to the refugees discussed in this verse. The "Scattered People" experience became an approach to which Lifeline's Social Inclusion team could unify and make allowance for diversity simultaneously. So what qualities of this approach are replicable? First, the democratic approach to making music within a defined framework – one that has to be respectful to each culture and allow the expressive qualities of each human experience to be heard. Second, the therapeutic and psychological value lies in the personal, social and cultural expression of the experience that is encapsulated collectively in one's mother tongue, the English language, through utterance and chosen musical style.

The ethical dimensions are important too. Music can be a repressive or coercive force and it can evoke powerful sentiments that may need to be kept private. Many refugees suffer post traumatic stress and songs that evoke nationalism or oppressive regimes can trigger anxiety as well as having the potential to heal. Osbourne's (2007) work with children's song and post traumatic stress provides compelling evidence of the effects these processes have on calm breathing and a normal heart rate. With performance however we have noted that a composition task like the one described cannot unravel years of low self esteem. Public performance can be a political propaganda device and trauma-inducing rather than being therapeutically effective. Community music workers encourage performances that showcase outcomes inherent in the appearance of cohesion and fun in performance. The question that arises is who is the performance for? Is it for the organisers to show an outcome or does it demonstrate a genuine benefit to the participants, or does it achieve both? The Sweet Freedom production team is attentive to these ethical aspects and seeks to remain sensitive to the purpose and democratic nature of the interaction.

Whilst singing a song can never wipe away a lifetime of abuse and violent trauma, it can provide a means to express the inexpressible and to share those feelings with others who know them and others who do not (Osbourne, 2007). Resilience for these people is evident in the "making sense" of their personal trauma with music as a kind of exorcism (Pavlicevic et al., 2004). Music making acts to reinforce the collective acknowledgement of shared struggles and provides a vehicle for recognising humanity across cultures in a compassionate, empowering way.

Finally, expressing collective experiences of human adversity while demonstrating the ability to rise up to conquer it in a compact form is empowering for all involved. In the light of a growing body of evidence across disciplines and circumstances, I suggest that whilst song may not erase trauma and tragedy, it can engage others to sing along and understand whilst other methods fall on deaf ears.

Verse 3: Aim High/From Little Things Big Things Grow Project

http://www.youtube.com/watch?v=Sc-o5TShG48

The Zillmere State School population is comprised of 30% Aboriginal children, 20% Pacific Islander, and a further 12% from a non-English speaking background. Zillmere is located in the lowest socio-economic

10% of the State of Queensland. The "Aim High" project was designed to give the children a sense of pride in their capacity to achieve as well as to mobilise the broader school population, including parents and local community members, into more effective relationships with one another.

Zillmere State School Principal Angela Wilson spoke of the students as having to navigate their young lives within what she described as the "corridor of deprivation" – high levels of unemployment and public housing, single parent families, cultural conflicts, child abuse notifications, etc. Angela said that the students unfortunately seemed to suffer from a collective "low self esteem" – and were embarrassed to be identified with Zillmere. It was considered by many to be a *loser* suburb that suffered from postcode discrimination.

We in the Lifeline Counselling & Community Development team had just moved into the area and were anxious to help in whatever way was appropriate. We brought our brochures – family counselling, personal counselling, financial counselling, etc. Wilson was warm and courteous but indicated that the offer of professional counselling was not likely to invoke a rush of appointments and suggested "people within this social demographic talk to one another, their families, their communities – not usually to a stranger." It was a reality check for us. The tea was finished – there was nothing much more to say. However, I had a sudden thought as we were shaking hands to leave, prompted no doubt by our "Scattered People" experience. I asked, "By the way Angela, does your school have a song?"

The side-to-side shaking of the head and the bewildered look beckoned an explanation. "I'm not talking about the style of song that we had when we were at school – generally a plagiarised melody with an overlay of lyrical clichés – an embarrassment to sing once we were over the age of ten. I'm talking about a song that the entire school community – students, teachers, parents, families, etc., would have input into."

Angela liked the idea, took it to her teachers and then to her students. The response was enthusiastic. An advisory committee was formed of teachers, parents and community workers, a project plan was devised and a funding application to the Brisbane City Council was submitted.

We worked closely with the music teacher Rachel Templeton who allowed us a segment of time each week with every class and guided us as we asked our questions of the children. "What is it about this school that you'd like other people to know about?" "What do you have at this school that is possibly different from other schools?"

Responses were memorable:

> We have a swimming pool, we have an oval, and we have a garden.

We responded, "Sure guys I can see that you have those things – you're very fortunate but other schools have got those things too – what have you got that is unique to your school?" Eventually the children looked around at one another – somebody said it – it was the answer that we were hoping for …"

> We all come from different places and here we are in the one room – most of the time we get on pretty well with one another.

Once the theme was identified, students, teachers and parents had ideas to contribute. Much acclaimed Aboriginal performer and recording artist Kev Carmody was a friend of Bev the Grade One teacher. She asked for his cooperation – he agreed to join our advisory committee. We all met at her place in Ashgrove. Kev said "You can use the song that Kelly & I wrote if you want." He was referring to the Australian classic "From Little Things Big Things Grow" he had composed together with Australian legend, Paul Kelly. It was an amazing offer but triggered an awkward moment. "Thanks Kev – that's very generous of you – it is the best song. However, it's your song – we need to use the ideas of the kids to put together their song." Kev understood perfectly.

The school motto was "Aim High." It was to become the title of the new school song. I brought in draft #1 and played it to the advisory committee. I could tell from their faces that it didn't have the magic. This was a collaborative process – getting precious about one's own input would be inappropriate. Back to the drawing board. Producer Simon Monsour came up with another melody. People loved it – especially the students – and Indigenous & multi-ethnic instruments were used to capture the cultural flavours that reflected the diversity within the school.

Kev Carmody's offer was tantalizing and proved too good to let go. We, the project coordinators, decided to take it to the students. They would love it and want to record it alongside their "Aim High" track. They didn't. It was another awkward moment. I asked "what can we do with this song so that you would feel that it belongs to you?" They responded *"we like rap."* The powerful lyrics telling the story of Vincent Lingiari had minimal resonance with the students. If they were in high school, it may have been a different story. This was their project and I had to make the uneasy phone call to Kev. "Mate I wonder how you'd feel if we made a few changes to your song to adapt it to the young ones who will be singing it." His response was unforgettable, *"let the kids rule."* The children were then asked "Look at this big world of ours – there are good things and not-so-good things happening in it – someday soon you'll be grown up and out there with the chance to make some changes. What would you like to do that will hopefully make a difference?"

Every child had a response, all communicated well and we promptly noted it. Some of them would raise a few eyebrows. There was to be no editing. The rap song "From Little Things" was recorded in a borrowed hall next to the school.

The launch was an occasion of great excitement. Government representatives, Brisbane City Council officers, non-government agencies, local businesses, residents, families, relatives – all were there to be entertained by Kev Carmody himself, the Waka Waka dance troupe, by Samoan boy band the Oti Brothers, by Indigenous story-tellers and lastly by the combined school community singing their songs. Radio 4KQ and Triple J were there interviewing the students. ABC radio sent it to their 55 nation-wide radio stations. The Indigenous radio network loved it and also took the song of the Zillmere community to the national airwaves. It wasn't long before the phone calls from different parts of Australia came into the school office:

> Congratulations to all. I clock up many hours as an itinerant teacher travelling to support behaviour-disordered children, hearing your students sing on Triple J was certainly a highlight of my week, indeed of my year. All of the social skills which I attempt to teach were beautifully demonstrated, co-operation, teamwork, inclusion, respect for others, and a celebration of faith in and hope for the future. (J. Smithhurst - Tuncurry NSW)

> May I commend the kids from Zillmere - as the radio stations announce it - for their very, very catchy song. Had you the opportunity to have this released for general sale, I'm sure it would have been a number one hit! To quote many of the on-air guests on the ABC in Perth - "they're playing that song again, and we spend the whole day humming and singing it to

ourselves." Congratulations - you have taken the radio waves by storm. (D. Stevens - Cooloongup, WA)

To the students and Staff of Zillmere State School and everyone involved in the making of the "Aim High" CD. Congratulations on a wonderful job. The CD has had quite a thrashing at home and at my daughter's school. It sounds really good. Thank you. (Paul Kelly)

Affirming comments from strangers in other parts of the country were shared each morning at assembly with the students. That was a new experience. The children were invited to perform at a national conference on "Health Promotion in Schools" to be held at the Marriott Hotel on the Gold Coast. A bus was hired. It was another occasion of great excitement. The Pacific ocean lapping the Gold Coast is 88 kilometres from Brisbane. Most of the students on the bus had never seen the ocean. None of the children had been inside an environment like the Marriott Hotel at Surfers Paradise. The school won the Showcase Award for Excellence from the Queensland Government – a prize of $40,000. Sales of their CD amounted to a similar figure. This was all new for students from a "loser suburb" suffering from a collective low self -esteem.

Chorus: From Little Things Big Things Grow

Urban cultures are complex. The demographics represented at Zillmere present challenges for those attempting to enable access to human rights and education. Zillmere State School was part of a large government funded study of resilience (Lemerle & Stewart, 2004; Lister-Sharp et al., 1999; Stewart & Dillon, 2007; Stewart, 2006). Essentially music was the glue that bonded these diverse communities in enabling access to "common ground" and shared interests. Resulting from that fledgling initiative, today there is a multicultural festival located in Zillmere that attracts crowds of 10,000 people. More than ten years on, the school choir still sings these songs that celebrate their diverse identity and collective struggle against adversity.

The same struggle with ethical approaches to intercultural understanding is apparent in this verse. The impact of the intervention by the agencies involved was compelling, but the lack of acknowledgement, at an academic research level, that the music making contributed to the process or indeed provided the vehicle for the interventions to take place is perplexing. The problem lies in the need for ways to capture the critical moments or most significant changes (Davies & Dart, 2005) and strategies.

We need to place them alongside the empirical evidence and present a thick description of phenomenon that has both immediate and compelling views that link to rigorously conducted methods (Dillon, 2006). We also need to collect large numbers of these kinds of verse, identify how they contribute to resilience, describe the ethical ways of engaging with communities, and disseminate this information widely. The beginnings of this kind of documentation and compiling of project summaries have just begun with a United Nations initiative to create a compendium of project summaries and outcomes. The projects listed above have been invited to submit to this collection.

Sweet Freedom provides a long-term example of how songs of resilience function in marginalised communities and how the simple act of encouraging people to create music together can be refined into a quality expression of personal significance. These personal utterances and feelings are then shared across diverse demographics and used as effective communication of their collective and individual condition. The songs when heard and seen speak for themselves. Resistance factors to adversity are both encouraged by these experiences of collective creativity, as they become a public statement about the suffering of adversity and how it can be overcome. These approaches are sustainable and develop through being consistently alert to ethical ways of proceeding – using democratic and inclusive approaches to making music and culturally sensitive methods of presentation. To identify a causal link between music making and human resilience we must constantly strive to identify the qualities of music making that serve the cause of social justice and offer opportunities for the voices of the unheard to both educate and beckon a compassionate response from all.

References

Antonovsky, A. (1996). The salutogenic model as a theory to guide health promotion. . *Health Promotion International* 11:11-18.

Bartleet, Brydie-Leigh, and Carolyn Ellis, (eds). (2009). *Music Autoethnographies: Making Autoethnography sing/ making music personal.* Brisbane: Australian Academic Press.

Bartleet, Brydie-Lee, Peter Dunbar-Hall, Richard Letts, and Huib Schippers. (2009). *Sound links*: community music in Australia Brisbane: Queensland Conservatorium Research Centre.

Bittman, Barry B, Lee S Berk, David L Felten, James Westengard, and et al. (2001). Composite effects of group drumming music therapy on modulation of neuroendocrine-immune parameters in normal subjects. *Alternative Therapies in Health and Medicine* 7 (1): 38.

Davies, Rick, and Jess Dart. (2005). The "Most Significant Change" (MSC)Technique: A guide to its use.
http://www.mande.co.uk/docs/MSCGuide.pdf (accessed   April   20, 2010).

Dillon, Steve. (2006). Assessing the positive influence of music activities in community development programs. *Music Education Research* 8 (No. 2): 267-280.

Dillon, Steve C, Deidre Seeto, and Anne Berry. (2010). Ezine and iRadio as knowledge creation metaphors for scaffolding learning in physical and virtual learning spaces In *Physical and Virtual Learning Spaces in Higher Education: Concepts for the Modern Learning Environment*, edited by M. Keppell, K. Souter and M. Riddle. Perth: IGI Global.

Feldenkrais, Moshe. (1990). Awareness Through Movement: health exercises for personal growth. London: Arkana.

Lemerle, K., and D. Stewart. (2004). Health Promoting Schools: A Proposed Model for Building School Social Capital and Children's Resilience. Paper read at 18th World Conference on Health Promotion and Health Education Conference, 26th - 30th April, 2004. at Melbourne,.

Lister-Sharp, D, S. Chapman, S Stewart-Brown, and A. Sowden. (1999). Health promoting schools and health promotion in schools: two systematic reviews. *Health Technology Assessment* 3 (22):1-209.

Leitschuh, Carol A, and Melissa Brotons. (1991). Recreation and Music Therapy for Adolescent Victims of Sexual Abuse. *Journal of Physical Education, Recreation & Dance* 62 (4):52.

Mithen, Steven (2005). The Singing Neanderthals: The Origins of Music, Language, Mind and Body. London: Weidenfeld & Nicolson.

Osborne, Nigel. 2007. Music for Children in Zones of Conflict and Post Conflict. Open University Press

Pavlicevic, Mercedes, and Gary Ansdell. (2004). *Community Music Therapy*. London: Jessica Kingsley Publishers.

Reid, Kerry. (2005). Makaton Signing for Children with Down Syndrome. *DSAQ Digest*

Stewart, D, Sun J., and Hardie M. (2006). "An Ounce of Prevention ..." Final Report of the "Resilient Children and Communities Project". In *Health Promotion Queensland*. Brisbane Queensland Health.

Stewart, Donald, and Steve Dillon. (2007). The social ecology of music, health and well-being: a song of resilience. *The Journal of the Royal Society for the Promotion of Health*

Strauss, Anselm L. (1990). *Qualitative Analysis For Social Scientists.* New York, USA: Cambridge University Press.

CHAPTER NINE

WE SHALL OVERCOME:
TRANSCENDING THE CHALLENGES OF AUTISM
USING A RESILIENCE FRAMEWORK

DONALD DEVITO

Introduction: Gabriela Barber

Imagine having little control over the coordination of your body, no apparent ability to speak in a coherent manner, and as a result little meaningful connection with anyone in your community or school. Gabriela Barber is an African American high school music student at the Sidney Lanier Center in Gainesville, Florida. "Gaby" also happens to be on the severe end of the autism spectrum. Thought to be able to communicate only by responding to visual aides and specific "yes" or "no" questions, Gabriela's other primary method of communication is through behavioral responses to stimuli presented in whatever home or public environment she is placed. One environment that has led to social inclusion and connectedness with other people is Gabriela's public school music class.

United States (U.S.) public school systems use a common tool with students who cannot speak due to the challenges of autism – augmentative and alternative communication (AAC) devices. These devices come with a variety of switches that teachers can program and couple with visual aides. The AAC device allows Gabriela to indicate a myriad of responses to questions related to academic lessons, preferences in normal daily experiences (food and recreation requests) and basic needs. Yet documentation on their usage to provide equitable access in U.S. public school music education is non-existent. Partly this is because participation in public school music ensembles is based on an audition, which often precludes access for students with disabilities as severe as Gabriela's – a student unable to read music or control her body, mind and soul into one coordinated whole. One social practice that allows her opportunities for authentic communication and participation is singing. In fact, this is the only time that Gabriela uses spoken language in a communicative manner. These short-lived musical activities provide her relief from the challenges associated with autism. They also provide her with the opportunity to be recognized as a singer rather than simply a person with autism. In this chapter I illuminate the path that led Gabriela's stereotypical autistic behaviors towards her current singing ability through the use of AAC devices.

Context

Gabriela is not among the stories you often hear of students with autism. Newspaper headlines and news clips are mostly reserved for people with autism who are classified as savant. Gabriela will not sit at a piano and replicate a Chopin etude after one listening. She does, however, represent the public school students with autism who should be given the opportunity for a sequential and adapted opportunity for inclusive music education. In a single day, as exhibited in the three video clips on the Songs of Resilience WIKI (http://songsofresilience.wikispaces.com/ We+Shall+Overcome), Gabriela will alternate between exhibiting stereotypical repetitive movements and verbalizing in syllables that are incoherent, to singing a beautiful rendition of *We Shall Overcome*. The middle ground between these extremes occurs when Gabriela presses the visual aides and switches of the AAC device to respond to questions and to indicate her needs and preferences. The videos on the WIKI demonstrate the sequence of events that led to the exhibition of her resilience through music, which allows her for a short time to break through the communicative barrier of autism. These findings are discussed more fully in the data and analysis section of this chapter.

Gabriela almost never initiates interaction with others due to the severe social challenges she experiences. However, in her music education class, the AAC device provides her with the communication tool necessary to select the music she prefers to sing with others. This empowerment allows her to initiate – for the first time – a communicative path for social interaction. Gabriela will not instigate singing until she is prompted to select a preferred song or is invited to sing with another person. I have observed that the social challenges associated with autism preclude Gabriela from commencing singing with others without this technology.

Once initiated, Gabriela will sing alone or with others and retain the lyrics and melodies of the songs. These brief moments give Gabriela respite from the challenges of autism and provide her life with experiences of pure joy.

When it comes to her high school syllabus, her instruction is divided into curriculum and learning, social and emotional needs, independent functioning, related services such as speech language therapy, daily living skills, post school adult living and basic vocational skills. The clearest general evidence of her resilience through music comes from teaching staff who indicate her three most likely employment skills are: folding, sorting and singing in a band. One would hope the latter is the primary method, but alas it is not likely to happen. Her educators and service providers characterize the intensive adaptive services that she receives to overcome her communicative and social limitations as: a) understanding verbal language, b) being happy, c) having a good selective memory, and d) a love of music. The references to music as a possible occupation, and as a communicative strength, were indicated and documented through the enactment of her statutory planning sessions with care providers and fellow educators. Her Individualized Educational Plan (IEP) defines Gabriela at level five – in greatest need for educational support.

With a focus on strengths, Gabriela demonstrates a keen selective memory through music choice, which both motivates and feeds her love of singing. Preference is of the utmost importance when it comes to her music performance. For Gabriela, positive affective responses shape her overt behaviors, which indicate joy, excitement and a desire to sing and interact with others. Through empirical evidence I infer that this is as a direct result of her preference for *music* that acts as stimuli. My video evidence shows that when she rises from her seat to sing with a microphone she is indicating songs that speak to her through positive affective responses. Her selective memory allows her to remember the lyrics to these songs and retain her list of music favorites, and the ACC device assists her to indicate a preference. Recognizing these positive affective responses and continually exploring the songs that speak to Gabriela is the basis of instruction during her music lessons with myself – as her music teacher. This preference information, when put in the hands of her family, school and community, provides opportunities to share her resilience through music and increases opportunities for social interaction and self-expression.

It is Gabriella's experiences with music that lead to the development of her personal preferences. We all have a favorite song, activity or book. Literacy teachers often choose stories they believe will interest their students, motivate them to read or affect them in a manner that will engender interactive classroom discussions. One area that music educators could explore further is their students' knowledge and communication of music preference. Gabriela's case provides a clear example of a student with autism and profound speech language challenges who communicates musical preference through overt behavioral responses. Educators could easily dismiss such behavioral indicators as problem behaviors associated with autism. Individuals with problem behaviors, cognitive disabilities and/or autism place tremendous demands on the support capacities of teachers. An important question to ask is, how do students with autism use behavior to communicate musical effect in the public school music classroom? Public school behavioral specialists in the U.S. assess non-verbal communication in public schools for a variety of students with special needs. Little documentation exists or is applied that connects the association of the behaviors they observe to music education. The following review of literature informed the development of the approach I used with Gabriela.

Review of the literature

The U.S. Department of Education defines autism as "a developmental disability significantly affecting verbal and nonverbal communication and social interaction, generally evident before age 3, which adversely affects educational performance" (Turnbull et. al., 2002, p. 91). The variety and degree of challenges displayed by each person with autism are along the autistic spectrum. Autism spectrum disorder (ASD) comprises several categories of autism. *The Diagnostic and Statistical Manual of Mental Disorders*, Fourth Edition, contains three essential features for identifying autism spectrum disorder:

> Subject impairment in social interaction, manifested by (a) impairment in the use of nonverbal behavior; (b) lack of spontaneous sharing; (c) lack of socioemotional reciprocity; and/or (d) failure to develop peer relationships.

> Impairment in communication, manifested by (a) delay in or lack of development in spoken language and gestures; (b) impairment in the ability to initiate or maintain conversation; (c) repetitive and idiosyncratic use of language; and (d) lack of pretend play.

A restricted repertoire of activities and interests, manifested in (a) preoccupation with restricted patterns of interest; (b) inflexible adherence to routines; (c) repetitive movements; and/or (d) preoccupation with parts of objects. (DSM-IV-TR, APA, 2000, pg. 70)

This diagnosis of ASD assumes that no other primary behavioral causes for the symptoms exist. The definition provided in the Individuals with Disabilities in Education Act (Turnbull et al., 2002, p. 337) classifies seven characteristics of ASD including (1) challenges in language development; (2) social interaction; (3) repetitive behavior; (4) impeding behavior; (5) the need for environmental predictability; (6) sensory and movement disorders; and (7) challenges in intellectual function. An impediment to social interaction is noted as significant in both definitions yet neither acknowledges a diminished personal identity, or sense of self, associated with ASD.

Autism and preference research

The ability to communicate needs and interests and to engage socially in interactive experiences varies for each person with autism, due in part to the fact that autism is a spectrum disorder. As a result, the social, behavioral and communicative challenges associated with autism vary in degree for each person (Wetherby & Prizant, 2000). Research dealing with preference communication covers almost all areas of everyday life. Fisher et al. (1992) discuss preference research for populations with severe and profound disabilities. In their approach a limited number of stimuli are offered to the client, and behavioral responses to preferred and non-preferred stimuli are documented. The use of limited selections (similar to those used in the ACC's with Gabriela), result in higher-level responses for preferred items. More recently, Ropar and Peebles (2007) researched the sorting preferences in children with autism based on abstract or concrete features. Schreck and Williams (2006) studied the food preferences and factors influencing food selectivity for children with autism spectrum disorders. Mechling and Moser (2010) studied video preference assessment of students with autism between themselves, adults and peers. The practice of developing and itemizing preference inventories for people with autism is another method of providing support that is gaining credibility. Schreck and Williams (2006) developed a food preference inventory (FPI), which provides a caregiver with a checklist of preferred or accepted food items by children with autism. The use of these inventories can be useful in music education to provide the student with desired items, whilst attempting to diminish undesired behavior through the use of a reward system.

Another challenge for a person with autism is the development of a sense of self. Due to communicative disorders, parents have difficulty expanding their child's repertoire of preferred music (DeVito, 2009). Communication, both verbal and written, is often difficult for students with autism especially when coupled with a high degree of speech language impairment along the autism spectrum. These students often have difficulty conceptualizing and communicating an answer to the question "What kind of person am I?" Music education helps develop a sense of self in relation with their own and other cultures, and self-expression through music performance and composition (DeVito, 2009).

Students with autism face varying speech, cognitive, and behavioral challenges in their daily life, as well as when listening to and participating in music listening activities. When Gabriela responds to preferred music, she is crossing a communication divide that disables her in most aspects of daily life. Students without these preference and communication challenges can enjoy quality of life activities such as playing a CD of their favorite musical artist, attending a local orchestral concert of a preferred symphonic composition, or turning on the radio with ease and changing the dial to an interesting new music selection. For students on the severe end of the autism spectrum, these simple tasks can be potentially daunting.

Augmentative and Alternative Communication devices

Speech language impairments are one of the characteristics found in varying degrees across the autism spectrum. As a result, gathering information related to a preference inventory cannot always be accomplished simply by awaiting a verbal response to a question. When this occurs, augmentative devices can be used to cross the communicative divide. Augmentative and alternative communication (AAC) refers to communication techniques that an individual uses in addition to (augmentative) or instead of (alternative) the naturally acquired speech, gestures or vocalization ability the person may possess (Mirenda & Erickson, 2000).

Common AAC devices in the U.S. are Cheaptalk and GoTalks. These hand held devices can be programmed to provide students with the opportunity to distinguish between multiple visual and verbal responses to a given question through the use of switches. In *Meaningful Experiences for People with Autism*, Cafiero (2005, p.26) indicates multiple benefits for the use of AAC in a variety of educational settings. Benefits include: increasing complexity with devices as communication skills increase, visual learning, accommodation of the need for repetition that is associated with autism, provision of a method of exchange in interpersonal communication, and language recognition rather than an over reliance on memory. Additional benefits associated with AAC devices include (p.33) increased access to social settings, functional spontaneous communication, interaction and greater independence in the home, school and community.

Functional Behavioral Analysis and positive behavioral supports

According to the U.S. Office of Special Education Programs, Functional Behavioral Analysis (FBA) has been an effective approach to diminishing undesired behavior (Sugai et al., 2000). "Among the most important changes in applied behavioral analysis in the past 20 years has been the development of FBA. The development of positive behavioral interventions and plans that are guided by FBA is the foundation on which the Positive Behavioral Support (PBS) approach is delivered (Sugai et al., 2000)." In order for a behavior change intervention to be effective, Sugai et al. (2000) indicate the need for identifying the events that reliably predict and maintain undesired behavior (Carr, 1994; Horner, 1994; O'Neill et al., 1997; Repp, 1994; Sugai, Lewis-Palmer, & Hagan, 1998).

According to Fox, Dunlap and Buschbacher (2000) challenging behavior by children with autism can prove to be a primary barrier to not only education but community engagement and peer relationships. One approach to reducing these behaviors is through positive behavioral supports:

> Positive Behavioral Support (PBS) is a general term that refers to the application of positive behavioral interventions and systems to achieve socially important behavior change. Positive behavioral support is not a new intervention package, nor a new theory of behavior, but an application of a behaviorally-based systems approach to enhancing the capacity of schools, families, and communities to design effective environments that improve the fit or link between research-validated practices and the environments in which teaching and learning occurs (Sugai et al., 2000).

The generally accepted belief is that challenging behavior has a purpose for students with autism and serves a specific function (Carr et al., 1994). The function of the behavior is specific to the student and can be meant to communicate any specific need or response to stimuli in their daily life. In my experience, this is evident with students who have profound speech language impairments who utilize behavioral responses as the immediate and primary method of communication. Research since this statement deals primarily with determining the communicative purpose of challenging behavior and developing the supports necessary to reduce this behavior (Fox, Dunlap & Buschbacher, 2000). In Gabriela's approach to music education, behavioral responses are identified based on their communicative function with positive overt responses being highly valued as a path to inclusion.

Focusing on positive behavioral communication

The term "positive" in positive behavioral intervention does not necessarily mean the identification of positive behavioral responses, but rather a non-invasive and non-demeaning approach to reducing undesired behavior. A functional behavioral analysis for Gabriela centers on identifying the undesired stereotypical behaviors (demonstrated in the first video clip) rather than entering the music class to identify the positive behavioral communication being exhibited in clips two and three. My theory informed approach was to use the ACC devices to help students with speech language impairments to communicate their needs and preferences in everyday settings. The approach centers on the identification of behaviors that communicate positive affective responses to music to create a music preference inventory for Gabriela. In an education plan incorporating positive behavioral supports, this preference information can be used as a reward system for minimizing undesired behavior, but this is not the purpose of music education for Gabriela. My search for preferred music for Gabriela improves the quality of her life by increasing the moments when she is able to transcend the challenges associated with autism.

Wetherby and Prizant (2000) indicate that most published intervention studies lack measures that overcome barriers to learning. They often fail to provide meaningful lifestyle changes for the individual or family of children with autism. These statements by Wetherby and Prizant and the previous review of literature support my focus on Gabriela's positive behavioral communication.

Autism and music listening

An important goal of public school music listening activities is to provide students with an appreciation of music that permits them to develop and communicate preferences within a variety of musical genres and styles. Music listening is a presentation of sounds that have the potential of being meaningful for the listener (Reimer, 2003). According to Reimer, the meaningful nature of these sounds is dependent upon the listener's ability to absorb sound gestures. The listener can then share the musical significance of the given sound. Perhaps most significant for Gabriela is Reimer's belief that the need for improvement in these listening skills is a "major obligation" to the music education profession. Reimer states:

> The entire body of music, historically and culturally, can be directly experienced and more fully shared by even young children through listening. Very little of that music will ever be encountered by most people in any other way. The development of every student's listening intelligence, therefore, is a crucial obligation of music education. Listening-think, as much as any other way to think musically, deserves the fullness of respect and cultivation that all musical intelligences require (2003, p. 225).

Elliott (1995) developed a theory of music listening based upon the premise that listening is a process of attention, awareness and memory. The individual listener's human consciousness determines the selection of music and the allocation of time to this process. Student participation in this process is the principal reason why music listening is a "thought-full" activity. An example of Elliott's (1995) theory in practice would be two individuals attending an orchestral performance of Leonard Bernstein's "Maria" from *West Side Story*. As the two individuals listen, they receive auditory signals, or *acoustic energy*. This energy stimulates the auditory nerve endings, which transmit information to the brain. When received, the brain responds, resulting in sensations throughout the body. With Gabriela, overt behavioral responses from these sensations that correspond with music preference are identified as positive affective responses.

Elliott (1995) stipulates that cognition and memory of the listening experience result in more than sensations alone. He explains the recall of the characteristic auditory patterns from previous listening experiences of "Maria" influenced the present sonic event. When this takes place, the two listeners "know" the auditory patterns comprising the song "Maria." The individuals know "Maria" because they are familiar with the sound patterns that comprise the song. According to Elliot, familiarity by the listener with specific harmonic theory is not required. Evidence of an individual's ability to "know" a piece can be determined through (a) the ability to hum or sing along with a degree of accuracy; (b) the ability to discriminate, construct, and organize auditory events of the "Maria-kind"; and (c) the knowledge of how Western orchestral auditory patterns are presented (Elliot, 1995). He specifies that the listener is then said to possess knowledge of the "style-specific cognitive process" and he demonstrates discrimination through the "thought-full" nature of music listening. In this context, Gabriela indicates discrimination between sonic events through the communicative function of positive affective responses and the demonstration of musical preference utilizing AAC devices.

Music educators aspire to help students comprehend musical concepts, to perform music through singing, dancing, and to use instrumentation and an individual preference developed from a variety of musical genres and styles. Preferences result from the music's effect on the listener. Behavioral interaction between the music and listener is often one of the direct ways students with autism and profound speech language impairments can indicate preferences to stimuli. These communicative challenges result in the need for AAC devices to indicate a desire for participation and preferences. Music education, AAC devices and behavioral communication provide an opportunity to establish a music preference inventory through Gabriela's planned involvement with music from a variety of cultural and historic backgrounds.

Method

Iwata and Dozier (2008) state that a functional analysis methodology is a well-established standard for assessment in applied behavior analysis research. This includes clinical (non-research) applications and is applicable in these settings for the treatment of problem behavior. Dr. Iwata's University of Florida graduate students conduct a significant amount of their training in Gabriela's Sidney Lanier School environment. Gabriela's homeroom and music class represent one clinical non-research setting to document a behavioral analysis of responses to preferred music. The first video clip (in her homeroom) represents a quasi control setting, while the second and third represents the test setting.

In this method analysis included the communicative functions of behavioral responses to musical stimuli in the form of selected musical works presented during public school music classes. Gabriela used AAC devices as a mechanism for selecting preferred music. A music preference inventory was developed through her selection of the preferred song using an AAC device programmed with the melodies of the songs presented in the lessons, and the behaviors that signify enjoyment for her through documentation on observational checklists. The methodological benefits of developing a music preference inventory to document the communicative function of behavioral responses related to musical preference aim to enhance the music listening repertoire of students with autism throughout their lifetime.

Procedure

A Functional Behavioral Analysis (FBA) determined the communicative function of Gabriela's behaviors. In other words, which behaviors indicated musical preference and which did not? To accomplish this, I categorized her overt behaviors using behavioral checklists and compared them with her selections using the AAC communication device. Specifically, these checklists included the perceived communicative function of a variety of behaviors, the manner of identifying behaviors, and types of behaviors encountered in a variety of settings outside of the music classroom.

At the end of Gabriella's music lessons I programmed an AAC device with the melodies of each song we auditioned. She presses the programmed switch that indicates her preferred song after hearing each option. Gabriela is fluent in the use of the programmed switches on the AAC device because they are a daily part of her school curriculum. The phrasing of my questions is consistent with terminology used for preference requests by the homeroom teacher.

For Gabriela, communication of preferences is indicated through alternative communication devices throughout the school day. Specifically, a visual aid representing the desired item is attached to a switch that activates a recorded message by the teacher – the message matches the item in the picture. For example, if the pictures represent a variety of foods and she presses the picture of the ice cream, the device is programmed to state, "I want ice cream" and her indicated desired item is provided. When used throughout the day, a template of behavioral communicative function and preferences becomes clear. In Gaby's music lessons, overt behaviors that she exhibits to the music presented in the lessons are compared with the preferences indicated on the device. The names of the songs are placed over the musically programmed switches as a visual aid.

Data

The aforementioned video clips are exemplars of the empirical evidence I have gathered using this method. The information that follows is a basic description of the environment in which Gabriela is placed – including the setting, materials used and structure.

Video clip 1

The first video depicts Gabriela in the classroom on a typical day. She is exhibiting stereotypical repetitive behaviors for a child on the severe end of the autism spectrum. The video was created in her homeroom classroom and the behavior indicated is a typical reaction to stimuli. The classroom is supplied with the same AAC devices that I use in the music classes. The device collates responses that inform preference inventories. In this clip Gabriela receives services from a speech language pathologist and is being taught concepts that can lead to basic vocational skills with assistance.

Video clip 2

In the second video clip, Gabriela is using an AAC device that is pre-programmed with four melodies used in our music lesson. A visual aide with an icon that matches each melody corresponds to the switch on the device that activates the recording of the melody. The music room is supplied with a microphone, CD player, percussion equipment, risers and space for dancing and movement activities, which are all a part of her curriculum. After building our educational relationship I presented Gabriella with a lesson that incorporated four selections before asking her to discriminate between the songs. In this clip Gabriela is being asked to indicate her preferences between four music selections and she displays clear recognition of the theme of *Appalachian Spring.*

Video clip 3

In the third clip, Gabriela is in the school auditorium during an African American History program. There are approximately 200 people in the audience as she holds a microphone. She was asked to come to the stage to sing *We Shall Overcome.* This is one of several songs on her music preference inventory due to its relevance to the theme of the performance. Her experiences with music performance now include performing with the school world music ensemble, but her primary method of performance interaction with others is through singing.

Analysis

The following analysis focuses on the behaviors that are exhibited in each of the three video clips in relation to the environment in which Gabriela is placed.

Video Clip 1 – she is exhibiting stereotypical repetitive behaviors for a person on the severe end of the autism spectrum. Her hands are raised in front of her eyes, which are fixed on her finger snapping in a repetitive manner. Afterwards her outstretched palms are shaking in relation to her verbalization. The pitch level of her voice changes to indicate an attempt at verbal communication, but as in every attempt at communication, there is not an indication of verbal language acquisition. This is the key reason for the use of the AAC device in her daily routine.

Video Clip 2 – rather than looking away as in the first clip, she's looking directly at the AAC device and pressing the correct switch in a clear response to the question posed by the music teacher. She looks directly at the device, which is programmed with four visual aides placed on switches to represent the four melodies presented in the lesson. It should be noted that there are four additional switches that are empty and potentially could also have been pressed by Gabriela. Her stereotypical verbal behavior from the first video has changed to singing the melody on the syllable "du." Her repetitive hand movement has changed to indicating the rhythm of the melody. The tapping between the thumb and index finger matches the tempo of the music. The overall positioning of her body and movement patterns of her head matches the upbeat nature of the phrasing of the melody.

Video Clip 3 – demonstrates what happens when the positive affective responses to preferred music lead Gabriela toward her resilience – to break the communicative barrier of autism through singing. She is being handed a microphone and singing *We Shall Overcome* with excellent pitch and accuracy, including smiling and clapping for herself at the end. It turns out she can verbalize in complete and clear English when she is singing music that inspires her to overcome the outer shell associated with her autism.

Discussion

Gabriela's story of discovery as a singer, and in turn her finding a coping strategy for the challenges of autism, aligns with arguments in Lemerle and Stewart's resilience chapter in several ways. In this section I have taken three statements from the Songs of Resilience WIKI and applied them directly to Gabriela's outstanding communicative progress. This application of Gabriela's story to the resilience framework provides a practice-led view of educational services in music to outline implications for the "outside lives" of students with autism.

Songs of Resilience invites researchers and practitioners to examine the often disruptive and challenging efforts of diverse cultural contexts and new technology on music making and learning.

The AAC devices used by Gabriela in music education classes constitute a new technology for music learning in U.S. public school ensembles. The companies that provide this technology are continually adapting their product to changing trends and student needs. While common in the clinics of speech language pathologists and homerooms of special education teachers, the application of this technology in music classrooms and ensembles is a new approach for music making and learning. In the U.S., it is not a requirement that high school students like Gabriela receive music education. Other electives can fulfill the *fine art* requirement. As a result, students with disabilities may not have access to arts instruction unless they are fortunate enough to receive it in their local communities. One reason this may occur is the false belief that if a student cannot verbally respond to questions and instruction then they do not possess the cognitive aptitude for arts instruction. If the first video clip of Gabriela were used as an aptitude test for inclusion in arts instruction, she would not have received training to use the AAC devices in her music lessons. As a result, the music preferences that led to her singing of "We Shall Overcome" would never have been identified because it was only through music instruction that she began to sing. Through continued use of this technology and arts instruction I can apply the hopeful final lyric of the song to Gabriela's battle with autism, "Deep in my heart, I do believe, we shall overcome someday."

Shifting the focus to social factors of music making, on sound communities ranging from aged choirs to refugees and the disabled.

In order for a social event between two people to have shared meaning, there needs to be interaction between parties. The development of a community music ensemble at the Sidney Lanier School has provided social inclusion for Gabriela and other children with autism, cerebral palsy, Down syndrome and developmental disabilities to share a music experience with their families and neighbors. The type of music incorporated in each gathering shifts because the music teacher turns the reigns of the program over to a "music coach" or leader in the community. In one gathering, Lansana Camara, a local community musician originally from Conakry, Guinea-West led the performance. His family created an ensemble in Africa called Group Laiengee, which accommodates children with disabilities by providing food, resources, and an opportunity to enhance their standing in the community through music performance. For another month, a neighbor in the school community who performs with the didgeridoo shared Australian music with the ensemble. The Santa Fe College Jazz Band (Gainesville, Florida), under the direction of Dr. Steve Bingham, has performed with the students with each child having an opportunity to sing and perform on percussion instruments to a variety of jazz music. Regardless of music background or expertise, these inclusive opportunities incorporate everyone – from maintaining a steady beat to improvisation. The method of involvement is up to the Sidney Lanier students themselves.

This interactive music ensemble provides Gabriela and all of the students in the school the opportunity to participate in inclusive family drum circles and singing groups. These music evenings are always concluded with a food social so the families can get to know each other, share stories, experiences, and provide mutual support to each other regarding the care of children with disabilities. Having a music preference inventory allows Gabriela and other students at the school with autism to attend these evening events and have an integrated experience with their community because the songs are already known and are shared with everyone at the event.

Shifting the focus to resilience factors of music making

Gabriela's responses in the second and third clips replicate items that match her music preference inventory. Preferred activities indicated via a preference inventory have several benefits for determining resilience factors as I have shown that they directly relate behavioral communicative function with overall wellbeing. Through fourteen years of experience, providing opportunities for students with autism from community music ensembles to Carnegie Hall, I have witnessed students along the autism spectrum generate behavioral indicators of communicative function during music activities. Options presented through alternative communication devices, in conjunction with visual aids, empower students with autism to select music examples that inspire them to respond and engage with others. These preferences can often be the one communicative function that transcends the challenges associated with autism, and the use of these devices provides a specific method for Gabriela to select a music pathway out of her autistic shell. Even if this is for minutes at a time, the potential benefits to her continued wellbeing are clear.

We discovered Gabriela's love of singing in 2009. After she sings, she reverts to behaviors seen in the first video example. The video of her singing amazed the whole school population as she exhibited resilience through music; we strive to give her opportunities to repeat these experiences whenever possible. These moments, when Gaby is relieved of the challenges of autism, allow her to briefly interact and communicate with others. She provides an inspiration for educational practitioners to search for additions to her preference inventory in ways that have potential to demonstrate her resiliency beyond music education. For Gabriela and all of those whose resilience and uniqueness inspires them to DIScover their ABILITIES and change the world around them.

References

American Psychiatric Association, (2000). Diagnostic and statistical manual of mental disorders text revision (4th ed.). Washington, DC

Cafiero, J. (2005). Meaningful exchanges for people with autism: An Introduction to Augmentative and Alternative Communication. Bethesda, MD: Woodbine House, Inc.

Carr, E. G., Levin, L., McConnachie, G., Carlson, J. I., Kemp, D. C., & Smith, C. E. (1994). *Communication-based intervention for problem behavior: A user's guide for producing positive change.* Baltimore: Paul H. Brookes.

DeVito, D. (2006). The Communicative Function of Behavioral Responses to Music by Public School Students with Autism Spectrum Disorder. University of Florida: Dissertation.

—. (2009). The Communicative Function of Behavioral Responses to Music: A Precursor to Assessment For Students with Autism. *The Practice of Assessment in Music Education: Frameworks, Models and*

Designs. Proceedings of the 2009 International Symposium on Assessment in Music Education, 239-252. Chicago: GIA Publications.

Elliott, D. (1995). *Music matters: A new philosophy of music education.* New York: Oxford University Press.

Fisher, W., Piazza C., Bowman, L., Hagopian, L., Owens, J. & Slevin, I. (1992). A comparison of two approaches for identifying reinforcers for persons with severe and profound disabilities. *Journal of Applied Behavior Analysis,* 25(2), 491-498.

Fox, L., Dunlap, G., Buschbacher, P., (2000). Understanding and intervening with young people's problem behavior: A Comprehensive Approach. In A.M. Wetherby and B.M. Prizant (Eds.), Autism Spectrum Disorders: A Transactional Developmental Perspective (pp. 307-332). Baltimore: Paul H. Brookes.

Horner, R. H. (1994). Functional assessment: Contributions and future directions. *Journal of Applied Behavior Analysis,* 27, 401-404.

Iwata, B., & Dozier, C., (2008). Clinical Application of Functional Analysis Methodology. *Behavior Analysis in Practice,* 1(1), 3-9.

Mechling, L.C., Moser, S.V. (2010). Video Preference Assessment of Students with Autism for Watching Self, Adults or Peers. *Focus on Autism and other Developmental Disabilities,* 25(2), 76-84.

Mirenda, P., & Erickson, K. A. (2000). Augmentative communication and literacy. In A. M. Wetherby & B. M. Prizant (Eds.), Autism spectrum disorders: A transactional approach (pp. 333–369). Baltimore: Paul H. Brookes Publishing Co.

O'Neill, R. E., Horner, R. H., Albin, R. W., Sprague, J. R., Storey, K., & Newton, J. S. (1997). Functional assessment and program development for problem behavior: A practical handbook. Pacific Grove, CA: Brooks/Cole.

Reimer, Bennett (2003). *A philosophy of music education: Advancing the vision.* Upper Saddle River, NJ: Prentice Hall.

Repp, A. (1994). Comments on functional analysis procedures for school-based behavior problems. Journal of Applied Behavior Analysis, 27, 208-412.

Ropar, D., Peebles, D. (2007). Sorting preferences in children with autism; the dominance of concrete features. *Journal of Autism Developmental Disorders,* 37 (2), 270-80. 0

Sugai, G., Horner, R. H., Dunlap, G. Hieneman, M., Lewis, T. J., Nelson, C. M., Scott, T., Liaupsin, C., Sailor, W.,Turnbull, A. P., Turnbull, H. R., III, Wickham, D. Reuf, M. & Wilcox, B. (2000). Applying positive behavioral support and functional behavioral assessment in schools. *Journal of PositiveBehavior Interventions and Support, 2*,131-143

Sugai, G., Lewis-Palmer, T., & Hagan, S. (1998). Using functional assessments to develop behavior support plans. Preventing School Failure, 43(1), 6-13.

Turnbull, R., Turnbull, A., Shank, M., Smith, S., & Leal, D. (2002) (3rd ed.). *Exceptional Lives: Special education in today's schools.* Columbus, OH: Merrill/Prentice-Hall.

Wetherby, A. M., & Prizant, B. M. (2000) (Eds). *Autism spectrum disorders: A developmental, transactional perspective*. Baltimore: Paul H. Brookes Publishing Co.

CHAPTER TEN

A LIFE-LONG SONG OF RESILIENCE: IN PURSUIT OF ABRAHAM HAGHOLM

PETER BERRY

Photo of Hagholm circa 1860

Introduction

I work at Lund University in Sweden as a librarian who enjoys playing the violin. Many years ago, whilst looking for a repertoire of traditional music from the area of southern Sweden where I lived, I happened to hear a tune that has stayed with me ever since – a waltz in the key of G minor that reminded me of medieval long dances. Later I learned that it had been recorded in a manuscript by a 19th century schoolteacher in a remote parish of the province of Östergötland. This was the first time Hagholm had appeared in my life.

Abraham Hagholm (1811-1890) could not walk. He lost the use of his legs when he was a young boy due to an undefined illness. Years later, as he did some gardening in his little plot by the church, he died suddenly. He fell down, his life ended and one remarkable story received its measuring stick. The local newspapers wrote about him with approval and appreciation – offering the occasional anecdote. There is one word present in the majority of the media accounts: Hagholm was original. The evidence I present in this chapter aims to make a compelling argument that the term "resilient" would have been an equally appropriate description of Hagholm's character.

I started my study of Hagholm twenty years ago. Through archival research I discovered that he was a poor and disabled man in a society where it was difficult to make ends meet. Hagholm's whole life is an interesting story of how he established his identity and how music was a central theme in this struggle with adverse circumstances. He sang, played the violin, led a choir, participated in men's quartet singing, played the *psalmodikon* (a bowed box zither), taught and recorded music in his notebooks. And he survived. My historical analysis of Hagholm and his music denotes that this man sung a life-long song of resilience.

My study of Hagholm would have taken a different turn if I had not met Steve Dillon, a visiting academic at the school where I work, the Malmö Faculty of Fine and Performing Arts. He brought to my attention the "Songs of Resilience" project in his lecture about young underprivileged Australians being helped to find their identity through music (Dillon, n. d.). That music could have such a wholesome effect was a revelation to me. I started thinking of songs of resilience in relation to Hagholm and discovered new and interesting questions to ask.

I am frequently asked the question, what is resilience? Partly this is explained by the fact that there is no single translation of this word into Swedish. Instead, I offer the following brief definition – the ability to survive under difficult circumstances. I add that this ability could be thought of as ranging from a physical condition to aspects of a particular culture. This I tell my friends, is not my own invention, but the research focus of many scholars, some of whom operate within the fields of education, health, and, sometimes, music education with a focus on health.

I describe this study as an historical autoethnography – the study of a culture through an individual's self-study (Bartleet & Ellis, 2009), where I use archival records available to myself as a librarian. Using this approach to explore historical records I will address the following questions: In what sense was Hagholm's journey through life a life-long song of resilience? Could Hagholm show us how to foster resilience in others? Could his music be used as a source of creativity and emancipation? Is it possible to study resilience using a historical/biographical approach?

The main challenge for my research was to rearrange my informal and historical knowledge of Hagholm to suit an academic public. I decided to create a serious presentation that would benefit my study without losing touch with my personal objectives. I felt compelled to undertake this study as I was fascinated by the landscape of Godegård, and the music of Hagholm's notebooks. It became clear every time I connected to Godegård – my violin skipped out of its case and prodded me to play at once. My reasons for bringing this tale to the attention of others have to do with resilience: how it sustains others and how my creativity helps to alleviate physical and mental hardship. The recent earthquake in Haiti has reminded me of the need to address motor disabilities therapeutically (Bayard, 2010). In the future could treatment based on movement and rhythm make the victims of these catastrophes become "whole" human beings again?

I have tried to investigate a research territory, which I define as historical and biographical as it concerns an individual and his journey through life in the 19th century. I found studies in many different subject disciplines useful. Magnus Gustafsson (2004) cleverly describes the infrastructure of popular music of the period, whilst Aaron Antonovsky (1987) offers a salutogenic analysis of the human ability to cope, which he defines as *sense of coherence*. Oliver Sacks (2007) provides a neurologist's perspective describing music and the human brain, and Ruud (1997) has written extensively about the building of identity through music. Historically, the study of disability has an action orientation, similar to resilience research. A dissertation on the history of disabled people was recently defended at the University of Umeå (Olsson, 2010), which outlines attempts to improve material and environmental conditions in Sweden. Bredberg (1999) writes about current disability research and calls for less focus on institutional histories and more experiential studies about the micro history of each person. Together these historical and contemporary arguments support studies such as the one I have conducted about Hagholm.

I start my research journey commenting on available source material. Since this study is intended for an international audience I present an overview of the time and place that we will be visiting. It is also necessary to include a few words on the history of Swedish popular music. I will then present a summary of events in Hagholm's life-long journey, and offer my analysis that found traces of resilience in Hagholm's life and music. Finally I will discuss Hagholm and his music as possible sources for resilience interventions today.

The historical record of Hagholm

There was no particular source that provided all the information I needed about Hagholm. Making sense of his life was similar to putting together the pieces of a giant jigsaw puzzle. Bits and pieces appeared in different documents. The best available biography consists of a few pages in *Svenska låtar*, the national inventory of Swedish folk music (Andersson, 1922-1940). This is also where a large selection of his scores are published. A few years ago Hagholm's notebook was photographed and presented in its entirety on the Internet by the Centre for Swedish Folk Music and Jazz Research (Folkmusikkommissionens, n. d.). The records of The Church of Sweden, which used to be responsible for population data, are an obvious source of pertinent historical research and the minutes of the parish council are another important source – the "sockenstämma." In addition, collections of notes by A. T. Engholm, one of Hagholm's nephews, have proved helpful. Most of the remaining material I have used helps to paint a broader backdrop of the history, economy, politics and culture, both locally and on a national level. More sources would have made speculation and informed guesswork less necessary. The most impressive source of information, of course, has been the records produced by Hagholm's own hand: his collections of fiddle tunes and songs.

Hagholm spent nearly all his life in the parish of Godegård. It is still a vast and sparsely populated area with woods, lakes and mountains, located far from any larger cities. The closest city is Linköping, the capital of Östergötland. In the 19th century, the local landlord owned the entire parish more or less. He and his family operated a successful manufacturing business. During odd hours and at home, people made nails and scythes from iron produced at the manor forgeries. Most of the small villages were hard to reach on the poor roads that stretched through forests and across mountains.

When I started my study I was stranger in this environment, meeting people and surroundings that although sometimes looked familiar, turned out to be full of surprises. Today I can discern the contours of 19th century Sweden, a country that was recovering from centuries of warfare and political power struggles in Europe – it licked its wounds, turning into a modern state. Sweden was in the process of abandoning a society with roots in the Middle Ages, changing into the country that we are familiar with today. Political and social reform was introduced in the middle of the 19th century, and one outcome of this was the establishment of a national public school system in 1842. Hagholm became one of its first public funded music teachers.

It is necessary to say a few words about popular music in Sweden during the 19th century (Cf. Ling, 1997). The most appreciated popular music instruments of the period were the violin and the clarinet. Music and dance were an important and integrated part of everyday life. Popular music in the countryside was a mixture of influences; it was reported that many people, including court musicians, composed tunes. Most of the tunes were known in several of the Swedish provinces. Academic interest in this music started early in the 19th century with the goal of discovering the roots of Swedish music. Some music collecting did take place and this activity boomed at the end of the century. The academic collectors created a framework for the study of this popular music. They were responsible for defining the music in a way that did not always reflect its multi genre character and the traditions of performance. One possible reason why Hagholm was not well documented in these academic collections was that he did not fit easily into their categories.

Hagholm did not record music belonging to one specific genre and he did not inherit his musicianship as many countryside fiddlers believe they did. The fiddle music that Hagholm collected was that used in communities to which he belonged. This music is today referred to as folk or traditional music. These concepts were unknown to Hagholm and I will avoid them here. I have chosen to use "popular music" as an inclusive term, reflecting the width of Hagholm's collection as well as the origin of the tunes.

Hagholm's journey through life

The best introduction for this section relates to an incident that occurred when I first became interested in Hagholm. At that time, as I learned later, there still existed a sack of personal memorabilia from Hagholm's home.

When his late relative died, it was all thrown in the garbage since no one appreciated or knew of the value of this material. The fact that I was not able to lay hands on it forced me to broaden my study and learn things that I otherwise would have neglected. Perhaps, what I finally achieved was different and in some respects a better study. Of course, I have wondered about the contents of this sack and what might have been preserved over the years. I do not think scores would have remained in tact, yet some of those originals were saved from other sources, and as I shall explain later in this chapter, they are now being reinterpreted by contemporary fiddlers around the world.

Hagholm was born on the 16th of October 1811. He was the first child of Jan Persson and Magdalena Karlsdotter, crofters and residents of the small village of Hagen. The family income was low and supplemented by their manual manufacturing of nails. This type of cottage industry was common in pre-industrial societies and it involved long, unsocial hours of labour. Hagholm's mother, who eventually reached the age of 94, was born out of wedlock, a stigma at this time. She later married and became the mother of many children of which Hagholm was the oldest. Several of Hagholm's relatives, including his father, reached similar longevity to that of his mother.

There is no evidence of singing or music in the Persson home but Magdalena, as most other women of that time and place, was likely to have known the traditional songs, of which there were many (Ling, 1965). We may also take it for granted that locals heard hymns performed at Hagen at regularly catechetical meetings conducted by the vicar. These songs and hymns were probably the first traces of music in Hagholm's life.

When Hagholm was 10 years old his life took a turn for the worse. Illness reduced his leg movements to crawling. He never regained the ability to walk unaided. The parish council of Godegård regularly sent a small number of patients to the neighboring spa and hospital of Medevi, a half-day's journey from Godegård. Hagholm had the good fortune to receive this help a number of times. This is where Hagholm was taught to walk using crutches, and also where he was likely to have made his first contacts with popular dance musicians.

The spa of Medevi is situated in the northwest corner of Östergötland. It remains a small village, and its function as a health institution ended in the late 20th century. Medevi is famous for its wells of Middle Age origin, and the health routines focused on the drinking of its wholesome water.

An important part of the health regimen at Hagholm's time was the emphasis on regular movement: not only long walks and parades but also dance and music. The choice of music was decided by "dietary ethics," stating that rhythm was essential and that it should be steady, without jumps or skips (Levertin, 1892). Tempo, melody or key was not mentioned, yet it is possible to discern this even character in the authentic brass band music that is provided at the spa today. Music in Hagholm's era was mostly played on the violin or the clarinet, and the historical record suggests that some of the players appeared at the spa only temporarily, being employed in several different places in the region.

After his "cure" in Medevi, Hagholm sought ways to make himself useful. He was unfit for daily hard work as well as for manufacturing nails. Hagholm found other opportunities, which I learned from the minutes of the parish council. When the local sexton became too old to teach, there was a chance for Hagholm to fill his place. He had already – through his own initiative – gathered children around him after church to teach them how to read. Hagholm accepted the teaching responsibilities of the sexton and was appointed School Master in 1830. He kept his position as a teacher until 1871 when he retired. During this entire period he worked as a so-called ambulatory teacher, travelling to the different small villages, stopping for a few weeks, then returning after a year. This is how Hagholm became well known to generations of Godegård parishioners.

Hagholm continued to visit Medevi as a teacher, but with a considerably higher status than before. He was even allowed to write his name on the back of one of the large sitting room tables, an honor only granted to guests of higher standing. Medevi was not only a hospital where the poor and ailing were allegedly cured; it was also a place where the bourgeoisie mingled. Yet strict class barriers of the time were less guarded at the spa than in the cities (Mansén, 2008), and it was a place where people from different backgrounds could meet and muse. It was a place where Hagholm could be accepted with his new identity as a teacher.

In the 1830s Hagholm decided to learn to play the violin. He probably learned this with the support of the sexton's son, who also learned to play violin at this time, and who was a collector of fiddle tunes. His teacher was the organist in a neighboring village. Assuming that Hagholm had the same teacher as the sexton's son, one might deduce that his approach to musicianship and reliance on scores was reminiscent of classical training, as it differed from the training of village fiddlers who mostly, but not always, learned by ear rather than by reading scores. Hagholm later on played at weddings and dances, but it is not clear how often and how well he played. He was at the very least a gifted amateur.

Hagholm started to assemble his collection of popular dance tunes for the violin in the middle of the 1830s. He continued adding to his collection till the 1850s until eventually his collection consisted of close to 400 tunes. Hagholm's is one of several fiddlers' notebooks that were saved in a national inventory conducted at the end of the 19th century. These notebooks consist of popular dance music scores. During this period there seems to have been an accepted practice of copying from other fiddlers' notebooks. Some of Hagholm's tunes probably entered his notebook in this way. There has been a debate concerning the extent to which the fiddlers' notebooks reflected the actual repertoires of the fiddlers. It has been argued that one did not transcribe the music with which one was familiar. In terms of Hagholm's use of his notebook, this remains an open question. I believe that some of the tunes were indeed part of his playing repertoire and that at least four were his own.

Let us take a look inside Hagholm's collection of fiddle tunes. His collection is one of the largest at this time from southern Sweden. It also appears to be one of the most accurate. Unfortunately, Hagholm added very few comments to his scores. He described all the tunes in the first part of his collection as "polonaises." It seems that he used this as a catchall phrase for all tunes except waltzes and quadrilles, which belonged to a pre-19th century tradition. Instead of polonaises, I call them "polskas" which is the common way to describe them today. Many of the polskas have an 18th century baroque flavour. The second half of the collection consists of more waltzes similar to music composed in a classical 19th century style. Inserted between these collections are a few quadrilles that probably belong to the first half of the 19th century.

The polskas constitute the core of the collection and were amongst the first tunes Hagholm collected. They dominate the collection in terms of quality transcription. They are in 3/4 time signature, mostly in major keys and typically consist of phrases of sixteenth notes suggesting an even rhythm. According to Hagholm's own comments, he composed four major pieces that appear in his collection. One of them is a polska in the smooth sixteenth note tradition; the three remaining compositions are waltzes in a classical style.

The historical records show that most tunes in Hagholm's collection were played in other parts of Sweden as well. Their use in the area of Godegård and Medevi reflect two local repertoires. The polskas appear to belong primarily to the parish repertoire, particularly in the keys of A and D major. The waltzes, the quadrilles, and the polskas in the keys of F, Bb and E (probably played on the clarinet) are likely to have belonged to the Medevi repertoire. Judging from the scarce comments in his notebook, I can only assume Hagholm collected his tunes both at the spa and during travels in his own parish. At Medevi Hagholm was likely to have made friends with travelling musicians from different parts of Sweden. In his own parish he almost certainly met musicians primarily of local origin. In this collection Hagholm mentions only one of these local musicians, the blind fiddler Nyberg. In the minutes of the parish council we can read how Hagholm rose above his standing, obtaining a stable position as a school teacher and, as mandated by liberal reforms in parliament concerning education in 1842, attended the new teacher training college in the regional capital of Linköping. He became one of the first accredited public school teachers in Sweden.

As a schoolteacher Hagholm was responsible for teaching music, and he did this with more energy and imagination than was common at this time. In the 1850s he became even more involved in singing, at which time he and his school choir received a compliment from the bishop of Linköping. In school Hagholm taught different vocal parts of the hymns using *psalmodikons*. With the aid of this bowed, single-string instrument, it was possible to rehearse different vocal parts before singing them in church. Hagholm also sang in men's quartets, probably with the other guests he met in Medevi. Hagholm sang second tenor, "accurately but not beautifully" (Andersson, 1936).

Hagholm's singing was of a secondary interest to me for a long time, but was brought to my closer attention by a friendly villager of Godegård who asked me if I wanted to see some notebooks by Hagholm's own hand. Naturally, I was taken aback since there is so little left directly attributable to him. Answering "yes please," I then received eight small books of carefully printed notes and texts, scores for men's quartet divided into parts. These scores were copies of published songs that were composed in the early 19th century. They were popular among university students and since the 1840s, also among the upper and middle class. The texts consist of much praise for history and nature. The first date Hagholm provided in his collection of songs is 1858, indicating that they were written after Hagholm finished his collection of dance music. This second set of songbooks included work after 1858. The collection ends suddenly without any explanation in the middle of the latter set of notebooks. The last few entries were clearly made by somebody else's hand. Hand written collections of songs, similar to Hagholm's, are known from many areas of Sweden. Hagholm's notebooks stand out because they appear relatively early in the 19th century and because they constitute a representative selection.

In the late 1850s Hagholm became a clerk at the newly founded library of the Godegård parish. This was the time when several such libraries were established in Sweden as mandated by the public school reform. The Godegård library was a mid-sized library with book collections consisting of all genres, even popular. These books, including the library catalog, were recently discovered in a shed belonging to the church in Godegård.

Hagholm devoted his last years to his job as the new parish librarian. He is said to have appeared punctually, regardless of weather. If it snowed, and crutches were useless, he crawled from his house to the library. He took a keen interest in practical matters such as keeping the books neat and in order. He appears to have advised people about good reading, in the manner of a modern librarian. It does not seem that his interests were above his community, which is clearly evident in the library catalogue where he noted the books he had donated to the library himself. Among the titles he donated were serious items such as *Excerpts of Swedish history*, but also more frivolous such as *The mysteries of Russia revealed by an old diplomat*, and *The ridiculous babble mouth or funny anecdotes*. Hagholm worked in the library well past his pension age until his sudden death in 1890. A second stroke may have caused his death.

In what sense is Hagholm's journey through life a life-long song of resilience?

I have found traces of resilience in Hagholm's life, which I have tried to connect to his music. I am now going to investigate areas pertaining to the workings of the brain, the establishment of identity and the impact of different environments, which is the most concrete assertion I can offer about how these areas of resilience complement each other.

Sacks (2007) studied the relationship between the functioning of the brain and music, and in particular rhythm. He suggests that people with motor disabilities, such as those who suffer from Huntington's disease, "may benefit from dancing – and, indeed from any activity or sport with a regular rhythm or kinetic melody" (Sacks, 2007, p. 281). Sacks points out the therapeutic value of music for patients suffering from Parkinson's disease, noting that this music should be of an even character in order to induce relief in these patients (2007, pp. 270-283). The key words are dance, rhythm and evenness, which are reminiscent of the music that Hagholm heard in Medevi, where the orderly and even structure of dance music was emphasised therapeutically. In terms of musical treatment for patients with motor disabilities, Sacks further suggests that the simple act of listening to music also stimulates motor centers in the brain (2007, p. 262). Is it too far-fetched to apply this to Hagholm? Maybe he could not dance due to his condition, but the aspect of motor disabilities research concerned with the loss of movement and the feeling of "phantom" movement comes to my mind. Sacks argues that the brain can compensate for a disability such as blindness by stimulating other sensory abilities (p. 175). Is it possible that people with impaired movement could be compensated neurologically by extra sensory stimulation? Does Hagholm provide a case in point? I will leave these questions to the scientific experts.

I also interpret Hagholm's struggle to establish his identity as an expression of resilience. He was a poor and disabled man for whom it was critical to make an impact on his communities in order to survive. I believe his identity was intimately tied to his music. In his home parish, coming into close contact with many people in the small isolated villages, his capacities and capabilities as a travelling teacher grew. It must have become part of his work as well as leisure, i.e., music and dance that took place frequently. Fiddlers were sought after entertainers of the period and there is reason to believe that Hagholm was a welcome patron, particularly because of his familiarity with a large repertoire of dance music originating both locally and in the spa of Medevi, where new music from other parishes and provinces probably made its way into the local areas. It is plausible that Hagholm was accepted at these local dances also because of his status as a disabled man, who by adding a few *kronor* to his limited earnings, made it less necessary for the villagers to pay collectively for his upkeep.

The establishment of his personal identity was conceivably an important part of Hagholm's visits to Medevi. It is possible that he was considered an asset at Medevi because of his talents as a fiddler, as dances were an important part of the health regimen and amusements. I have shown that the nature of Hagholm's involvement in music changed as he became an accredited teacher and an established visitor at the spa. It was likely that he chose to become engaged in music such as the men's quartet repertoire because it better represented the more distinguished visitors.

I believe that Hagholm also experienced the impact of different resilient cultures. The system of treatments offered in Medevi represent such a cultural resource. One might also consider the generally held view of disabled people in 19th century society, and in the culture of social and political development, as expressions of resilient cultures. When I first thought about health in connection to Medevi I admit that I did not find this particularly relevant. Who believes in a treatment consisting of drinking water that tastes bad? Since then I have realised that one could conceive of Medevi as a locale for resilient cultural resources. The spa treatments there are somewhat akin to modern music therapy with its emphasis on movement (not only for the disabled) in the shape of music and dance.

The view of disabled people at the time was heavily influenced by a rational conception of man represented by 18th century Enlightenment, which emphasised people's usefulness and function. In terms of disability, it was a matter of disabled people being used to serve society as efficiently as possible. Thus, people with disabilities were encouraged to make a living in any way they could, as there were few resources available, and their access to them was also problematic. Some might then end up in professions where their disabilities did not stop them, as was the case within the teaching profession. It may also have meant a privileged access to certain ways of making a living, such as playing at dances in the small villages in the countryside. One might interpret all this as a general positive attitude in 19th Century Sweden to disabled people who displayed an individualist or self-reliant approach towards resilience.

In significant ways I believe the social and political developments of the 19th century implied a culture that emphasised belief in the individual, thus supporting an enterprise approach towards resilience. This is reflected in a central tenet of liberalism, which was to offer poor people betterment through education. Schools were established and teachers received professional training, and so a person's identity was increasingly defined in terms of profession. Music might have been recognised as a professional pursuit, but from what we know about Hagholm's case, it was first and foremost his personal interest.

Resilience in Hagholm's old age is evidenced primarily by his work in the library as someone who encouraged wider access to public resources. But what happened to his music? I believe two things happened. First of all it became less important for Hagholm to manifest his identity as he became older. He had already achieved what he wanted in this sense. He did not need music to confirm his status anymore. My other thought is to interpret Hagholm's songs of resilience as an expression of an intellectual process, a theoretical preference, where music eventually became less important to him. The theoretical aspect of Hagholm's relationship to music early in his life is reflected in his collection of fiddle tunes, which show how he learned music informally by reading scores and was later taught the classical method of playing the violin. His musical interest then changed and he became more interested in scores, as witnessed by his large collection of songs. This can be considered as an increased interest in an institutional aspect of music that had less to do with melody than the intellectual status of the songs. Hagholm's last scholarly effort was a collection that consisted of no music at all - the catalogue of books in the parish library. Is it possible to interpret this collection as the final stage of a development where music, to some extent, represents his intellectual position? Hagholm experienced disability and turned to music in an environment that acknowledged his personal struggle and his resilience. I found that his journey through life ended in relative comfort. His community appreciated him and he was no longer a poor man. He certainly experienced personal, social and cultural meaning through music making (Dillon, 2007).

What can we learn from Hagholm?

If I were to use Hagholm in a project to stimulate and replicate resilience, I would concentrate on him as an agent, a person who selected music in a special way, and show how his activities might guide action today. I would then examine Hagholm's music in a search for elements that one might consider of particular importance to the latest resilience research findings, and use these to inspire people. Permit me to present an outline of the important parts of such an undertaking with a short reflection on my own resilience project.

Lessons from Hagholm as a resilient agent

Lesson 1: inclusive not exclusive.

Most significant is the populist characteristics of Hagholm's music - he did not address an exclusive public but involved everybody surrounding him who were in the habit of "using" music at dances and at celebrations.

Lesson 2: personal involvement

Hagholm's success as a musician would not have been possible without his very personal investment.

Lesson 3: awareness of your community

Music also served Hagholm's purpose, establishing him on the social map, but he arrived there well aware of the importance of a nurturing community.

Lesson 4: openness to different genres

Hagholm's music was characterised by a certain degree of openness to genre. Whatever was available seems to have been considered and re-used.

Lesson 5: select "quality" music

Hagholm made careful choices with his music.

Lesson 6: : Knowing how music fits into your life

Hagholm's involvement in music had an intellectual and spiritual emancipation overtone that tied all of his musical activities together.

Lessons from Hagholm's musical record

It is possible to dismiss Hagholm's collection of music as mere trivia as the melodies are neither complex nor spectacular. The notation is correct but not pretty. There is little of the favoured minor tone in his music, supposedly so typical of Swedish folk music, and valued highly by many. Yet what looks so ordinary has the potential to stir deeper feelings. The characteristics of Hagholm's music show that a man who spent his life overcoming difficulties in some sense has the imprint of resilience. The emphasis on rhythm with a pumping even pulse. The emphasis on dance, "an ideal combination of music and movement" (Sacks, 2007, p. 279); an evenness and predictability of structure, the key to the whole tune seems to be located in the first bar and; a preference for major keys, for a relatively slow tempo for the polskas, and a faster tempo for the waltzes.

Lessons from Hagholm enacted today

My feeling that there are rich possibilities to express resilience in Hagholm's music prompted me to start my own "Songs of Resilience" project. My goal is to collect interpretations of Hagholm's music that will support and spread the use of his music to promote resilience. So far it has taken the shape of an interactive project on Wikispaces. I have selected what one might consider Hagholm's most obvious contributions to resilience, his own compositions. I have made scores and midi files available on my online forum and have invited the public, some people by personal invitation, to play these tunes and then share their interpretations. I ask contributors to explain how they have arrived at their interpretation and what part resilience played. I have now received a small, but interesting, number of replies.

I would like to share some of the responses I have received so far. I was surprised to see the appearance of a multicultural angle, showing a keen understanding resilience globally. A "world music" interpretation was one of the first contributions. Then followed Peruvian and Greek versions. There were clear indications of different music languages in these interpretations. Besides the flavours of different musical languages and different instruments, including the Quena flute, I was made aware of the importance of musical ornaments and how they colour these interpretations. One of the contributors pointed out the orderly structure of these pieces, comparing them to children's building blocks that one might put together in different patterns. He even suggested playing these "blocs" backwards, which interestingly enough, had guided my own interpretations some months earlier. It seems as if my Wikispace has slowly taken on a life of its own. I now follow it with great interest. At the same time I make use of Hagholm's music at festivals and in my own band. Making sense of resilience in Hagholm's music is now a long-term commitment for me.

What can historical cases add to the current resilience debate?

Since this is a study of history it is not possible to measure or analyse it in a laboratory to decide whether it is resilient or not. We are looking at a place and a person, distant in time and locality. Life then was different in so many ways. A study of people in this seemingly remote world is a question of interpretation and imagination. Because of my subjectivity as the author and researcher, I have felt a concern that the experiences of Hagholm are so unique that they lack relevance as a source of understanding anything, except for Hagholm's few living relatives and myself. In spite of all this, I believe that a study of an individual's life, be it distant in time and locality, add to our current understanding of resilience and help us to figure out efficient ways to share resources focused on resilience.

Let me end by returning to a more imaginative way of describing my study. I started this chapter describing my research as a journey in the company of Hagholm. At this point we are both exhausted by the extensive probing that has been necessary when subjecting Hagholm's historical record to examination. I believe we are reasonably happy about the way things turned out, although our conversation sometimes tended to become disconnected and abstract. We will now go on with our less demanding ramblings and I am sure we will play some music.

Sources and literature

Stockholm
Musik- och teatermuseet:
Pollonesser och vals-bok primo för violen sammanskrifven af A. Hagholm
Vadstena
Landsarkivet i Vadstena:
Godegårds socken: sockenstämmoprotokoll.
Medevi brunns arkiv
Svenska kyrkan: folkbokföringsarkiv; husförhörslängder.

Private collections
Engholm, T A. Utur minnet... [copy of manuscript]
Hagholm, A. Catalogue of the Godegård parish library [manuscript]
Hagholm, A. Music for men's quartets, a collection of scores [manuscript]

References

Andersson, N. (Ed.) (1922-1940). *Svenska låtar*. Stockholm: Norstedt.
—. (Ed.) (1936). *Svenska låtar: Östergötland*. Stockholm: Norstedt.
Antonovsky, A. (1987). *Unraveling the mystery of health*. San Francisco: Jossey-Bass.
Bartleet, B.-L., & Ellis, C. (Eds.) (2009). *Music Autoethnographies: Making Autoethnography sing/ making music personal*. Brisbane: Australian Academic Press.
Bayard, D. (2010). Haiti earthquake relief, phase two – long term needs and local resources. *New England Journal of Medicine*, 362, 1858-1861.
Bredberg, E. (1999). Writing disability history: problems, perspectives and sources. *Disability & society*, 14(2), 189-201.
Dillon, S. (n. d.). *Exploring new kinds of relationships using generative music making software*. Retrieved 6 April, 2010, from QUT Digital Repository: http://eprints.qut.edu.au/18148/1/c18148.pdf
—. (2007). *Music, Meaning and Transformation* (Vol. 1). Newcastle: Cambridge Scholars Publishing.
Folkmusikkommissionens notsamling och Musikmuseets spelmansböcker. (n.d.) Retrieved 7 April, 2010, from Svenskt visarkiv, Centre for Swedish Folk Music and Jazz Research: http://www.smus.se/earkiv/fmk/index.php?lang=sw&PHPSESSID=5c 58789fb95107bdba5a20c9ba75cea4
Gustafsson, M. (2000). *Småländsk musiktradition*. Växjö: Smålands spelmansförbund.
Levertin, A. (1892). Svenska brunnar och bad: med en kortfattad badlära och dietetik. Stockholm: Svenska.
Ling, J. (1997). *A history of European folk music*. Rochester, N. Y.: University of Rochester Press.
—. (1965). Levin Christian Wiedes vissamling: en studie i 1800-talets folkliga vissång. Uppsala: Uppsala universitet.
Mansén, E. (2008). Kurorter och vattenkurer. In G. Broberg (Ed.), *Til at stwdera läkdom: tio studier i svensk medicinhistoria* (pp. 285-301).
Olsson, C. G. (2010). Omsorg och kontroll: en handikapphistorisk studie 1750-1930. Umeå: Umeå universitet.
Ruud, E. (1997). *Musikk og identitet*. Oslo: Universitetsforlaget.
Sacks, O. (2007). *Musicophilia: tales of music and the brain*. New York: Alfred A Knopf.

CHAPTER ELEVEN

CD PRODUCTION FIGHTS SCHOOL FAILURE: SOCIALITY THROUGH MUSIC

EVA SÆTHER

Introduction

In Malmö Sweden, the percentage of school "dropouts" from year nine is 20%; this situation creates a challenge on many levels. In a multicultural city like Malmö, it poses questions about how segregation co-varies with school problems, and what political measures can be undertaken to address this. It also asks for pedagogic creativity – how do you motivate students who detest mainstream school and only associate it with disappointments, dreariness and gloominess? How do you motivate students to study the subjects successfully they have consistently failed for 9 years?

One of the most successful Swedish programs to remedy low or incomplete marks, thereby opening the door to continued studies and access to a sustainable future, is a unique school program called: Save the Children's Music Project. In this project the collaborative composing and playing of music is a method teachers use to increase students' self-confidence and self-esteem. It is a process-oriented program where the students learn how to cooperate and solve conflicts within a group. Apart from reaching the necessary standards in core school subjects, the students learn a positive learning model to which they can relate in future schooling and work. This chapter builds on the stories and songs of two ex-students from the music project, including interviews with the projects leaders, to show how the musical end product – an audio compact disc (CD) – is envisioned by one young woman and one young man, both of whom now enjoy increased confidence and competence.

Musical resilience

The research of Norwegian music therapist Even Ruud has shown that music strengthens vitality, providing experiences of competence and a sense of belonging. From his professional experience he also draws the conclusion that quality of life is intertwined with vitality, agency, belonging and meaning (Ruud, 1997, p.41). In this context agency is about possibilities to direct your own life, and vitality is used here as a concept to describe the connection between emotional status and how emotions are perceived and expressed. In other words, how open are school systems to students? – especially in terms of blocking and/or encouraging dynamic learning relationships. In this chapter I argue that through sharing their stories, students who "dropout" can increase both their vitality and their agency through the experiences of producing an original music CD.

Belonging and meaning refers to identity, the sum of all the stories we create about ourselves. Construction of identity also relies on memory, where raw data consists of experiences and understanding, and coherence is created by language metaphors. In this context, music is significant because it is typically connected to emotions that mediate processes where we acquire the social and personal experiences we choose to include in our constructed selves. Thus music can help us draw a flexible map of our lived world (Ruud, 2002). Another metaphor that depicts how music can be used in identity construction is the instrument: our personal and specific performance, our life praxis and agency can be perceived as an instrument tuned in many different ways. We can change the strings; we can even change the genre (Ruud, 1997, 2002).

Ruud (2002) concentrates in his research on understanding what it is that promotes health, the connection between health and the art of coping with life. Drawing on earlier research, for example Antonovsky (cited in chapter two by Lemerle & Stewart), he argues general resources that can be mobilised against sickness, or rather the absence of good health, are available to those who experience emotional coherence in life. It is not enough to associate quality of life with economical growth and material welfare as meaning and coherence are also crucial in this respect. Ruud (1997) underlines the strong and intense peak experiences that music offers, and argues that these experiences can contribute significantly to quality of life. He calls for an "expressive identity" that actively exposes itself to such experiences, and for a society that allows room for experiences that promote self-respect and recognition, creates social networks and advocates agency (Ruud, 2002).

Fredrickson (2000) presents arguments along the same line. She shows that positive emotions can not only reduce effects of negative emotions, but also help us to gain control over life. Positive emotions, created for example through musical experiences, create possibilities and new orientations, leading to more constructive actions. In this chapter, music stored on students' Mp3-players and mobile telephones further emphasises musical influence on young bodies, thoughts and feelings. Ruud (2008) calls it a "musical pharmacy" to be used for comfort, positive experiences, and to recall good memories. The therapeutic uses of music, however, need to be complemented by culturally aware practitioners to show how art can be inclusive. In this chapter I aim to show the musical resilience of students Ibbe and Viktoria, who make active use of such positive emotions by more or less constantly exposing themselves to music from their Mp3-players, rehearsals and recordings, inside and outside the classroom.

Resources and results

National trends in Sweden for the percentage of school dropouts increase in spite of efforts at local and national levels that seek to reverse this tendency. One of the largest interventions was carried out in Malmö 2005 – 2008, when 148 million Swedish Kronor (14.2 million Euros) of public funding was directed towards schools with the poorest test results and the highest percentage of students with foreign backgrounds. A school "dropout" is here defined as a student who has failed to reach the required goals in at least one of the three core subjects (Swedish, English, Mathematics), prerequisites for acceptance in further studies at "gymnasieskolan," or upper secondary school. Research shows that the grade differences between schools only represent 5% of the schools' teaching, organisation, resources and leadership, whilst 50% can be attributed to the demographic composition of students. Generally it is difficult to achieve high marks when you come from a family with poor economic circumstances and a foreign background. Typically, boys also tend to achieve lower marks than girls (Skolverket, 2009).

This was a much-needed project. At national level 15.3% of the students in year nine are excluded from further studies (Skolverket, nd). In Malmö, the most multicultural town in Sweden, the situation is extreme. While some schools show 0% dropouts, the schools that shared the 148 million

Kronor had between 7.9% and 58.5% dropout rates at the end of the project period, 2008. The evaluation of the project shows how difficult it was to locate any difference when looking only at the statistical data (Enö, 2009). The evaluation also shows that many teachers and school leaders were critical of the investment, as they would have appreciated more consultation about how to use the extra resources. For example, it was stated that all schools should organise "study workshops" even though there was no evidence that this was needed. The report gives a clear picture of a segregated Malmö, where the schools have a very complicated commission. One of the school leaders spoke about children who have to take their younger brothers and sisters to nursery school before they come to class as an example of the different lifestyles of these students. In such situations it is often unproductive to insist on order and rules. Teachers and school leaders often talk about how crucial it is to maintain good communication with the parents and carers, but in these circumstances this is difficult to achieve.

Most of the Malmö schools used the extra resources to divide the classes into smaller groups. That approach proved to be one of the most efficient measures. Individual student's self-confidence grew; the teachers could develop customised pedagogical activities and also communicate with the parents and carers. However, as the author of the evaluation states, continuity and long-term actions are needed to obtain results. When the project ended in 2008, many of the newly employed teachers did not continue their employment, and things returned to normal. When the project started, one of the schools had 65% dropout rate, at the end of the period the figure had fallen to 58.5%. The research shows that the most important variable is the socio-economical background of students and their peers, family and carers, and that it is very difficult to see any clear connection between additional resources and school results (Enö, 2009).

Learning to be able

The individual programme (IV) in the Swedish upper secondary school is an addition to the 17 regular national programmes. It is aimed at pupils with particular educational needs, and was introduced as a result of a system shift in 1994. The national curriculum Lpf-94 introduced the requirement that all students in compulsory schooling must pass the core subjects of Swedish, English and Mathematics. Originally Lpf-94 was designed for the few individuals that were expected to fail, but soon it grew to be one of the largest secondary school programmes in Malmö.

Approximately one fifth of the students from year nine in the compulsory school now opt for the individual programme IV as their only choice. Thousands of students come to these IV-programmes where the teachers are faced with a difficult situation; they are expected to encourage students to cope with something they have learned during nine years of repeated failure. As expressed by a former teacher at a IV-program:

> After having taught at an IV-programme for more than five years I still have not seen a general plan for how to receive these thousands of pupils that start every year. On the contrary, it seems as if these programmes are growing like shantytowns; fast and unplanned, without any guarantee that even the most fundamental needs will be met (Lorensson, 2006, p. 7).

Based on personal experiences Lorensson (2006) has studied and adapted the Rädda Barnens Musikprojekt (Save the Children Music Project), an IV-programme that takes a different approach. While most programmes attempt to introduce more of what the students have learnt already that they cannot do (i.e., Swedish, English and Mathematics), this programme promotes an experience of success, in this case with music. The students' energy for working with music can then be exported to other areas like their core subjects. The simple idea here is that success at one thing encourages the student to experiment and achieve in other areas – learning to be able.

The driving spirit of this programme was Mikael Svennerbrand, who started the pilot model of Rädda Barnens Musikprojekt (RBMP) in 1992, and after two years it was integrated with the local municipal school organisation. His own background as recreation instructor at Rosengårdsskolan (the school with a 58.5% dropout rate) had shown that his experience as a musician served as an effective tool for communication with students who had difficulty concentrating in school. He aspired to use his tools on a larger scale by starting a music school for marginalised teenagers based in the town centre rather than the suburbs.

Today the RBMP is located in the heart of Malmö at the former chocolate factory – positioned alongside the municipal music and culture school activities. The RBMP programme lasts one year, and normally receives about 15 pupils, many from families with drug problems, and others with post-traumatic stress as a result of experiences with war or political oppression in their home countries. Many of them have received special tuition in smaller groups, but with little success. It is typical for a student in this cohort to have an absence rate of 80% in their classes during the last years in the compulsory school. Their dreams for the future are either non-existent or quite unrealistic (Lorensson, 2006) and repeated negative experiences tells them that in a meeting between two human beings there is always one looser. Svennerbrand (2008) takes it as his task to show that in any meeting there might be two winners. He uses their interest for music as a vehicle to increase confidence and social competence. Consequently, the main practical task for the class during the RBMP year is to produce a CD containing their own compositions. The metaphor Svennerbrand uses when talking about a typical school year at RBMP is "pregnancy." In the conception phase you "fill up" yourself, then follows the sometimes-painful delivery, and finally the baby is there. In this case the baby is the original music CD that students produce during the school year. Two thirds of school time is dedicated to music that is supervised by musicians and followed up by band meetings with the teachers. At the end of the school year each group is given a day in a professional studio to record their tracks for the CD. The rest of the time is devoted to the core subjects, and with this positive framing, most of the students pass. In 2002 the RBMP was awarded the honour of being "the best school in the region" and in 2004 Swedish television showed a documentary about the school (Lorensson, 2006).

Adder and stand-by

Svennerbrand and his colleagues have developed a teaching method as a result of meetings with the pupils; the "Adder and stand by method" (the metaphor here refers to the Death Adder snake).

> In the Adder mode you strike when you are given an opportunity. Using fingertip sensibility you feel when it is time to sow good seeds that can grow into something useful later. As there are not many openings, you have to be quick as an Adder when it is time to strike. In the stand by mode you simply wait. The pupils in the music project have so many bad experiences with teachers and other grown ups that it takes time to build up confidence (Svennerbrand, 2009).

When Svennerbrand summarises his experiences from the RBMP he uses nine words, grouped in three. As the students start the programme they are experts in 1) *falseness, cowardice* and *falsity*. They meet the teacher who gives them 2) *love, demands* and *consequences*, with the help of 3) *music, meetings* and *humanity*.

Lorensson's (2006) study *Musical Manners* refers to a sense of coherence as one of the most important factors for success at RBMP. The teachers talk about how they frame the activities with rules, times and structures. The CD itself is a goal, but more important is the students' ability to learn how to work in a group, to trust other people and to strengthen self-esteem by taking responsibility. The time and opportunity taken for each teacher to see each pupil is crucial. This time and opportunity is created for the individual's creative goals to become meaningful. It creates a sense of coherence that gives the pupils the chance to succeed in the other subjects that used to be so impossible. The following section provides the stories of two ex-pupils at RBMP, Ibbe and Viktoria, accompanied by their songs.

The music is located online at:

http://web.me.com/evasaether/Egen/Songs_of_resilience.html

Ibbe

When I met Ibbe he was studying auto mechanics at a regular upper secondary school programme. Far from musical on the surface, almost everything in his life story refers back to music, and sometimes in our conversation he uses his poetic abilities, as if he was composing another song text:

> I can sit like this, and I see different things, and then I think, look at those two for example (points at an old couple that cross the school yard). I think of old love. You see what I mean? I check the branches of the trees, it is green outside, the sun is shining. I used to sit on the balcony, I saw little children, they are our future, and I am one of them. You see what I mean? A lot of thinking, but it is in my system, how I shall catch my thoughts, by writing (Ibbe).

Ibbe started to write songs as a tough little nine-year-old hip-hop fanatic. "Every day, every day I listen to music. I can't live without music." He remembered a horrible night when he didn't have access to an Mp3-player, so he had to find someone to borrow from, as he couldn't stand his life without music. "I love listening to music…maybe you find yourself in the tune, somehow…"

Finding himself has been crucial to Ibbe. His parents come from Macedonia and moved to Sweden to find work. When Ibbe was born his parents invited his grandmother to help with the children. "When I came home from school, she was always there I could see her standing behind the window, waiting for me…" Unfortunately, she died from cancer when Ibbe was 10 years old, and this started a negative spiral of events. Ibbe started to smoke and drink and gave up most of the schoolwork. He went to the music lessons, but since the music teacher was lost in an historical approach, and Ibbe was not too fond of Beethoven, he did not pass music either. "It was about composers and things like that, you know, but now it is 2008, we have to accept that we can't go backwards, if you get stuck in history it's boring."

After one year at RBMP, Ibbe knows that music could have saved him even earlier. "If all music teaching was like at RBMP I would have left school with the highest marks in every subject. Because I love music, it was the only subject where I did not play truant." The turning point came with the structure and rules introduced at RBMP. There he had no problems working on his mathematics or language lessons since he knew that in the afternoon he would go to the studio and continue working on his tunes. It gave him an idea about where he was heading, and what he wanted to achieve in his life: "Because I can't just fuck everything. Next year I am 19, I can't continue with school until I am 25, I need to earn my own money, not always ask mother."

Attending the music project also had an additional benefit that Ibbe made new friends, and lost contact with old "friends" from the gang. Many of his old friends from compulsory school have not been able to repair what they missed during the school years such as lack of complex language and literacy skills. In Ibbe's class there were no Swedish-speaking children over the last three years. All children spoke in their mother tongue and tried to communicate between themselves with the Swedish spoken in Rosengård, the segregated area where they lived. "Not much, like hey, what's up, see you…our Swedish." At RBMP Ibbe met new people and developed confidence with other teachers and grown ups. "Still, they know a lot, and they can supervise us, so after all, it is good to have a music teacher. They know how hard it is to communicate what you really want to say." With the help of the teachers from RBMP, Ibbe started to build new networks, competencies and visions. Soon he was fighting for a new life, not only for the CD production where he sang on four of the tracks, but also for membership in his society.

In this process, music has been the catalyst that provided the necessary resources for his resilience. Resilience came from the memory of his grand mother, and the musical expression of shared moments with her, his role model. For her sake, he is determined to achieve success at upper secondary school, because she wouldn't like to see him as he was before RBMP. This is the song for his grandmother – and himself:

Om Du Inte Fanns (Mormor Låten) (translated by Linda Schenck)

If I hadn't had you (Grandma song)

Verse 1
A woman, a grand old woman
Part of my life I never expected to leave
She had cancer and I grieve
Saw her eyes go dim as we held hands
Drowned in tears as I felt my heart stand
Can't breathe I'm hurting so bad
She was more than my grandma, we were friends
Oh now I know she'll never be home again
Look up at heaven blue sky, white clouds
Wonder if we'll meet again, head bowed
'Cause I'm so sad, it feels so bad
Gran, I remember what you taught me, be cool
And patient, I remember every single word
Red rose on your grave, don't want you underground
Feels so short but time goes fast though you're not around
I'll never forget what you meant to me.

Refrain
Where would I be today
If I hadn't had you
What would I know of life
If I hadn't had you
Where would I go
No way to know
I'll miss you forever
Hold you in my heart
Oh how it hurts when we're apart.

Verse 2
Shit how I hate when you're not at my side,
Tears fall on my papers, I just can't abide
How my heart aches with each word I write
The pain is with me day and night
Lots of memories both good and bad
Being little not knowing what love I had

Remember when you taught me to make eggs
Finding you on the floor, unable to get on your legs,
I know you were sick and all worn out
Sitting at your side not knowing what it's all about
I held her hand thinking about all she gave me
Telling myself she'd always be there to save me
But your time had come to say farewell
Tears on my cheek, I couldn't take it well
You breathed your last breath and I was there
I'm so lonely now wanting someone to share

Hook
I hope we'll one day meet again
Meet again where we'll be friends
We'll hold hands walk side by side
You'll tuck me into bed at night
We've all got dreams and this is mine
When I dream of you then things are fine
'Cause I miss you and I love you
Be with you's what I want to do

Refrain

These ecologically linked emotional and physical resources, love from his grandmother combined with experiences from RBMP, has helped Ibbe resist destructive forces in his life. Ibbe has many close friends who didn't make it at school, and who now face greater problems. He is most afraid that his little brother is now exposed to the same risk factors, so tries his best to protect him from bullying and bad role models. This tune expresses both his concern and hope:

Min Brossa (Lillebror Låten) (translated by Linda Schenck)

My bro

Verse 1
In 1993 you were born on the sixth of May
Hard to believe you're so big today
Hear me now, what your bro has to say
Family must always come first, dad and mom
You may not get all you want but live with what you got
The day will come when you've got to take life seriously
You'll be grown up and take responsibility
Think it through now and you'll make a better way
You saw me skipping class day after day

Sitting around not caring about school
Starting to smoke and playing being a fool
That's not how I wanted you to be
But maybe you learned from all you could see
Oh I'll be there and speak up for you
My bro I'll be around to see you through

Refrain
My bro I'm here for you day and night
I remember the times we did nothing but fight
We lost our grandma, couldn't believe it was true
My bro be a man now I'm counting on you
So, bro, I'm here for you now, wipe your eyes
Anybody hurts you I'll knock them down to size
Yeah, I hear you, yeah, whatever you need I'll do
My bro, I love you, you can count on me too

Verse 2
Both feet on the ground now wherever you go
And if I go to heaven no tears you should show
Okay I know it will cause you pain
You're my flesh and blood we're one and the same
I know we argue and fight and are mean
But when we've got trouble our joint strength can be seen
I have no big brother but you've got me
I can answer your questions, just ask and you'll see
There are weirdoes out there, out there on the streets
Don't get blood on your hands when they assess you meet
Don't find yourself locked in a prison cell
Making lots of mistakes in a criminal hell
Don't get into that world, you're only thirteen
Try to live your life without all that pain
Again I'll be there and speak up for you
My bro I'll be around to see you through

Refrain
Verse 3
Get yourself an education
And a job, police protection
Bro, violence is no solution
Kid criminal's no situation
Soon you'll see guys out of it, minds blown
Doin' drugs is no way to get yourself known
I spend a lot of time with those dudes
Come along, listen, get yourself clued
Lots of guys vandalize wreck stuff and then

Beat up and rob, find themselves in the pen
It's a bad crazy world out there, you can bet
And it's your choice about what life you'll get
If you take risks you'll find a knife at your throat
Don't get involved, keep your own self afloat
Once more I'll be there and speak up for you
My bro I hope this song helps see you through

Ibbe has managed to build his capacity for resilience using the human
capital available to him within the education system (teachers at RBMP),
and the resources provided at family and community levels. He has
performed on local stages, but since he started upper secondary school he
has stopped because, as he says, "I need to concentrate on my
education…now, now it is all about education. I have to give everything.
Yes, that is what I am doing."

Viktoria

Unlike Ibbe, Viktoria has continued to write songs after her RBMP year
and even now that she is concentrating on her studies at catering school.
She seems to be more or less constantly composing. "They just come to
me," she says, when I ask about her songs.

After nine years at school Viktoria had failed the three core subjects. She
says she never liked school, and rarely bothered to attend. At RBMP
however, she never missed a day. She explains, "the teachers offered their
hearts and souls for us to make it – and then you make it. I used to think
that mathematics was too difficult for me, but with Jalle (the teacher at
RBMP) it was easy. No teacher has ever cared or had the patience before."

When Viktoria tells her life story, music is the common thread. She
remembers from her early childhood that she used to sing all the time, and
that the teachers at her nursery school wanted to send her to a music
school. But her mother thought it was too far away for her to go there on
her own, so she never started. It is something she regrets, as she never took
any extra music lessons, either at the municipal school or privately. But
she and her friends took every opportunity to perform at concerts in school
(when she was there). Most of the time she spent outside school, as she felt
that the teachers had given up on her. She had definitely given up on
school.

When she came to the music program, a radical shift in her attitude towards her future and her life took place. I asked her to explain why playing music in the afternoons made studying easier in the mornings? "It is an interest. I mean, we were there for the same thing, so things fall into place. That's how it works. Everyone came because of one thing, and that was music. It is like Jalle says – when you arrive your suitcase is very small, and almost empty. At the end of the project your suitcase is filled with knowledge, everything you want and need."

Coherence and the ability to express her emotions grew during the process. In the beginning she didn't know what to be and whom to be with. But through the music ensembles she made new friends and opened up emotionally. "Then they get to know you in the deep of your heart and see your tears, laughter and everything"…

The expectations and demands from the teachers also helped. Viktoria feels that it was a relief to have strict rules and had no problems adapting to them because of her passion for the music. She thinks that it would have been possible to work like this at the comprehensive school as well, if teachers only knew…."Well, you can find the child's interest at young age, and leave them to explore it, work with it, instead of just going to school all the time, it gets boring. Nine long years."

The music that is so important to Viktoria played only a minor role during her ordinary school years. She says that was because most music teachers didn't know what they were doing. During her year at RBMP she developed strong views about what a music teacher must know and do, "they must know a lot about music. And give us a lot of space. The music teacher I have now is like that. She allows us to give her ideas, for her development as well. We are encouraged to make our own songs, and play what we like. It is great to be given that opportunity. That is how you learn yourself."

At RBMP peer education is the normal procedure. The teacher's assist with the technical aspects of the CD-production, and lessons like drumming or singing are given when the students demonstrate a need. The song "Nevermind" that Viktoria produced for the CD grew like a collective improvisation. Someone was inspired on the drums, the bass player joined in, and then the guitar player started with their own ideas. "Then I just wrote down the text that came to me. The melody comes when I start to sing, it always works." The song meant a lot for her own development. When she wrote it she thought of everything that had happened in her life, and she now believes that her own experiences are relevant to many other youngsters in Malmö. "I think that when they listen to it, they hear themselves in it. Many people in Malmö listen to it now, all the time."

This song of resilience is transmitted from friend to friend, from Mp3 player to Mp3 player, often via online social networks. It is not possible to buy the CD on the open market but local distribution is no problem for Viktoria. Good things spread anyhow, and with new media there are many ways to share important experiences. Victoria's Mp3 song is almost always playing at her home because she needs it when she is happy, when she is sad, all the time. Music is important, and with the CD-production, new visions for the future took shape:

> Before I just wanted to quit school, quit everything. But now, it is about education, get a good job, and travel, maybe around the globe. Then come back and work again. But I would like to continue studying, and be a music teacher. I think that would be really great.

I have chosen to let Viktoria and Ibbe represent the five students I interviewed from this project. All of them have managed to access protective resources and used them as buffers to counteract the contextual risk factors they have been exposed to through their school years. Their stories reflect individual variations, but there is a common denominator: their capacity for resilience has been increased by RBMP, which has an effect on many levels apart from the individual; on the social system level by linking different members to each other; on the community level by providing access to resources and; fostering a sense of belonging. As Lemerle and Stewart argue in chapter two, more attention must be paid to the cultural determinants of resilience, especially when investigating complex multicultural societies.

Discussion

The concept of culture can be interpreted in many ways, some of which are confusing. If it is interpreted as art, the RBMP example shows how music can provide positive learning experiences, enhance social capital and affirm how it can lead to new actions and perceptions. If culture is interpreted as norms, values, symbols and patterns for action, expressed in daily life and giving meaning to daily life, a school culture for example also influences personal identity. The identities of the young people at

RBMP have been formed by many factors, but their nine years of failure in comprehensive school is significant. The school culture presented at RBMP presents contrasting norms, values and patterns for action, which these pupils have used successfully in their personal identity constructs.

The concept of sociality can be likened to that of social capital to look at connections and belongings, mutual trust between people and communal activities. Putnam (2000) has shown how important social capital is for societal integration and connections, and further quantitative proof for his argument is found in medical research. With theoretical inspiration from Dewey's theories on aesthetic experiences and art, Konlaan (2001) carried out a study on the relationship between health and participation in cultural life. Based on a random sample from a cohort of 10,609 individuals from the adult Swedish population, he found that attending cultural events (film, concert, art exhibition or museum visit) co varied with health outcomes. The study shows that art "culture" does not provide us with escape from this world, but rather with possibilities of deeper understanding and appreciation of the world in which we live.

The inclusive school culture at RBMP has given Ibbe, Viktoria and the other ex-students the needed impulse to change habits, and also to believe in their own capacities. The teachers at RBMP use music in a way that resembles music therapy, even if they do not label it as such. They also invest a lot of energy in building strong relationships with students. Their methods serve as an example of what Aspelin (2005) calls "the third route for pedagogy" where students are not left to find a path and direction on their own, neither are they directed by the teacher on a prescribed highway. The third alternative, attributed to the philosopher Martin Buber, acknowledges that teachers and students follow different directions, and that the teacher has to adjust to the student. Human being to human being, in a true relationship, based on personal and active presence, s/he builds up an atmosphere where the students are able to achieve what they are striving for (Aspelin, 2005). This emphasis on face-to-face relationships is a mutual approach, which covers a broad stream of ideas and styles from areas like sociology, social psychology and anthropology. In anthropology we also find the concept of sociality used as an analytical tool to interpret how RBMP explains its success. Carrithers (1992) argues that it is sociality, our ability to socialise, which makes us human beings, and explains why we have cultures. It is how people interact with each other, how we produce knowledge about ourselves, how we develop our societies that decides our history, not technological inventions. Just as

Viktoria and Ibbe uncover personal knowledge through their songs, the finished product also reveals knowledge and resources to them – sociality through music.

References

Aspelin, J. (2005). *Den mellanmänskliga vägen. Martin Bubers relationsfilosofi som pedagogisk vägvisning.* [The human direction. Martin Buber´s philosophy as pedagogical guide.] Stockholm/Stehag: Symposion.

Carrithers, M. (1992). *Why humans have cultures. Explaining anthropology and social diversity.* Oxford and New York: Oxford University Press.

Dewey, J. (1934). 11th ed. *Art as experience.* New York: Capricorn Books.

Enö, M. (2009). *Resurser, framgång och mångkulturella skolors verksamheter och strategier* [Resources, success and multicultural schools activities and strategies]. Utvärdering Malmö stad 2009. Malmö: Malmö stad. Retrieved December 20, 2009, from http://www.malmo.se/mangfaldiskolan.

Fredrickson, B. L. (2000). Cultivating positive emotions to optimize health and well-being. *Prevention & Treatment, 3.* Retrieved December 12, 2009, from http://psycnet.apa.org/journals/pre/3/1/1a.pdf.

Johannisson, K. (2008). Kultur och hälsa. Två besvärliga begrepp. [Culture and health. Two awkward concepts]. In G. Bjursell & L.V. Westerhäll (Eds.) Kulturen och hälsan. Essäer om kulturens yttringar och hälsans tillstånd. [Culture and health. Essays on the relationship between culture and health.] Stockholm: Santérus förlag.

Konlaan, B. B. (2001). Cultural experience and health: The coherence of health and leisure time experiences. Umeå University Medical Dissertations. New series No. 706. Umeå: Umeå University.

Lorensson, J. (2006). *Musical manners. Music for life.* Master (year 1) thesis. Malmö: Malmö University.

Putnam, R.D. (2000). *Bowling alone: The collapse and revival of American community.* New York: Simon & Schuster.

Ruud, E. (2002). *Varma ögonblick. Om musik, hälsa och livskvalitet.* [Warm moments. Music, health and quality of life] Göteborg: Bo Ejeby förlag.

—. (1997). *Musikk og identitet.* Oslo: Universitetsforlaget AS.

—. (2008). Hvorfor musikk som terapi? [Why music as therapy]. In G. Bjursell & L.V. Westerhäll (Eds.) Kulturen och hälsan. Essäer om sambandet mellan kulturens yttringar och hälsans tillstånd. [Culture and health. Essays on the relationship between culture and health.] Stockholm: Santérus förlag.

Skolverket (2009). *Resultat från ämnesproven i årskurs 9 vårterminen 2009.* [Results from subject tests in year 9, springsemester 2009]. Retrieved December 14, 2009, from http://www.skolverket.se/publikationer?id=2289.

Svennerbrand, M. (2009). Personal correspondence, 24th April, Malmö.

CHAPTER TWELVE

MUSIC IS A WORDLESS KNOWING OF OTHERS: RESILIENCE IN VIRTUAL ENSEMBLES

STEVE DILLON

Introduction

Music making affects relationships with self and others by generating a sense of belonging to a culture or ideology (Bamford, 2006; Barovick, 2001; Dillon & Stewart, 2006; Fiske, 2000; Hallam, 2001). Whilst studies from arts education research present compelling examples of these relationships, others argue that they do not present sufficiently validated evidence of a causal link between music making experiences and cognitive or social change (Winner & Cooper, 2000; Winner & Hetland, 2000a, 2000b, 2001). I have suggested elsewhere that this disconnection between compelling evidence and observations of the effects of music making are in part due to the lack of rigor in research and the incapacity of many methods to capture these experiences in meaningful ways (Dillon, 2006). Part of the answer to these questions about rigor and causality lay in the creative use of new media technologies that capture the results of relationships in music artefacts. Crucially, it is the effective management of these artefacts within computer systems that allows researchers and practitioners to collect, organize, analyse and then theorise such music making experiences.

In this chapter I describe these ideas and provide evidence as they apply to generative music making. I also focus on what generative systems offer to the maintenance of cultural and artistic relationships with self and others. Generative music and art are relatively new phenomena that use procedural invention as a creative technique to produce musical and visual new media artefacts. These systems present a range of opportunities that facilitate new kinds of relationships with music performance and production. The network jamming systems that are the subject of my research provide users who possess little formal musical or artistic expertise with access to collaborative ensemble experiences. Put simply, they provide a virtual "band like" instrumental performance experience. Multiple players perform through a screen based and/or physical interface that involves simple gestures such as moving an icon vertically and horizontally on an X-Y axis, or manipulating sliders dials, pads and joysticks to generate a real time change in pre-sequenced musical arrangements. These methods of interacting are common in computer games and are familiar to many children and young people. Yet jam2jam's networked ensembles also allow novice users and the disabled to interact with each other in a virtual band and record their creative performances – a wordless knowing of others.

The questions that arise from these experiences with virtual music and media performances are about the extent to which they are meaningful and engaging, and whether they lead to changes in social and cognitive behaviour that have long-term positive effects on participants.

Protective factors in music experiences

In the first book in this series: *Music, Meaning and Transformation* (Dillon, 2007) I suggest that the location of music making experiences needs to be personal, social and cultural. Experiences of making, performing and sharing music resonate with notions of resilience; they build competencies that act as protective factors with positive implications in other aspects of life. Personal engagement with music making is an expression of self if attended to in a structured way. It can have the effect of developing expressiveness and habits of mind that develop commitment and personal problem solving skills.

In terms of resilience, my jam2jam research is specifically looking for the presence of protective factors that encourage learned competencies, a repertoire of social skills, and access to social networks and resources in response to adversities (see Lemerle & Stewart's review of definitions in chapter two). There are also innate qualities that enable an ability to respond positively to adverse challenges, which correspond to the idea of an autotelic personality (Czikszentmihalyi, 1994). Autotelicism describes a personality type in individuals who can create their own challenges so that they remain engaged with a task and maintain their "flow.' There is congruence between this psychological concept of flow – the point where challenge and ability intersect – and the current debate about resilience in public health research.

Play, as a way of learning through discovery and experience, is also important in this context (Bruner, 1966; Dewey, 1989), as is the connection between these kinds of playful interactions and ensemble music making. Yet these experiential and collaborative structures are only beginning to be recognised as valuable in public health (Dillon, 2006) beyond their application in music therapy (Pavlicevic & Ansdell, 2004).

I have also described the social interactions within large ensembles, where players with a diverse range of skills and abilities blend into a unique character of sound. This kind of musical experience provides structures for relationships facilitated by symbolic representations such as notated scores, physical gestures from a conductor, or within the music itself through rhythmic pulse or groove. The player in a small ensemble potentially experiences the challenge of one person – one part dependence on each individual meshing to make a cohesive whole. Participants valued these small ensemble experiences because of these challenges and "the wordless knowing of others" gained in these experiences (Dillon, 2007).

Connection to a culture and ideology is very much part of performance and production of music. I suggest that whilst these qualities are recognised within music therapy, the salutogenic (Antonovsky, 1996) application of these ideas and the connection to community music making (Bartleet et al., 2009; Koopman 2007; Sun & Stewart, 2005) is not well established. This is partially due to the newness of these non-therapeutic contexts and concepts as well as the development of research that measures social and cultural capital. Evidence of these outcomes were recorded in Australia in an examination of community music in Australia (Bartleet et al., 2009) and in the United Kingdom in the "Power of Music" study that reviewed and presented a substantial literature review positing the effects of music making (Hallam, 2001). Further evidence is found in Bamford's "Wow Factor" presenting a global sketch that recognised the transferability of these concepts across cultures and across arts (Bamford, 2006). Broadly speaking, this literature implies that it is reasonable to suggest musical relationships have the potential to affect the human capacity for resilience.

A wordless knowing of others

Participating in music making provides an opportunity to communicate with self, with others, and with cultures in ways that are not necessarily dependent on spoken language. Whilst language is present and a significant source of meaning in song lyrics, its utterance also contributes to significant shifts in timbre – one of the musical structures that provide a location for meaning making. These semiotic aspects are further enhanced by music devices, which trigger distinctive neurological factors and cultural belief systems (Sachs, 2008). Drone and repetition, for example, are common musical devices used to induce transcendental experiences.

There is also an aspect to music making within a given cultural framework that gives participants permission to act differently, either as an individual or as a unified group.   The act of making music collaboratively involves participation in a set of defined cultural rules that focus and bind together what can be achieved, whilst interactions provide a sense of belonging that can transcend otherness. Yet this same act can also delineate and exclude. National anthems, battle chants and hymns are musical practices that do this. In ancient Indigenous Australian culture certain songs are "restricted" because the custodians of the knowledge embedded in the music require that the songs be made available to the specific person that needs said knowledge in their lives. Equally, songs for particular places are often delineated by relationship, gender, and age to sustain and pass on knowledge to others (Mackinlay, 2005).

Music, meaning, and relationships

Mass musical systems such as choirs or large ensembles contain multiple skill levels embedded in musical parts that enable these kinds of interactions. These systems form part of cultural ceremonies in both secular and sacred events where large bodies of people perform symbolic interactions (e.g., congregational singing in churches or football chants in stadiums). In *Music, Meaning and Transformation* I identified three areas where meaning was located in the act of music making. I suggested that music making experiences facilitated relationships with *Self* through the personal interaction, with peers through ensemble/band - *Social* interaction - and with *Culture* through performance, exhibition and publishing work. These areas feed back into a transforming self, and consciously grow the human condition.

The philosopher Martin Buber suggests humans are made by their interactions with others, and that education worthy of the name is "the education of character" (Buber, 1969). He also described human relationships in terms of equality and reciprocity, ones which he called "I and Thou," with physical things denoted as "I and it" relations (Buber, 1969; 1975). At the core of these relationships is the recognition of humanity in others. Musical relationships are particularly important because they provide common ground so that every act of music making acknowledges the humanity of others. This recognition of humanity is at the core of what I describe as cultural meaning. In the act of music making the "I-it" relationship is between music maker and instrument; the instrument becomes invisible in the process. We often see a merging of the human and technology into an expressive being capable of complex communication and communion.

Many musical instruments are complex and require a high skill level to be expressive. Yet with generative music making we have focused on the maintenance of ensemble relationships. We have utilised a computer process based on Sorensen's *Impromptu* language and placed a simple gestural interface on top of complex expressive interactions. "Impromptu" is a language used by Live Coding Performers who generate algorithmic music and visual images in real time (Brown & Sorensen, 2009). Using this language, our jam2jam interface allows players to select musical and visual transformations of music and to enact them immediately in real time and in collaboration with others, similar to performing in a band.

In the development of a generative music making application we have considered and observed thousands of interactions displaying immediate engagement with varied musical styles. For eight years now I have been working with a team of researchers to examine and develop generative media in the form of computer software that has a "game like" interface (see figure 1). During this time the Network Jamming project has collected many hours of video data of participants using these generative systems. What follows is a presentation of three critical moments that occurred whilst testing our generative software. I aim to show how these moments act as additional evidence that demonstrates a form of resilience that builds capacity through virtual ensembles.

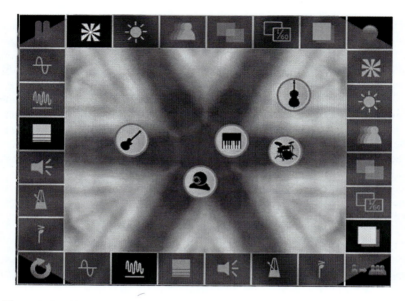

Figure 1. Jam2jam interface

Methodology

The methodology used here is Software Development as Research (SoDaR) devised by (Brown, 2007). It involves the simultaneous development of software alongside pedagogical and experiential approaches to design. We have gathered multi-camera recordings of participants' faces, their creative work via screen capture, and filmed the interaction within classrooms and other venues. Stimulated recall and interviews have also been captured and transcribed. These data sources have been synchronised using Transana analysis software so that the researcher could retain the musical process in an audiovisual form, coding relationships between incidences and critical moments in a way that maintains the compelling nature of these experiences. The identification of critical moments and compelling examples of symbolic interaction between participants using jam2jam has provided us with insights into meaningful engagement with generative systems. This method has allowed us to focus multiple lenses on relationships that take place in the act of generative making music.

Here I examine three critical moments drawn from the Network Jamming project data as examples of resilience-building relationships in a virtual setting. The question I raise here is: what kind of therapeutic or pedagogical approach might we design to take advantage of these quality experiences?

The following three purposively selected accounts constitute incidences, where we as researchers identified something unique in the data. Since our first observations, these experiences have been replicated across age groups, gender and country. Whilst their limited replication provides an element of rigour, they do not present concrete answers as to why the phenomenon exists or the purpose it serves. To rectify this, I propose a set of "what if ?" scenarios that refer to personal, social and cultural meanings of experience. I proceed to identify qualities that have potential to be considered and researched further as virtual protective factors.

Our first vignette comes from a Health Information Technology (HitNet) project that examined an Indigenous mental health arts program in a school community in suburban Brisbane and in remote far North Queensland, Australia.

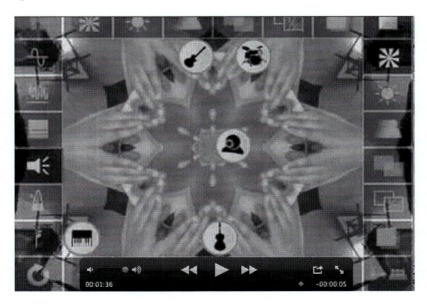

Figure 2. Fingers picture

Critical moment 1: A choreography of fingers
(Dillon & Jones, 2009)

In front of the computer in a suburban Brisbane primary school sits an 11-year-old Indigenous Australian boy. This is his first encounter with jam2jam. He seems oblivious to the other young people around him who are also playing with the interface, watching numerous screens around the room. He has explored his screen and worked out how to position the icons so that he hears a repetitive Hip-Hop groove. What is intriguing him most is real-time visual manipulation, not the music, though he is responding to it with his movements.

For forty-six minutes he sat in front of this computer completely engaged with a very simple process. He learned to shift the video icon so that the web cam function was operating; he then selected the kaleidoscope effect from the video effects. From there he proceeded to perform a sequence of "finger-choreographies" with the aesthetic qualities of a Busby Berkley dance sequence.

	Appreciate	Select	Direct	Explore	Embody
Personal					
Social					
Cultural					

Figure 3. Meaningful Engagement Matrix

We had already observed engagement with mutating faces in jam2jam videos and knew users were intrigued by it. We called it the "Andy Warhol factor" (Dillon & Jones, 2009), which acknowledges the popularity of the Photo Booth experience at a recent Warhol exhibition in Brisbane. We noticed the visual phenomenon in jam2jam had become a performance activity that blended media forms seamlessly. When examining the data against our meaningful engagement matrix (Figure 3), we noted that this experience was clearly a personal one. The young performer was becoming increasingly proficient at creating effective choreographic sequences. For a long time we have been concerned about the lack of a physical and tactile aspect to what we saw as a virtual experience. What we saw here was a kinaesthetic and visual-spatial experience directed by improvisation in music. When he *selected* the musical icons it produced a groove he *appreciated*. And when he *directed* visual media, *exploring* transformations of colour and form with dance movement, he *embodied* choreographed finger movements in clever and entertaining sequences.

This intrigued us as education researchers because we knew he had learnt something yet we didn't really know what it was. We knew he was demonstrating control over real-time media sequencing tools because he clearly improved each time he performed. This kind of learning is reminiscent of moving through levels in a computer game. From a teaching and learning point of view, the artefact of the experience – the recorded performance – is a representation of his *embodied* knowledge. This assertion has implications for learning in two ways: first, common in the arts is the notion of being able to capture experience that cannot (yet) be articulated in spoken or written language. Second, the intrinsic nature of the experience provides a safe training ground for the development of autotelic behaviours. In terms of resilience, these implications point to a virtual protective factor, a type of experiential resource, which has engaging qualities that encourage independent and self-actuated challenges. The experience is multi modal: visual, kinaesthetic, gestural and aural. Whilst the activity and software experience is similar to a computer game, the aesthetic dimension adds a different kind of challenge to the process of creating a product, and I believe that performance in this arena is more powerful than the extrinsic nature of learning embedded in most commercial video games.

Personal meaning and resilience

In terms of contributing to an individuals' capacity for resilience, solo experiences with jam2jam offer opportunities to compose a multimodal personal statement. Music therapists have expressed interest in using our interface as a solo activity to present a "how am I feeling today" statement. The act of choosing musical styles and visuals and then transforming them in an original sequence provides a fluid canvas for non-verbal transactions and for symbolic interaction that resembles singing in the shower, playing guitar in your bedroom, or even karaoke. These experiences are about selecting music that represents your state of mind in order to "get in touch" with a memory or to "amplify" your personal feelings. The potential for jam2jam in these kinds of personal statement experiences is profound, especially as it can move beyond music to recording the visual and kinaesthetic performance.

Each time we create a product that we value ourselves, or feel it expresses something about us, we affect our sense of self and our relationships with others. Jam2jam has much ecological potential in these areas. Even though a smile is difficult to measure as evidence, the sheer amount of smiles I have witnessed from users, doing much the same as the young man described above, suggests that access to happiness via real-time performance is a key protective factor. Over the past few years we have worked with thousands of so called "disengaged" youth; we have noticed that they are not disengaged whilst they are using our software. The experience itself cannot alter adversities such as years of abuse or solve social and educational problems, but it can provide access to critical moments of achievement, flow and happiness.

The provision of this engaging tool fosters a relationship with self and achievement. It promotes autotelic behaviour and gives access to an expressive medium that positively feeds self-confidence. It enables this through the diversity of media made available for expressive manipulation: audio, visual, gestural, kinaesthetic, as well as creative problem solving. It enables what Gardner called an "intelligence fair" experience (Gardner, 1993; 1993), and in this context jam2jam is an intrinsically engaging experience. I argue that it provides opportunities for self-expression and flow leading to feelings of satisfaction that act as a "virtual protective factor" with potential to affect an individual's capacity for resilience.

Critical moment 2: Common ground

The following vignette was not formally part of my research yet the incident has spawned an academic article (Dillon & Brown, 2009), and has become the basis of a research project about accessible interactions for people with disabilities.

In August 2009, at an International symposium called Jamskolan, I co-organised a workshop that examined external controllers for use with jam2jam. Within that workshop several researchers demonstrated wired and wireless controllers with jam2jam alongside some newly developed gestural controllers developed by Associate Professor Bert Bongers and his team at University of Technology in Sydney with Dr Adam Postula from the University of Queensland. Amongst the participants were a music therapist, a DJ producer, and a group of teachers, academics and researchers. On this day of the symposium I invited a young man to attend whom I knew was interested in music and who has Down Syndrome. The young man worked with the music therapist and DJ producer manipulating the controller's sliders to create a jam2jam performance. Initially we thought the controllers might be too complex and the software too abstract for him to be able to hear and relate sound and visual effects to slider movements. Yet despite problems we perceived in the design of our software, it did engage the young man considerably. The observations of researchers present suggested potential for common ground between professionals like the DJ, the music therapist and the young man.

The following evening we planned a showcase of network jamming for future community and education usage. We invited representatives from Down Syndrome Queensland, and what occurred that night was quite unexpected. The young man who had worked with us the previous day returned with four friends determined to perform at the showcase evening. Following a brief rehearsal, where each young person explored the controllers, listened and watched three screen projections of visuals, the group jammed live for the entire audience with the music therapist and DJ playing live instruments. One young lady became infatuated with dancing in front of the kaleidoscope web cam image, whilst others engaged enthusiastically and with great concentration on the audiovisual performance. The result was visually and aurally exciting. We recorded the visual output of the performance, yet we did not have a camera on the spontaneous performers. Distinction between the quality of sound and vision of the young people with Down Syndrome and the MT and DJ was not noticeable. Our generative technology had provided a safe common ground where the skills of the performers were perceived as equal and expressive.

I first thought of the idea of song as a common ground when I examined Indigenous Australian music (Dillon, 2007). In this research we identified that music making in song forms represent what a group values in sound and narrative content, and how this provides gel to bond a cultural expression of shared values. Green's (2008) idea of delineated meaning is pertinent here. When applied to group learning, a performance takes on new dimensions as groups feel connected with the music itself and the making of it with peers whom share values; they persist with tasks even when their prior efforts document recurring failure.

The complexity of the interface did not impair the group of young people engaging with the experience of music making in the vignette I presented above. What unfolded was an enthusiasm fuelled by the sound and vision, but also by the opportunity to engage with the music making process collaboratively. The "wordless knowing of one another" was profound. These young people's speech patterns were not articulate yet their engagement with music making and the process of collective expression was. Granted, a music therapist who understood how to structure the encounter, and a DJ who inspired their participation facilitated this experience, but what we witnessed was similar behaviour to any music ensemble rehearsal and performance. What effect could this experience have upon notions of self, other, confidence and resilience? We do not have longitudinal data to answer that question as yet, but hope that the Accessible Interaction project will illuminate affordances of these technologies with meaningful outcomes and positive relationships with self and others.

It is apparent that our technology provides a safe playground for exploring creative performance, and that it can connect people in a relationship that is not dependent on spoken or written language. This vignette documents an instance of collaborative music making with jam2jam, where the participants with an intellectual disability capability demonstrated inspiring human connection and performance. This poses questions about what generative systems might contribute to resilience research by providing a safe common ground for interpersonal relationships. The technology mediates the quality of the interaction whilst still providing an engaging and challenging task. It also leads us to ask what the Music Therapist and DJ provided that might lead to those outcomes, and how we might measure it.

Critical moment 3: Cultural fluidity

The idea of cultural fluidity with jam2jam extends from our research findings that assert both images and musical materials can be changed to suit a particular cultural environment. The image above comes from an Indigenous artist enrolled on a project where a series of artists' work was digitized. 11-year-old urban Indigenous children were given permission to improvise with the artwork, add music to it, and create new videos, which were then sent back to the artists for comment. The notion of relationships here is central. In Indigenous cultures the notion of relational knowledge – who you are in relation to others is critical, as is where you are from –

place. This project, represented here by the artwork (Figure 4), saw the young people respond to artworks with a sense of pride in their Aboriginality. The pleasure they expressed when given permission to be playful with the images, and to include hip-hop grooves, encouraged them to simultaneously represent their indigenous and urban affiliations through sound and image. When the movies were returned to the artists, there was a sense of virtual relationship through the artwork – a symbolic interaction. The artist recognised the cheeky and playful nature of the interaction with "remixing" the artworks and making new works; this process merged two communities – those of rural/remote adults with urban youths. In both locations there was genuine recognition of otherness, a connection via this generative experience amongst people whom have never met.

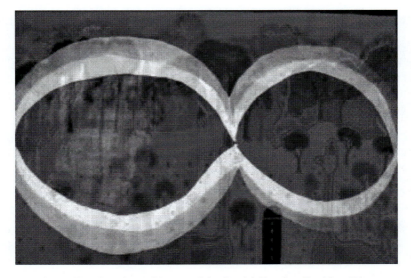

Figure 4. Jam2jam interface with artwork by Patrick Butcher, Lockhart River.

In relation to resilience research, the message that emerges from our thematic analysis of cultural fluidity is that jam2jam can provide multiple connection points between cultures by giving permission to artists to be playful with the materials. This is a relatively new kind of relationship between tools and artists that has a high level of reciprocity and interaction. This relationship has implications for resilience researchers examining a sense of belonging and well-being. It has potential therapeutic value as well, both within and between cultures in a safe and non-verbal way. Most certainly these kinds of experiences need to be considered in ethical ways appropriate to the culture of the participants, and generally should involve genuine "custodians" of those materials. As the developers of jam2jam we aspire to develop a direct, engaging pedagogy to enable reflection that makes sense of these experiences in both verbal and embodied forms.

Conclusion

This chapter has focused on the idea of virtual protective factors, which I have documented in observations using the jam2jam software in communities across the world. Clearly, there is potential to use such generative software to provide access to meaningful and expressive personal experiences with music making. Yet wordless, but structured relationships through collaborative ensemble performances require equitable access to resources. The idea of a culturally fluid system that provides access to both intense mono cultural experiences and syncretic-blended experiences is significant for resilience research. Whilst I have not presented evidence here in a scientific sense (which needs to be addressed through clinical trials), the indicators from these vignettes consistently present participants who demonstrate flow and engagement as evidenced by the smiles on their faces and their passion to continuously engage. Generative media systems present us with a technologically mediated environment. When deployed by skilled music practitioners, jam2jam can support resilience projects in cultural, social and personal ways.

Acknowledgments

The author of this paper acknowledge the work of Andrew Brown, Craig Gibbons, Barbara Adkins, Thorin Kerr, John Ong, Andrew Sorensen, and Kathy Hirche, each of whom contributed significantly to the research and development of jam2jam. We also acknowledge support for this project by the Australasian CRC for Interaction Design (ACID) through the Cooperative Research Centre Program of the Australian Government's Department of Innovation, Industry, Science and Research.

References

Antonovsky, A. (1996). The salutogenic model as a theory to guide health promotion. Health Promotion International 11:11-18.

Bamford, Anne. (2006). The Wow Factor: Global Research compendium on the impact of the arts in education. New York/ Munchen/Berlin: Waxmann Munster.

Barovick, Harriet. (2001). Drumming circles. Time 157 (18):6.

Bartleet, Brydie-Lee, Peter Dunbar-Hall, Richard Letts, and Huib Schippers. (2009). Sound links: community music in Australia Brisbane: Queensland Conservatorium Research Centre.

Brown, Andrew. (2007). Software Development as music Education Research. International Journal of Education & the Arts (6), http://ijea.asu.edu.

Brown, Andrew R., and Andrew Sorensen. (2009). Interacting with generative music through live coding. Contemporary Music Review 28 (1):17-30.

Bruner, Jerome, S. (1966). *Towards a Theory of Instruction.* Cambridge Mass: Belknap Press of Harvard University.

Buber, Martin. (1969). Between Man and Man. Trans and Introduction by Ronald Gregor Smith. London: Fontana.

—. (1975). *I and Thou.* Translated by T. W. a. P. b. R. G. Smith. Second Edition ed. Edinburgh: T & T Clark.

Csikszentmihalyi, M. (1994). *Flow: The Psychology of Happiness.* New York USA: Random Century Group. Original edition, 1992, Harper and Rowe.

Dewey, John. (1989). *Art as Experience.* (1st Ed.1934), 1980 ed. U.S.A: Perigree Books.

Dillon, Steve. (2006). Assessing the positive influence of music activities in community development programs. *Music Education Research* 8 (No. 2): 267-280.

—. (2007). Maybe we can find some Common Ground: Indigenous Perspectives, a music teachers' story. . *Australian Journal of Indigenous Education* 36 Supplement: 59-65.

—. (2007). *Music, Meaning and Transformation.* Edited by E. MacKinlay. 6 vols. Vol. 1, *Meaningful music making for life.* Newcastle: Cambridge Scholars Publishing.

Dillon, Steve, and Anita Jones. (2009). Exploring new kinds of Relationships using generative music making software. *Australian Psychiatry* 17 (Supplement).

Dillon, Steve, and Donald Stewart. (2006). Songs of Resilience. Paper read at Proceedings of the 27th World Conference of the International Society for Music Education, 16-21 July, 2006, at Kuala Lumpur, Malaysia.

Dillon, Steve C, and Andrew R Brown. 2009. *Jamskolan09: An International Workshop and Symposium on Arts Education through Network Jamming with Generative Media.* Brisbane Australia: Australasian Cooperative Research Centre for Interactive Design (ACID) Network Jamming Project.

Dreise, Mayrah. (2006). Common Ground. Caboolture

Fiske, Edward B. (2000). *Champions of change: The impact of the arts on learning.* Edited by E. B. Fiske. USA: Arts Education partnership, The presidents Committee on the Arts and the Humanities.

Gardner, Howard. (1993). Creating Minds: An Anatomy of Creativity Seen Through the Lives of Freud, Einstein, Picasso, Stravinsky, Eliot, Graham and Ghandi. USA: Basic Books.

—. (1993). Frames of Mind: The Theory of Multiple Intelligences. London: Fontana Press.

Green, Lucy. (2008). Music, Informal Learning and the School. London: Ashgate.

Hallam, Susan. (2001). The Power of Music. In *The strength of music's influence on our lives*, ed S. Hallam. Place Published: The Performing Right Society: MCPS-PRS Alliance. http://www.prs.co.uk/powerfofmusicreport/ (accessed.

Koopman, C. (2007). Community music as music education: On the education potential of community music. *International Journal of Music Education* 25:151-163.

Mackinlay, Elizabeth. (2005). Moving and dancing towards decolonisation in education: An example from an Indigenous Australian performance classroom. *Australian Journal of Indigenous Education* 34.

Pavlicevic, Mercedes, and Gary Ansdell. (2004). *Community Music Therapy.* London: Jessica Kingsley Publishers.

Putnam, Robert D. (2000). *Bowling Alone: The Collapse and revival of American Community.* New York: Touchstone Books: Simon and Schuster.

Sachs, Oliver. (2008). *Musicophilia: Tales of Music and the Brain.* New York: First Vintage Books.

Sun, J., and D.E. Stewart. (2005). Building social capital in the school community: the 'Resilient Children and Communities' project. Paper read at International Conference on Engaging Communities, 14-17 August 2005, at Brisbane Queensland.

Winner, Ellen, and Monica Cooper. (2000a). Mute those claims: No Evidence (Yet) for a Causal Link between Arts Study and Academic Achievement. *The Journal of Aesthetic Education* 34 (Numbers 3-4):11-75.

Winner, Ellen, and Lois Hetland. (2000b). The Arts and Academic Achievement: What the Evidence Shows. *Journal of Aesthetic Education* 34 (3/4 Fall/ Winter 2000).

—. (2000c). The Arts in Education: Evaluating the Evidence for a Causal Link. *Journal of Aesthetic Education* 34 (Numbers 3-4): 3-10.

—. (2001). An Arts in Education Research Compendium: California Arts Council Year of the Arts 2001.